The Literary and Legal Genealogy of Native American Dispossession

The Literary and Legal Genealogy of Native American Dispossession offers a unique interpretation of how literary and public discourses influenced three U.S. Supreme Court Rulings written by Chief Justice John Marshall with respect to Native Americans. These cases, *Johnson v. M'Intosh* (1823), *Cherokee Nation v. Georgia* (1831) and *Worcester v. Georgia* (1832), collectively known as the Marshall Trilogy, have formed the legal basis for the dispossession of indigenous populations throughout the Commonwealth. The Trilogy cases are usually approached as 'pure' legal judgments. This book maintains, however, that it was the literary and public discourses from the early sixteenth through to the early nineteenth centuries that established a discursive tradition which, in part, transformed the American Indians from owners to 'mere occupants' of their land. Exploring the literary genesis of Marshall's judgments, George Pappas draws on the work of Michel Foucault, Edward Said and Homi Bhabha, to analyse how these formative U.S. Supreme Court rulings blurred the distinction between literature and law.

Dr George D. Pappas is currently a practising lawyer in North Carolina, USA.

Indigenous Peoples and the Law

Series editors

Dr Mark A. Harris, La Trobe University, Australia;
Prof Denise Ferreira da Silva, Queen Mary, University of London, UK;
Dr Claire Charters, University of Auckland, New Zealand;
Dr Glen Coulthard, University of British Columbia, Canada

The colonial modalities that resulted in the pillaging of the 'New World' involved wholesale dispossession, genocidal violence and exploitation of their original inhabitants. It was not, however, until the latter part of the twentieth century that Indigenous peoples attained some degree of legal recognition. This book series focuses upon the manner in which Indigenous peoples' experiences of law have been transformed from an oppressive system of denying rights to a site of contestation, and the articulation of various forms of self-governance. Encouraging a range of theoretical, political and ethical perspectives on Indigenous peoples and the law, this book series aims to provide a comprehensive survey of the experience of Indigenous peoples and their changing relationship with national and international juridical frameworks.

Titles in this series:

Aboriginal Peoples, Colonialism and International Law: Raw Law
Irene Watson

Indigeneity: Before and Beyond the Law
Kathleen Birrell

Forthcoming titles in this series:

Human Rights, the Rule of Law and Exploitation: Blood Minerals
Mark Harris

Scales of Governance and Indigenous Peoples: New Rights or Same Old Wrongs?
Edited by Irène Bellier and Jennifer Hays

Indigenous Peoples as Subjects of International Law
Irene Watson

The Literary and Legal Genealogy of Native American Dispossession

The Marshall Trilogy cases

George D. Pappas

Routledge
Taylor & Francis Group
a GlassHouse Book

First published 2017
by Routledge
2 Park Square, Milton Park, Abingdon, Oxon, OX14 4RN

and by Routledge
711 Third Avenue, New York, NY 10017

a GlassHouse book

Routledge is an imprint of the Taylor & Francis Group, an informa business

British Library Cataloguing in Publication Data
A catalogue record for this book is available from the British Library

Library of Congress Cataloging-in-Publication Data
Names: Pappas, George D. (Lawyer), author.
Title: The literary and legal genealogy of Native American dispossession : the Marshall cases trilogy / George D. Pappas.
Description: New York : Routledge, 2016. | Series: Indigenous peoples and the law | Includes bibliographical references and index.
Identifiers: LCCN 2016000850| ISBN 9781138188723 (hbk) | ISBN 9781315642130 (ebk)
Subjects: LCSH: Indians of North America—Legal status, laws, etc.—History. | Indians of North America—Relocation. | Indians of North America—Land tenure. | Indians in literature. | Indians of North America—Government relations. | Discourse analysis, Literary—United States—History. | Marshall, John, 1755-1835. | United States. Supreme Court—History. | Land tenure—Government policy—United States.
Classification: LCC KF8205 .P37 2016 | DDC 342.7308/72—dc23
LC record available at http://lccn.loc.gov/2016000850

ISBN: 9781138188723 (hbk)
ISBN: 9781315642130 (ebk)

Typeset in ITC New Baskerville Std
by Swales & Willis Ltd, Exeter, Devon, UK

Contents

Acknowledgments vii

Introduction 1

PART I
Theoretical foundations and the Marshall Trilogy cases **5**

1 Theoretical framework 7

2 The Marshall Trilogy cases: an overview 24

3 Colonial knowledge: a unity of discourses 54

PART II
Refining the Native American **67**

4 Theory of discourse in a colonial context: Edward Said and the American eighteenth-century literary archive 69

5 The discourse of the vanishing Indian in literature 96

6 Fenimore Cooper's *The Last of the Mohicans* 105

7 The wilderness in American art and literature 124

PART III
Resistance to colonial discourse **159**

8 Law and literature 161

9 Cherokee resistance: mimicry as deception 178

Conclusion 209
Bibliography 222
Index 234

Acknowledgments

This research could not have been possible without the support and encouragement of my wife, Ellen P. Pappas. Scholars may be seen to work in splendid isolation at times, but I can attest that but for the devoted support my wife has given me over the course of this research, I could not have completed it.

Special thanks to Patricia Tuitt, Professor of Law and Executive Dean at Birkbeck School of Law, University of London, and Dr Piyel Halder, Senior Lecturer in Law and Acting Director of Graduate Studies, for their support.

Professor Tuitt's consistent engagement and review of my work over the past six and a half years was essential to the development of my book. Her advice and encouragement, especially during the depths of difficult moments during my journey, were priceless to the ultimate completion of this research. Professor's Tuitt's review of the theoretical elements of this thesis, among numerous other discussions, provided vital insights on the integration of my theoretical foundation to the entire work.

Dr Piyel Halder provided important suggestions on the post-colonial sections of the book. His insights helped me to develop important comparisons between such theorists as Michel Foucault, Edward W. Said and Homi K. Bhabha. His suggestions were especially helpful on the research dealing with Cherokee resistance.

To my son, Alexander Julian Pappas, a special thanks for his profound literary expertise in providing a valuable sounding board to help me explain and articulate my research. I was blessed to have access to his literary and historical mind. Indirectly then I must also thank Goldsmiths College, University of London and Kings College London for their important contributions to my son's education in Early Modern English Literature. As editor, Alexander was exceptional in his ability to improve the clarity and consistency of my book throughout.

I would also like to thank Cherokee (Eastern Band) Supreme Court Justice J. Matthew Martin (retired) for allowing me the opportunity to introduce and discuss my research and to Steven Newcomb, author of *Pagans in the Promised Land*, for his valuable comments, in particular, for helping me appreciate that American Indians, while dispossessed from their numerous ancestral lands, are not a conquered people—for this important reminder, my appreciation.

Last but not least to my daughter, Natalie Youlan Pappas, for reminding me that I am blessed to have a loving and supportive family.

Special thanks also go to the following museums for their kind permission to reproduce the following images in this work:

Cover image of *Sequoyah*. Dr. Barbara Duncan, Education Director and Ethan Clapsaddle, Program Director, Museum of the Cherokee Indian. http://www.cherokeemuseum.org/

Figure 7.1 Thomas Cole *"The Last of the Mohicans"*, Cora Kneeling at the Feet of Tamenund, 1827 oil on canvas. Wadsworth Athenaeum Museum of Art, Hartford, CT. https://thewadsworth.org/

Figure 7.2 Thomas Cole. *The Oxbow* (*View from Mount Holyoke*), 1836. The Metropolitan Museum of Art, New York, N.Y. http://www.metmuseum.org. Image source: Art Resource, New York.

George D. Pappas
Asheville, North Carolina
December 24, 2015

Introduction

> Bosque Redondo: Homage to Yevgeny Yevtshenko
> . . . Oh, my American people!
> I know the melting pot is your guiding metaphor.
> But those with unclean hands—stained with the blood of people
> Who will not melt—besmirch your own clean name:
> the "Indian fighters" and their great battles, their Washitas
> and Sand Creeks, reputations written with the blood of women and children and old men, the missionaries who broke our connections and took our souls in exchange for names in Spanish and English,
> the Indian agents who stole us blind in both the buying and the selling,
> the politicians who say we're extinguished, distant history and garbled fiction, Squanto and Tonto.
>
> (Russell 143–144)

The Anglo-American view that the dispossession of American Indians from their land was inevitable, even ordained, has dominated many historical narratives, not least a particular history of law. Today, the American Indian is reoccupying the discursive space that was created and dominated by Spanish, French, English and later American narratives. It is perhaps a testament to the fortitude of the Indians and the poverty of dominant platitudes woven together by those who engineered the attempted conquest of the Indian that the indigenous Americans survived to reclaim their story, their identity and their culture. While the complete disavowal of the American Indian did not come to pass, their virtual erasure was well within reach by the time of the massacre at Wounded Knee of 1890. If anything is distilled from this research, it is that the virtual demise of the Indians by 1890 was never an inevitable outcome, but could only have been achieved by discursive myths that served, for too long, to provide justification for the attempted conquest of dominant European and American forces bent on appropriating Native Indian land.

The dispossession of Native American lands in North America incorporates a vast array of actors and agents. This book explores the agency of colonial literatures in the actions of explorers, settlers, frontiersman,

U.S. Presidents, religious missionaries, religious zealots, the Vatican, kings, queens, judges, legislators, ministers, gold diggers, traders and hunters. Of the various actors who went about the business of transferring Native lands to colonial stewardship, none had more important a role than the judges who fed upon colonial literature to produce now highly contested legal doctrines.

This book is an analysis of the complex relation between colonial literature and the Trilogy of cases produced by U.S. Supreme court Chief Justice John Marshall: *Johnson v. M'Intosh* (1823), *Cherokee Nation v. Georgia* (1831) and *Worcester v. Georgia* (1832). More than that, it relates a shameful period of shared European and American history, which still impacts on the distribution of lands between peoples across the globe.

Structure of research

This book is divided into three parts. Part I (Chapters 1–3) provides a largely theoretical account of how a particular subject—the Native American Indian—was formed through what Foucault describes as a unity of discourses. This part sets the theoretical framework of the book in the works of Michel Foucault and demonstrates how statements about law, art, literature and a range of others converged to create knowledge about a colonial subject that has served to dispossess that colonial subject of land and other valuable possessions. Part II (Chapters 4–7) substantiates the theory in Part I with particular compelling examples of art literature and law in defining the Native American Indian. In this part, Fennimore Cooper's *The Last of the Mohicans* is examined in detail. Also, Foucault's theory of discourse is specifically applied to the colonial context, drawing upon the work of Edward W. Said. The final part (Part III: Chapters 8–9) demonstrates how and why the colonial knowledge explained in the first part is being interrogated and challenged. In Chapter 8, we examine the law and literature movement as an instance of a re-distribution of discourses that has served to present alternative depictions of the Native American subject. Chapter 9 returns to the Trilogy cases and draws on Homi K. Bhabha's demonstration that even the most oppressive regimes are incapable of preventing resistance.

Chapter 1 establishes the theoretical foundation of the research. The first part of Chapter 1 provides an overview of Michel Foucault's account of how objects of knowledge are produced through discourse—that is, through the circulation, distribution and re-distribution of statements. Such statements take numerous forms—discourse is thus word, image and sound. Foucault's notion of discursive formation and the formation of archives of knowledge is examined in order to provide the framework for the book that argues that the Native American Indian—the subject of the Marshall Trilogy cases was precisely produced through statements, especially statements in art and literature, all trained toward one objective, the objective of producing a special body of knowledge, which we refer to as colonial knowledge. The second part of Chapter 1 explains how Foucault's theory of discourse is worked through the various chapters of this book.

Chapter 2 introduces the cases that comprise the Marshall Trilogy; namely, *Johnson v. M'Intosh* (1823); *Cherokee Nation v. Georgia* (1831) and *Worcester v. Georgia* (1832). It outlines the facts and judgments in these cases and places them in their popular contexts—within the context of American federalism. The purpose of this chapter is to provide the basis for the alternative reading of the Marshall cases with which this research is mainly concerned. The goal of federalism is less prominent as the motivating spur to the Trilogy. Rather, the research argues that the Trilogy cases represent an important landmark in which the legal discourse was joined with other discourses with the 'unified' objective of defining the colonial subject as other.

Chapter 3 introduces for the first time the contours of this alternative reading of the Trilogy cases. It applies Foucault's theory in an effort to demonstrate that what is ostensibly conveyed as legal fact or legal knowledge about the habits and capacities of the Native American Indian owes itself to largely fictional accounts that are disguised in the judgment as objective fact. The conventional writing of legal judgments of the higher courts demands that facts are deemed settled and no longer open to dispute. This feature of legal judgment allowed Marshall free range, with a range of statements about the Native American Indian which, whilst having the potency of settled fact, were not capable of supporting truth claims.

Chapters 4 to 7 provide situated accounts and elaborations of the argument that is sketched in Chapter 3. These chapters examine popular fictional works and other literary narratives of the day (Chapters 5 and 6) and popular landscape paintings in order to demonstrate the convergences between Marshall's account of the habits and capacity of the Native American and accounts of artists and writers. These three illustrate Foucault's notion of a unity of discourses.

Chapter 8 is one of two chapters that focus explicitly on resistance to the colonial archive detailed in the preceding chapters. Arguing that it required a radical redistribution of discursive statements for the colonial archive to unravel, it examines the law and literature movement as one such discursive revolution. Drawing on Peter Goodrich's *Law and the Courts of Love*, it follows that the great value of the law and literature movement is its recognition that literature and other sources (minor jurisprudences) have always haunted legal judgment. It is precisely this recognition that enables a re-reading of the Marshall judgment to reveal its literary sources (those illustrated in Chapters 5–7).

Chapter 9 brings the book to a close by examining Bhabha's work in *The Location of Culture* to demonstrate how the nature of discourse enable the colonized to resist—even against a solid colonial archive. It returns to the Marshall Trilogy in order to reveal and apply Bhabha's notions of mimicry and hybridity.[1]

Note

1 Mimicry as Bhabha describes it is an "exaggerated copying of language, culture, manners, and ideas. This exaggeration means that mimicry is repetition with difference, and so it is not evidence of the colonized's servitude. In fact, this mimicry is a comic approach to colonial discourse, because it mocks and undermines the ongoing pretentions of colonialism and empire" (Huddart 57). Hybridity by contrast refers to the fact that cultures are not discrete phenomena, but instead always in contact with each other, which leads to mixed-ness. Bhabha insists less on hybridity than on hybridization. In other words, Bhabha examines hybridity as an on-going process (7).

Part I

Theoretical foundations and the Marshall Trilogy cases

Chapter 1

Theoretical framework

> I would like to show with precise examples that in analyzing discourses themselves, one sees the loosening of the embrace, apparently so tight, of words and things, and the emergence of a group of rules proper to discursive practice. The rules define not the dumb existence of a reality, or the canonical use of a vocabulary, but the ordering of objects . . . A task that consists of not—of no longer—treating discourses as groups of signs (signifying elements referring to contents or representations) but as practices that systematically form the objects of which they speak.
>
> M. Foucault, *The Archaeology of Knowledge* 54

In this book I argue that literary texts—fiction and non-fictional works—informed the subject with which Judge Marshall's Trilogy of cases was concerned: the Native American. Outside of literature and other discourses there never was an individual, or group of individuals, out there in the American wilderness that announced themselves as Native American. As the quotation from Foucault demonstrates, both subject and object are not simply the *a priori* matter on which discourses speak, comment or critique. The existence of subject and object is instead a function of the circulation of discourses.

Initially inspired by Edward Said's analysis of the invention of the colonized subject in both *Orientalism* and *Culture and Imperialism*, this research seeks to produce a similar account of capture by the European Americans of those in prior settlement of lands.[1] Chapters 4, 6, 7 and 8 draw upon nineteenth-century fictional writings and pictorial landscapes to demonstrate how the aesthetic forms produced a figure of the native that resonates today—as child rather than steward etc.[2] This chapter sets the theoretical framework by examining Michel Foucault's theory of discourse; precisely, his claim that discourse cannot simply be relegated to the sphere of words and other signs.

Michel Foucault: discourse and discursive formations

Although it may be desirable to 'search discourse for' a unifying meaning in Michel Foucault's work, this is not possible since Foucault has several uses for the term. In several instances Foucault has used discourse to 'signify' a body of statements about an object: "we shall call discourse a group of statements in so far as they belong to the same discursive formation" (M. Foucault, *The Archaeology of Knowledge* 131):

> Discourse is constituted by a group of sequences of signs, in so far as they are statements, that is, in so far as they can be assigned particular modalities of existence. And if I succeed in showing, as I shall try to do shortly, that the law of such a series is precisely what I have so far called a *discursive formation,* if I succeed in showing that this discursive formation really is the principle of dispersion and redistribution, not of formulations, not of sentences, not of propositions, but of statements (in the sense in which I have used this word), the term discourse can be defined as the group of statements that belong to a single system of formation; thus I shall be able to speak of clinical discourse, economics discourse, the discourse of natural history, psychiatric discourse.
>
> (121)

For Foucault then the distribution of statements creates seemingly distinct spheres and operations of discourse, such that we can discuss scientific discourse, for example, and in a manner that enables this research to claim that literature has affected the law. This statement presupposes the distribution of statements in such a way as to form a body of discourse that we can call law, ostensibly as distinct from a body of discourse called literature.

Michel Foucault has produced the most comprehensive account of the discursive concept. According to Foucault, discourse denotes how *statements* are dispersed, or redistributed around particular subjects such as madness, education or history. The particular object that forms the focus of my research can be thought of inclusively as legal capacity, but more specifically, the capacity of people defined by ethnicity, or nationality, to manage their own land and resources. Statements about the capacity of people abound, but literature (fiction and non-fiction) has, at least until the twentieth century, been the dominant source. Statements about *legal* capacity are to be found in legal texts; however, this book explores the way these statements are 'dispersed' and 'redistributed' between legal and various other texts.[3]

Foucault's use of the term 'discourse' is important not only to this book, but to other diciplines beyond law. Whether economics, politics, medicine or law are subjects of discussion or analysis, Foucault's varied uses of the term provide an important analytical framework to inform the institutional rules that constitute the perception of objects. Such objects may be a definition of insane versus sane, criminal behavior versus non-criminal behavior or civilized versus uncivilized.

Thus far we have merely relied upon a simple definition of 'discourse' as statements. Such statements, of course, are not contained or produced solely in words but can be formed in paintings or musical notation. Yet this definition fails to explain how a statement or discourse oscillates between sign and object. The definition fails to tell us why discourse, according to Foucault, is more than a statement about an object in *prior* existence.

Discourse and discursive formations

> The discursive formation is the general enunciative system that governs a group of verbal performances—a system that is not alone in governing it, since it also obeys, and in accordance with its other dimension, logical, linguistic, and psychological system. What has been called 'discursive formation' divides up the general place of things said at the specific level of statements?
>
> (M. Foucault, *The Archaeology of Knowledge* 130)

The enunciative system governs statements. It is a system around those statements that can form legal discourse. This system is not a fixed unchanging one—how the system governs legal discourse is affected by alterations to the enunciative system itself—which is in turn a function of:

> it is a body of anonymous, historical rules, always determined in the time and space that have defined a given period, and for a given social, economic, geographical, or linguistic area, the conditions of operation of the enunciative function.
>
> (131)

That which determines the operation of the enunciative system—the context: historical, cultural, etc. is the archive. The archive establishes statements as events. The archive consolidates what are highly contingent and irregular statements into a seemingly given place.

In Foucault's *The Archaeology of Knowledge* we are introduced to an important analysis about how statements, or discourses, are affected by the context of the era so significantly that, given the same object, a new era might reconstitute statements to transform the object or subject. Interdisciplinary analysis is part of a context that can affect the archive and its regulatory effects on statements. Indeed, the cultural assault on the legal and literary archives of knowledge occurs in ways that impact on the way they are perceived as distinct domains of knowledge (see Chapter 3). This is precisely what enables me in this book to both demonstrate how discourse produced a debased legal subject in the American Indian and yet show how that same discourse can, through engagements such as Said's, represent the same object in ways that allows for his, or her agency and resistance to the very discourses from which they were originally repressed. In short, in *The Archaeology of Knowledge* Foucault introduces the concepts of the historical *a priori* and archive. Foucault states "they are all these systems of statements (whether events or things) that I propose to call *archive*" (145). Foucault introduces the concept of the archive as "systems that establish statements as events (with their own conditions and domain of appearance) and things (with their own possibility and field of use)" (145). Foucault sees the *archive* as an historical *a priori*, but here Foucault seeks to avoid splitting up so-called formal *a prioris* (those without contingence) and informal *a prioris* (those whose existence is purely empirical), but rather proposes a conceptual *a priori* that he describes as "the group of rules that characterize a discursive practice": but these rules are not imposed from the outside on the elements that they relate together; they are caught up in the very things that they connect [. . .] The *a priori* of positives is not only the system of a temporal dispersion; It is itself a transformable group" (144).

The archive represents a field within which statements are not only formed, but limited by their rules of discursive practice. Foucault, while interested in the discursive statements that collectively produce the knowledge about an object or subject, is uniquely interested in the archival site where the statements are derived from. The archive is neither universal nor timeless, but relative and subjective to the time and space of its geographical site. The archive is not a set of rules imposed externally, based on individual consciousness; it is a space of discursive rules that, whether conscious or not, limits the range of possibilities that discursive statements can interpret in a given historical period. Foucault states

> it is that which, at the very root of the statement-event, and in that which embodies it, defines at the outset the system of its enunciability [. . .] it is that which defines the mode of occurrence of the statement-thing; it is the system of its functioning.
>
> (146)

How can statements found in literature about the habits and sensitivities of American Indians become akin to sworn statements, or witness evidence in a legal setting, such as the Marshall Trilogy cases, that examines the legal capacity of American Indians? A starting point must be with Foucault's claim that such statements, formed through language, 'act on the body' in making this claim.[4]

This question only arises through an understanding of the social contingency of the archive—a contemporary archive of knowledge that precisely allows for the contamination of discourses that hitherto appear as independent and self-sufficient—the separate domains of law and literature (see Part III).

From formation to dispersal

As Foucault demonstrates in *The History of Sexuality* the multiplication and dispersal of discourses can never be a neutral, or benign effect of the object that is produced. Discourse is simply powerful—which is not to say that discursive power can never be deployed in resistance to repressive regimes. The regulation of sexuality could never have been effected through silence, or through a want of statements about sexuality. Was the discourse, for example, between doctor, parent and child on masturbation a result of the empirical event of child masturbation, or was that triad discourse precisely the one and only 'event?'

It is the opening up of a text beyond its founding that denotes the distribution and dispersion that Foucault identifies as the discursive space that arranges how subjects are perceived. Not a single defining text established the truth about a subject, but rather the originating text established a confined dispersal of discourses or meanings that over time, arranged how subjects are discussed, or perceived: "in this way we can understand the inevitable necessity, within these fields of discursivity, for a 'return to the origin.' This return, which is part of the discursive field itself, never stops modifying it . . . it constitutes an effective and necessary task of transforming the discursive practice itself" (Foucault, *What Is an Author?* 116). As Foucault argues, while the author and the text may initiate a shift or changing *episteme* about an object, the initiating text is not the totality of the discursive space being developed but rather exemplifies a beginning phase into a new discursive space. The initialing text is also part of the discursive dispersal. The author and text become part of the discursive formation that gradually defines an object through the distribution of varied discourses that relate back or "return to the origin" (116). The critical effect of the dispersion of the 'origin' over time becomes the anonymity of the discourse beyond the author; in other words, a transformation of an *a priori* emerges, or in the legal jargon of legal judgment, 'findings of fact.' Foucault stipulates that

> all discourses, whatever their status, form, value, and whatever the treatment to which they will be subjected, would then develop in the anonymity of a murmur. We would no longer hear the questions that have been rehashed for so long: Who really spoke? It is really he and not someone else? Instead, there would be other questions, like these: What are the modes of existence of this discourse?
>
> (119–20)

Marshall spoke about the Indian in disparaging terms in the Marshall Trilogy. While Marshall is, arguably, the ostensible author, the subject of his discourse—the Indian—had been formed long before his judgment. We can imagine the Native American as the "anonymous murmur" where those statements now circulate as empirical fact and become the source of an authoritative judgment that authorizes the dispossession of Native Indians of their lands. Contrary to the conventional interpretations of the Trilogy rulings, I shall argue how counter-discourses about Native Americans were excluded by judicial omissions; omissions that failed to highlight their expertise as farmers, peoples capable of political and social advancements that exceeded the cultural status of most frontier Americans. I shall argue that the institutional arrangement of legal judgment, an arrangement that builds legal doctrines upon findings of fact, distorted the image of the Native American in the Marshall Trilogy cases. How this history was excluded from the Marshall Trilogy findings exposes the power and knowledge relations that underscored how images of the Native Americans were formed. The collective colonial history of America, through the power of conquest and literature, was able to project discourses about the Native American which, over time, became what Foucault refers to as a "murmur," or as I propose, the natural state of things by the time *Johnson v. M'Intosh* was heard by the U.S. Supreme Court (119–20).

To continue to elaborate this process of dispersal, in describing how discourses about sexuality between the eighteenth and nineteenth century became, by Victorian times, an apparently taboo subject, Foucault reveals that rather than silencing discourses on sexuality, the attempt to regulate discussions of sexuality by official prohibitions had the opposite effect, generating an even greater distribution throughout society. This distribution derived from power sources such as parents, schools and church and between individuals to the extent that the discourses on children served to define how sexuality was regulated. In examining his 'repressive hypothesis' Foucault observed that:

> speaking about children's sex, inducing educators, physicians, Administrators, and parents to speak of it, or speaking to them about it, causing children themselves to talk about it, and enclosing them in a web of discourses which sometimes address them, sometimes speak about them, or impose canonical bits of knowledge on them, or use them as a basis for constructing a science that is beyond their grasp—all this together enables us to link an intensification of the interventions of power to a multiplication of discourse.
>
> (Foucault, *The Repressive Hypothesis* 311)

Foucault thus presents the 'intensification of power' through the manifestation and dispersal of discourse on a subject. Similarly, power regulates which discourses will be multiplied, thereby excluding some and accepting others.

The very articulation of a discourse about an object is manifested by the play between power and knowledge. Using Foucault's research on how child masturbation became a subject of concern in the nineteenth century, he identified the power relations between parents and children. He introduced the body of knowledge, during the nineteenth century, which derived from parental monitoring of child masturbation. The nexus between the power relations (i.e., parents and children) and knowledge (i.e., the knowledge obtained from parental monitoring) was brought to the attention of doctors, so much so that a new discourse on children's masturbation was developed as a result of the power relations between parents, children and doctors. The nexus between various power relations and knowledge formed where a discourse becomes a point of inflection or reference between the knowledge and power relations (Schirato 48).

Foucault states that knowledge is organized or arranged as a discourse according to a regime of rules that seek to limit the field as such. Is the exclusion of non-disciplinary knowledge a source of power and discourse? The two are joined rather than distinct parts. The transformative process that produces this regulated discourse is a synthesis of power and knowledge. It is here perhaps that Foucault's concept of power as productive is most illustrative. He states that

> we must cease once and for all to describe the effects of power in negative terms: it 'excludes,' it 'represses,' it 'censors,' it 'abstracts,' it 'masks,' it 'conceals.' In fact, power produces; it produces reality; it produces domains of objects and ritual of truth.
>
> (Fitzpatrick 15)

It is in this sense that the discourse of child masturbation became a domain of reality. Golder and Fitzpatrick were keen to pick up on this point about how Foucault sees power relations as a transformative process by institutions that regulate the individual. Here discourses about the individual within the context of a regulated discipline exemplify the transformative nature of objects or individuals resulting from power relations. Fitzpatrick notes:

> in formulating his concept of a disciplinary power which produced the subject upon which it acted through the articulation of a norm, Foucault was attempting to isolate a modality of power which exceeded the logic of the state and which transcended the usual theatres of sate power. He was searching for the exercise of power in places where the political theorist or the state had not been wont to look . . . he was searching for power's effects "at its extremities, at its outer limits at the point where it becomes capillary".
>
> (Fitzpatrick 21)

To illustrate Fitzpatrick's point, take Foucault's analysis of how a village laborer's playful encounter with a girl becomes transformed into an exercise of power and a broadside of discourses on sexual deviance:

> What is the signifant thing about this story? The pettiness of it all; the fact that this everyday occurrence in the life of village sexuality, these inconsequential bucolic pleasures, could become, from a certain item, the object not only of a collective intolerance but of a judicial action, a medical intervention, a careful clinical examination and an entire theoretical elaboration. [. . .] [S]o it was that our society—and it was doubtless the first in history to take such measures—assembled around these timeless gestures, these barely furtive pleasures between simple-minded adults and alert children, a whole machinery for speechifying, analyzing, and investigating.
>
> (Foucault, *The Repressive Hypothesis* 313)

The power relations between parent, village officials, judge, and doctor—a whole web of discourses—would now be formed to arrange how a simple gesture between an adult and a child would now constitute a new reality or perception about social deviance. Not only would a new arrangement of discourses about sexual deviance be constituted, but discourses that would otherwise speak about the subject, would now be hushed or regulated or excluded. "One can be fairly certain that during this same period the Lapcourt schoolmaster was instructing the little villagers to mind their language and not talk about all these things aloud" (313).

From these examples and analysis, it is hard to see how a discourse on the capacity of subjects to *own their land* was available to Marshall to apply as doctrine in the Trilogy cases. The discourse on the Native American was rather the production of that other domain of discourse—the discourse on *capacity*.

The research

Foucault's insights into the nature of discourse form the intellectual platform for this book. Starting with the Marshall Trilogy cases, this research uses Said *et al.* to bring to the fore the disorderliness of the colonial archive—the essential disarray as a contingent element of colonial power. Central to the colonial *archive* was a disaggregation of prior distinct and independent fields of knowledge. As so many post-colonial theorists have demonstrated, the colonial discourses saw an assertion of power on the cultural realm, more than by the use of guns and bullets. Neither literature, nor law were allowed against the exigencies of the colonial regime to demand and hold their distinctive places. We look to Foucault to explore the construction of the archive but we must also look to examine the precise characteristics and content of the colonial archive beyond Foucault. In Chapter 4, I discuss this by questioning the colonial archive, allowing this book to draw on numerous literary discourses from captive narratives, fiction, histories and poems of the Native American that reflect these images of the Native American that were accepted as sworn statements by the Marshall court. Applying Foucault and Said to the Marshall Trilogy cases, the discursive formations that helped to situate the privileged images of the Native Americans included discourses that portrayed them as noble savages, savages, helpless wards and finally as a "domestic dependent nation" (*Cherokee Nation v. Georgia* 18). The privileging of images about Native Americans in the Marshall rulings *excluded* any representation that cast the Native American as a farmer, a land owner or civilized human being. What is unique about this book is showing how these discourses were incorporated as findings of fact, or as *de facto* sworn statements in the John Marshall opinions. What I hope to illustrate is how the author of non-scientific, empirical statements about Native Americans disappears only to embed these as free floating *factual* statements that can be incorporated into legal judgments and, once within the judgment, to assume their authorship in the form of testimony. Discourses, in other words, about the Native American psyche and way of life were incorporated as mere findings of fact in legal judgment.

Conventional interpretations of the Marshall Trilogy cases focus on the political context of Federalism and challenges by such southern states as South Carolina over tariffs in relation to the Federal Government. These interpretations seek to cast the Trilogy cases as part of John Marshall's emerging Federalism and developing of Judicial Review. This research departs from this conventional approach by using Foucault's theory of *discursive* formations to examine the least contested areas of the legal judgment; namely, the findings of fact in the rulings themselves. By extension, an examination of Marshall's findings of fact opens up the influences of literature that would otherwise not be seen as affecting how the legal capacity of Native Americans was either undermined, or "impaired" by literary discursive formations that cast the Native Americans as uncivilized and savage.[5] Foucault's *discursive* formation is an important framework for assessing how disciplines like law, medicine, history and education, through their underlying rules or customs, can limit or reject some approaches to interpretation while accepting others. In Foucault's Inaugural Lecture at the College de France his essay "The Order of Discourse" elaborates upon how disciplines and professions can limit and exclude statements about a subject or object, thereby acting as a gate keeper as to what discourses (i.e., statements) will be permitted to help constitute the object:

> This will to truth, like other systems of exclusion, rests on an institutional support: it is both reinforced and renewed by whole strata of practices, such as pedagogy, of course: and the system of books, publishing, libraries: learned societies in the past and laboratories now. But is also renewed, no doubt more profoundly, by the way in which knowledge is put to work, valorized, distributed, and in a sense attributed, in a society.
>
> (Foucault, *The Order of Discourse* 55)

Foucault's 'will to truth' can only be realized at a specific time and only if it meets the rules of a given discipline. If a 'will to truth' fails to comport to a set of archival rules within a given set of power relations, it will not be allowed to occupy a discursive space:

> It is always possible that one might speak the truth in the space of a wild exteriority, but one is "in the true" only by obeying the rules of a discursive "policing" which one has to reactivate in each of one's discourses. The discipline is a principle of control over the production of discourse. The discipline fixes limits for discourse by the action of an identity which takes the form of a permanent re-actuation of the rules. (61)

Conventional interpretations of the Marshall Trilogy cases also exhibit instances of this mode of 'discursive policing,' according to which it is only permissible to read the cases in restricted ways. As an example of how interpretations of the Marshall Trilogy rulings provide an instance of 'discursive policing,' one can see the limited way these opinions are viewed and so serve to overlook how conventional interpretations of the Trilogy cases ignored important literary influences on the rulings.

Conventional readings of the Marshall Trilogy cases *Johnson v. M'Intosh* (1821), *Cherokee Nation v. Georgia* (1831) and *Worcester v. Georgia* (1832) for example, seek to interpret how U.S. Supreme Court Chief Justice John Marshall's opinions reflected his attempt to forge a place for Federalism through constitutional interpretations that limited state sovereignty in relation to the Federal Government. Tim A. Garrison cites various interpretative approaches to Marshall's opinion in *Johnson* that ranged from international law to Marshall's attempt to reconcile opposing opinions within the U.S. court. "First, and obviously, Marshall was influenced by the existing treaties on international law [. . .] It also seems rational to suggest, considering Marshall's mode of operation, that his opinion was the result of a compromise between extreme positions with the chamber of the Court" (Garrison 95). Garrison sums up his interpretation of the reasoning underpinng Marshall's opinion, as embracing a Federalist conception of Indian vs. the states.[6]

> the best way to explain Marshall's opinion is to return to his intellectual core: his conception of the Constitution as an expansive, flexible framework of government, his desire to promote the authority of the federal government and the Court, and a patriotic urge to act for the greater interest of the United States. (96)

Federalism was part of the social context in which the archive relating to capacity of the colonized was produced, refined, multiplied and dispersed.

By foregrounding the theoretical difference between this book and Garrison's explanation of Marshall's opinion in *Johnson v. M'Intosh* (together with other writers such as Norgren 2004; Robertson 2005; and Kades 2001 which this research distinguishes in my chapter on the Marshall cases), I demonstrate how conventional interpretations of *Johnson* limit the discursive field and exclude how literary discourses were absorbed as sworn statements or findings of fact by the Marshall Court. Conventional interpretations of the Trilogy cases link Marshall's opinions to his Federalist position on challenges between the U.S. Federal Government and southern states up to the mid-1830s. In Chapter 2 of this book, which situates the Marshall rulings, this research will foreground their political context, especially for the case of *Worcester v. Georgia* (1832), in relation to the political and constitutional challenges confronted by the U.S. Supreme Court and President Andrew Jackson.[7] From a theoretical viewpoint, conventional interpretations of the Marshall cases do not engage the structure of legal judgments and how judgments can be formed by literary discourses or, to use Foucault's term, the "archive" at a given moment in history.

Law and literature: knowledge and power

Foucault's discursive theory provides a framework to comprehend 'institutional'contexts that form, as Foucault describes, the *discursive formations* that constitute the ordering of objects as compared to language that merely identifies objects. The ordering of objects constitutes a critical part of Foucault's discursive analysis; namely, it reveals the limits and contours of discursive truths (for example, knowledge) during a given historical period, or context. This is what Foucault means when he states "the rules (or discourse practice) define not the dumb existence of a reality, or the canonical use of vocabulary, but the ordering of objects" (Foucault, *The Archaeology of Knowledge* 54). Foucault sees the normative arrangment of objects through discourse as constituting realities about objects. In particular, he identifies the 'institutional' arrangement of such discourses so as to constitute an image, or perception of reality of an object that would otherwise not exist. Stated otherwise, you can have words describe an object but how, or why those words are arranged is the focus of Foucault's discourse: what rules, what institutional practices and what historical contexts led to the formation of that specific discourse?

Foucault does not seek to explain how discourse describes 'things,' or 'objects,' but instead seeks to enhance our understanding of how institutional practices *regulate* how discourses are formed. It is not the 'things' that discourse forms that are the knowledge basis to Foucault's theory, but the rules and practices within discourse which establish the arrangement or perception of object, or things. "I would like to show that 'discourses,' in the form in which they can be heard or read, are not as one might expect, a mere intersection of things and words" (53). It is the "nexus of regularities that govern their dispersion" (53). Foucault identifies a connection between the 'regularities,' and practices, especially those by professional institutions, that implicitly govern how discourses will arrange objects. This implicit nexus revealed by Foucault's theory situates a relationship between discourses and knowledge.

A reading of Foucault seems to suggest that knowledge is not something to be discovered, but something that is "arranged" or discursively formed. "When one describes the formation of the objects of a discourse, one tries to locate the relations that characterize a discursive practice" (53). As a prelude to understanding Foucault's theory of knowledge and power, one needs to appreciate that discourse is the outcome of a regulated space that limits not only how knowledge of objects is constituted but the regulation of their dispersal; "[. . .] we must not forget that a rule of formation is neither the determination of an object, nor the characterization of a type of enunciation, nor the form or content of a concept, but the principle of their multiplicity and dispersion" (191). It is through the principle of 'multiplicity and dispersion' that we can next examine Foucault's power–knowledge nexus as it relates to the 'bio power' of bodies.

A further elaboration of Foucault's power–knowledge nexus is critical to our understanding not only of how a regulated discursive space limits the scope of statements, but also of how such statements reflect the power over bodies. Through the power that regulates the dispersion of statements through discourses, Foucault deciphers how bio-powers are formed to impact populations not only from institutional regulation but also on the individual level. In other words, Foucault describes the dispersion of power not only from the top but also between people at the individual level of society.

The law and literature movement is itself an important example of how discourses are formed and dispersed, transforming in important ways the perceived object of study. In Chapter 3 I demonstrate how the constitutive nature of the legal enunciative system has been put [into] question—as much as has been the question of the scope of [. . .] literary discourse[s]. The relationship between law and literature, the merging of a whole set of disciplines, is part of the 'conditions of possibility' of Said's *Orientalism* or Bhabha's *The Location of Culture.* It is that which enabled Goodrich in *Law and the Courts of Love* to speak of the silent fiction in literature—the aesthetic voice which the remnants of different discursive traditions and different sets of discursive regulatory practices aim (ultimately with only partial success) to silence. Goodrich was not attentive to the colonial archive, which I will argue had long infused the boundaries between law and literature that he exposes as being policed. The opposition of fact and fiction, truth and opinion was central to making colonial violence possible, as was indeed the placing into contestation of the civil versus the savage through slavery and servitude (Tuitt 95).

The structure of legal judgment

The legal judgment is an example par excellence of a structural and institutional incorporation of a particular set of discourses. The English Common Law tradition, which was incorporated into early American jurisprudence, has long adopted a deductive approach in cases of first instance starting in the twelfth and thirteenth centuries. The common law was developed initially by the courts of the Exchequer, the King's Bench, and the court of Common Pleas. Ultimately, these three courts were consolidated into Common Law Courts or Courts of First Instance. Courts of First Instance accept, or decide facts and information with respect to controversies. Judges can act as arbiters of fact and upon the close of the 'facts in issue' judges apply prior case law in the absence of statute or create legal doctrines where the law is silent on a given set of facts. Common law judges seek to follow precedent, or *stare decisis* when applying the relevant law to a given set of facts.[8] While judges can deviate from precedent if no law has been developed by prior courts, or the legislature, the structure of legal judgment strives to resolve disputes on the basis of prior judicial decisions. According to Bierce:

> **Precedent**, *n.* In Law, a previous decision, rule or practice which, in the absence of a definite statute, has whatever force and authority a Judge may choose to give it, thereby greatly simplifying his task of doing as he pleases. As there are precedents for everything, he has only to ignore those that make against his interest and accentuate those in the line of his desire.
>
> (Bierce)

Facts represent sworn statements received by a Court of First Instance. Appeal courts rarely review the facts *de novo* and instead review appeals in terms of whether the Courts of First Instance applied the law correctly to a given set of facts.[9]

A key feature of the appellate judgment is the assumption that the facts upon which important legal judgments are made are settled; i.e., they are no longer capable of being disputed. Only rarely would an appellate judge remand a case back to a Court of First Instance to revisit facts. In such instances the error of the lower court is the precipitating factor.

Judges seek to position themselves as adjudicators, or fact finders of information and evidence prior to formulating a "judgment" or legal opinion in relation to the facts in issue. According to *Black's Law Dictionary*, judgment is "conclusion of law upon facts found or admitted by the parties or upon their default in the course of the suit. Decision or sentence of the law, given by a court of justice or other competent tribunal, as the result of proceedings instituted therein, *Allegheny County v. Maryland Casualty Co*, C.C.A. Pa., 132 F. 2d 894, 897" (Black 842).

At the appellate level most rulings do not question the trial court's findings of fact but instead assess whether the law was applied correctly. At first glance it appears that the collection of facts is but an objective collection of information, or admission by sworn statements until a point is reached where the court can render its judgment or majority opinion.[10] It is at this seemingly objective phase, "the finding of fact" stage, of the legal judgment, before issues of jurisdiction and legal doctrines are introduced to support a judicial decision, that legal judgment's structure is critical to this research.

Where this book establishes a non-conventional approach to the Trilogy cases is in its examination of the *findings of fact*, as they relate to the Native Americans, as being anything but objective evidence. The literary archive, or discursive tradition, that contextualizes John Marshall's depiction of Native Americans in the Trilogy cases was shaped by many writers. Writers of varied literary genres transformed the Native American from a savage, menacing and uncivilized creature into a noble savage, a ward, a pupil, and to the status of "domestic dependent nations" (*Worcester v. Georgia* 18). John Marshall's judicial position in *Worcester*, for example, depicts Native Americans and their lands as 'domestic dependent nations' only after the judicial *findings* of the history and civilization dispossessed Native Americans of much of their lands east of the Mississippi. Through a stroke of judicial reasoning, Marshall had prepared the legal dispossession of the Native Americans from their land when he "impaired" the legal capacity of Native Americans from fee simple owners of their land to one of occupancy in his first ruling under *Johnson* (*Johnson v. M'Intosh* 574).

The dissemination of literary discourses with respect to the Marshall Trilogy cases exemplifies a non-conventional assessment of these rulings. The literary *archive* in this book will demonstrate how such discourses demonstrate a play within legal judgment between literature and legal judgment in ways that would otherwise be overlooked using the conventional methods that seek to interpret judicial decisions in the space of both political and legal discourses.

This book examines how judges' acceptance of legal judgment's findings of fact permit an elaboration of Foucault's role of discourses and his influence on such theorists as Edward W. Said and his *Orientalism* and *Culture and Imperialism* with their examination of colonial literature and Homi K. Bhabha and his theory of *The Location of Culture* on colonial discourses; this is where this book departs from a conventional interpretation of the Marshall Trilogy cases. The conventional interpretations about the Marshall judgments, for example, discounted the political, cultural and legal resistance by Native Americans. Bhabha's theory in *The Location of Culture* is useful in foregrounding the sites of resistance by Native Americans that are overlooked in conventional approaches to interpreting the Marshall judgments.

Foucault writes in *Power and Discipline* that "power produces knowledge . . . power and knowledge directly imply one another . . . there is not power relation without the correlative constitution of a field of knowledge, nor any knowledge that does not presuppose and constitute at the same time power relations (1995: 27)" (quoted in Schirato 48). Hence, power and knowledge are connected through discourse. For Foucault discourse is the point at which power and knowledge intersect: but what does this signify?

Unity of colonial discourses

The set of discourses that this book examines were united in their objective in defining the limits of colonialism. In discussing unity of discourse, Foucault argues

> Perhaps one should confine one's attention to those groups of statements that have one and the same object the discourses on melancholia or neurosis, for example. But one would soon realize that each of these discourses *constitutes* [my emphasis] its object and worked it to the point of transforming it altogether.
>
> (Foucault, *The Archaeology of Knowledge* 35–36)

It is interesting to note that Foucault sees the convergence of similar discourses upon a subject, or object, as the 'constituting' process by which the object itself is defined. Otherwise stated, it is not that the subject exists to be discovered independently of Foucault's discourse, but that reality is interpreted in a specific way (i.e., discursively) as to be constituted and transformed by its very *interpretation.* While the physical elements of a subject may exist outside of discursive spaces (i.e., trees, the body, etc.), the perception of that subject can be constituted based upon the convergence of statements that describe the limits or characteristics of that subject. Herein lies Foucault's discursive process that constitutes a reality at a given period in *history* [my emphasis]. It is also instructive to note that Foucault and Said diverge on this point; namely, where Said sees colonial discourses (real or imagined) as representing the Orient, Foucault, by contrast, situates his discourse within a historical *episteme.* Young states that

> the point about Orientalism, however, in Said's account, is that it develops initially as an imaginative and academic practice, involving a form of representation that misrepresents what is really there . . . Foucault is concerned with the way that knowledge was utilized as part of, a function in, a material practice.
>
> (Young 399)

For Foucault the historical, or *episteme,* produce statements or *enunciations* without any coherent plan or strategy, but simply by virtue of their historical creation as statements, they gather together through institutional filtering, such as medicine, or law, to create discursive spaces that constituted the perception and interpretation of a subject. This is not to state that Said's Orientialism is without utility for this research, but rather one begins to see that Said cannot be divorced from Foucault in order to understand how discourses work both in their formation and in their representation of either the Orient or the 'other.' Moreover, while Said focuses on the literary text as a precursor and enabler of nineteenth-century colonialism, Foucault expands the range of literary sites that extend beyond the text or its structure to include moments in history where statements include not only text, but also images and events. Taken together, Foucault and Said provide a valuable theoretical platform to investigate discursive formations that situated the findings of fact in the Marshall Trilogy cases.

In this work the discourse analysis articulated by Foucault and Said is utilized in arranging the statements that serve to situate discursive contexts or archives around the Native American subject. "The regularity of statements, both in general form and dispersion, come to represent a discursive field; a 'family of statements' that in betraying a certain 'positivity' can be (re)traced and linked to a constituting field of power–knowledge'"(Graham 10). From 1620 through the 1830s, American literary genres formed rhetorical images that served to create privileged readings of the Native Americans. Certainly these rhetorical images were established by the time the majority opinions in the Marshall Trilogy cases were written. The statements constituted a discursive grid that informed the Marshall judgments as to the meanings of the Native American. Foucault situates how statements can serve as literary or institutional platforms to inform later perceptions about an object "they are invested in techniques that put them into position, in practices that derive from them, in the social relations that they form, or, through those relations, modify" (Foucault, *The Archaeology of Knowledge* 139).

The effect of the literary discourses as sworn statements through the findings of fact in the Marshall judgments helped to constitute, in Marshall's mind, a perception of the Native American that would otherwise not be possible. This book will demonstrate that the early colonial literary genres, that is, the *archive* that preceded the Marshall Trilogy judgments, were incorporated as factual findings to the legal doctrines that informed Marshall's opinions. While the legal controversies that formed the subject matter in the Marshall Trilogy cases dealt with land titles, federalism and judicial review, historical and cultural sworn statements about American Indians were founded on assorted literary discourses—discourses that would not be identified as finding of fact but for this book's non-conventional approach to interpreting the judgments of the Trilogy cases.

Notes

1 Until 1815 the word *Americans* had generally been used to refer to Native Americans; after 1815 it meant European Americans (Loewen 123).

2 In his majority opinion in *Cherokee Nation v. Georgia* (1831), John Marshall described American Indians as 'hapless wards' and 'domestic dependent

nations' to emphasize a perceived Indian inability to survive without the assistance and benevolence of the American Republic.

3 "Statements do not exist in the same sense in which a language (*langue*) exists, and, with that language, a collection of signs defined by their contrasting characteristics and their rules of use; a language in fact is never given in itself, in its totality; it could only be as in a secondary way. In the oblique form of a description that would take it as its object" (Foucault, *The Archaeology of Knowledge* 95). "One should not be surprised, then, if one has failed to find structural criteria of unity for the statement; this is because it is not in itself a unit, but a function that cuts across a domain of structures and possible unities, which reveals them, with concrete contents, in time and space" (97–8).

4 Statements for Foucault, if repeated over time, accrue a 'truth' and 'materiality' that can appropriate certain truths. "Thus the statement circulates, is used, disappears, allows or prevents the realization of a desire, serves or resists various interests, participates in challenge and struggle and becomes a theme of appropriation or rivalry" (Foucault, *The Archaeology of Knowledge* 118).

5 Chief Justice Marshall described the legal capacity of the Native Americans in *Johnson v. M'Intosh* as "necessarily to a considerable extent impaired" (*Johnson v. M'Intosh* 575).

6 Federalists were led by Alexander Hamilton and John Adams. Federalists dominated regions in the North East and coastal regions of the United States. Federalists advocated a strong national government while at the same time imposing limits on state rights. A cornerstone of Federalism, at least with respect to an examination of John Marshall, was his judicial focus on demarcating Federal authority by way of U.S. Supreme Court *judicial review;* that is, the ability of the U.S. Supreme Court to declare a state law unconstitutional. John Marshall is known for his majority opinion in *Marbury v. Madison,* 5 U.S. 137 (1803).

7 See Chapter 2 "The Marshall Trilogy Cases," 54.

8 "Latin for 'to stand by things decided.' Stare decisis is essentially the doctrine of precedent. Courts cite *stare decisis* when an issue has been previously brought to the court and a ruling already issued. Generally, courts will adhere to the previous ruling, though this is not universally true.'" http://www.law.cornell.edu/wex/stare_decisis accessed March 5, 2016.

9 De novo "Anew; afresh; a second time. A venire de novo is a writ for summoning a jury for the second trial of a case which has been sent back from above for a new trial" (Black 435).

10 "A majority opinion is usually written by one judge and represents the principles of law which a majority of his colleagues on the court deem operative in a given decision" (Black 1092).

Chapter 2

The Marshall Trilogy cases

An overview

> John Marshall was the longest serving Chief Justice in Supreme Court history and played a significant role in the development of the American legal system and federal Indian law. He established that the courts have the power of 'judicial review' which is the authority to strike down laws that violate the U.S. Constitution. Marshall has been credited with cementing the position of the American judiciary as an independent and influential branch of government. The Marshall Court made several important decisions relating to federalism, shaping the balance of power between the federal government and the states. Among these decisions are the three cases that form the basic framework of federal Indian law in the United States, referred to as the 'Marshall Trilogy.'[1]

> It is tempting to quote *Worcester*'s assertion that state law has no "force" in Indian Country to the Supreme Court, but such an assertion doesn't implicate an important constitutional concern. In *Worcester*, it did—federalism.
>
> (Fletcher 695–6)

Collectively the Marshall Trilogy established the foundations of American Federal Indian Law. The Marshall Trilogy cases are comprised of the U.S. Supreme Court rulings of *Johnson v. M'Intosh* (1823); *Cherokee Nation v. Georgia* (1831) and *Worcester v. Georgia* (1832). In most accounts, these rulings are said to have pronounced upon land rights of Native American Indians. As outlined in the introduction to this book, my central claim is that the Trilogy is exemplary of a set of discourses from which subjects collectively known as Native American Indians were produced. According to that reading, Marshall was not simply engaged in the conferment or withholding of benefits from an objectively existent set of peoples. Marshall (with others) brought into being a community of people who were resolutely Other to the idealized American subject: unable to hold or cultivate lands, the Native American was born a marginalized subject.

Chapters 2 and 3 apply Foucault's theory of discourse to the Marshall Trilogy cases in order to demonstrate how legal discourses form and shape their own objects of study. The colonized subject has no objective existence outside of the statements (legal and others) that are circulated about him or her. As a prelude to my account of how discourse makes an object of study—specifically, the American Indian—I provide in this chapter an overview of the Doctrine of Discovery and the Marshall Trilogy cases, paying attention to the more conventional interpretations of the content and scope of the Trilogy cases.

The Doctrine of Discovery

The Doctrine of Discovery was the law of colonialism introduced in North America by the European powers in the early seventeenth century. The Doctrine was a legal fiction drawn up by colonial powers to divide the globe into spheres of influence. In its essence, it was a legal veneer to the appropriation of both lands and peoples while, simultaneously, maps were drawn up to manage potential conflicts between European colonial powers. By the symbolic act of planting a flag into the ground of newly 'discovered' lands England, France, Spain and Portugal laid claim to the territory not only in North America, but around the globe.

The Doctrine had its genesis in international law drawn up by the Holy See in the sixteenth century. It was based on several Papal Bulls issued in the fifteenth and sixteenth centuries. The Papal Bulls largely incorporated the language of domination and conquest. The Bulls were issued to the Kings of Spain and Portugal to 'convert,' 'subjugate' and 'enslave' non-Christian lands, first in West Africa and then in the Western Hemisphere. The Bull Romanus Pontifex (Nicholas V) January 8, 1454, stated in part to the King of Portugal, Alfonso V:

> We [therefore] weighing all and singular the premises with due mediation, and noting that since we had formally by other letters of ours granted among other things free and ample faculty to the aforesaid King Alfonso—to invade, search out, capture, vanquish, and subdue all Saracens and pagans whatsoever, and other enemies of Christ wheresoever placed, and the kingdoms, dukedoms, principalities, dominions, possessions, and all movable and immovable goods whatsoever held and possessed by them and to reduce their persons to perpetual slavery, and to apply and appropriate to himself and his successors the kingdoms, dukedoms, counties, principalities, dominions, possessions, and goods, and to convert them to his and their use and profit.
>
> (The Bull Romanus Pontifex (Nicholas V) January 8, 1454)

Further evidence of how the Papal Bulls provided religious legal cover to Christian monarchs and their servants is extracted from a close reading of the above Papal Bull. The Bull reveals the discourse of domination and subjugation. For example, use of the term "convert" clearly exemplifies a doctrine of domination; that is, to 'convert' said heathens to Christianity regardless of their possession of lands or culture "to invade, search out, capture, vanquish, and subdue all Saracens and pagans whatsoever, and other enemies of Christ" (The Bull Romanus Pontifex (Nicholas V) January 8, 1454). The phrase "Enemies of Christ" gave the European colonial powers Christian authority to subdue and conquer non-Christians' lands. Herein lies the nature of international law that underpinned the Doctrine of Discovery.

The rights created by the Holy See gave legal justification to Spanish and Portuguese explorers to seek out lands and, by the mere reading of Christian demands for religious conversion, established the pretense of legality to the appropriation of lands, their peoples and their cultures with the mere symbolism of "arrival." The alleged legal rights incorporated into the Papal Bulls were later used to establish the Doctrine of Discovery, a doctrine that formed the legal basis to the U.S. Supreme Court ruling in *Johnson v. M'Intosh* (1823).

The relationship between international law up until the sixteenth century and the decision in the *Johnson* ruling in 1823, cannot escape the accusation that it offered a pretext for conquest in the guise of Christian domination. Steven T. Newcomb in *Pagans in the Promised Land* de-codes the Papal Bulls to reveal how the framework of religious domination was sanctified as a legal doctrine, a doctrine which, while becoming law, was derived from religious assertions of what rights European colonial powers could impose on so-called 'heathen,' or 'non-Christian' peoples:

> the central premise of U.S. Indian law and policy—that the United States has plenary (virtually absolute) authority over Indian nations on the basis of the discovery of the North American continent by Christian people—will be revealed as truly bizarre. That premise, I contend, is fully in violation of the presumed separation of church and state in the United States, and in violation of the presumption that Christianity is not to be preferred in U.S. law over other religions.
>
> (Newcomb xxi)

Newcomb reveals the subtle yet profound decoding of the Doctrine of Discovery in the American context, a religious undercurrent that was imbedded in international law until 1823. The international Law of Nations up until 1823 accepted—whether directly via Papal Bulls or indirectly by orders issued by the King of England—that "heathen" lands were subject to conversion and domination based upon their non-Christian attributes. Robert A. Williams, Jr. in *The American Indian in Western Legal Thought: The Discourses of Conquest* connects the pragmatic English Acts in relation to their American colonies and the Law of Nations based on Christian domination over "heathens." Williams writes:

> As reflected in the Proclamation of 1763, this imperial discourse accepted the necessity of peaceful purchase of frontier Indian lands under strict pragmatic approach to Indian affairs, imperial policy ultimately rested on the ancient legitimating foundations of the superior rights of Christian Europeans in lands held by normatively divergent, non-Christian peoples. The English Crown, by virtue of English discovery of the infidel-occupied lands of North America, asserted the feudally derived prerogative rights of conquests over North America.
>
> (Williams 229)

The Doctrine of Discovery is a framework of colonial conquest transposed within the Holy See of religious piety and English legal justification. The sum of these two religious and legal sources underscored the nature of the Law of Nations up until the *Johnson* ruling in 1823. It is hard to avoid this harsh judgment of the Doctrine of Discovery as it founded the legal and religious justification of colonial conquest in North America by the major European powers during the sixteenth through the twentieth centuries. Not only did the Doctrine of Discovery provide a religious and legal veneer to colonial conquest, it also denied any rights of land or culture to the indigenous peoples who preceded the European incursions into North America. Williams writes:

> In the United States and in other Western settler-colonized states, the rule begins with the Doctrine of Discovery and its discourse of conquest, which denies fundamental human rights and self-determination to indigenous tribal peoples . . . In the United States, the doctrine has proved itself to be a perfect instrument of empire. Under the rules and principles of federal Indian law derived from the doctrine, the United States acquired a continent "in perfect good faith" that its wars and acts of genocide directed against Indian people accorded with the rule of law.
>
> (325)

A close reading of how the Doctrine of Discovery was incorporated by Chief Justice Marshall in the Trilogy cases is offered in this chapter. At this juncture, it is important to take a measured look at the Doctrine of Discovery as a basis of religious and legal domination over indigenous lands and people, not only in North America but throughout the world. Equally, once an understanding of what the Doctrine of Discovery meant and how it was derived are realized, one can also understand how European superstates clothed in the trappings of the Holy See and English law developed the discourse of the Law of Nations—a discourse that formed an important part of 'discursive archive' that situated the Marshall ruling in *Johnson* in 1823. Justice Story served on the U.S. Supreme Court as a contemporary of Justice Marshall. Story was a close friend and colleague of Justice Marshall. If anyone could explain Marshall's jurisprudence in the *Johnson* ruling, Story offered a rare glimpse into how Marshall incorporated the Christian Doctrine of Discovery. Story paraphrased Marshall's ruling as follows:

> The European nations found little difficulty in reconciling themselves to the adoption of any principle, which gave ample scope to their ambition, and employed little reasoning to support it. They were content to take counsel of their interests, their prejudices, and their passions, and felt no necessity of vindicating their conduct before cabinets, which were already eager to recognise its justice and its policy. The Indians were a savage race, sunk in the depths of ignorance and heathenism. If they might not be extirpated for their want of religion and just morals, they might be reclaimed from their errors. They were bound to yield to the superior genius of Europe, and in exchanging their wild and debasing habits for civilization and Christianity they were deemed to gain more than an equivalent for every sacrifice and suffering. The Papal authority, too, was brought in aid of these great designs; and for the purpose of overthrowing heathenism, and propagating the Catholic religion. Alexander the Sixth, by a Bull issued in 1493, granted to the crown of Castile the whole of the immense territory then discovered, or to be discovered, between the poles, so far as it was not then possessed by any Christian prince.
>
> (quoted in Newcomb, *Pagans in the Promised Land* 82)

As will be shown in this chapter, Marshall's opinion in *Johnson* upholds the Doctrine of Discovery and the historical interpretation upon which the Doctrine was based:

> he vigorously defends it, pointedly upholding the medieval premise that the primacy of Christianity and Western "civilization" justifies seizure of lands from non-Christian peoples. Accordingly, he finds Great Britain's New-World claims, passed on to the newly independent United States, legal and binding in U.S. law. The federal government's title, he ruled, was subject only to the fatally tenuous, as the later *Cherokee* case would prove, "Indian right of occupancy."
>
> (par. 6 Engle)

The medieval premise of Christian versus non-Christian, "civilized versus non-civilized" drawn up in the centuries preceding *Johnson*, was formally incorporated in the Trilogy cases as a doctrine of international law. This chapter examines how Justice Marshall incorporated medieval notions of Christianity and Western civilization; namely, employing the Doctrine of

Discovery to legally dispossess Native Americans of their land and culture under the guise of U.S. jurisprudence.

Johnson v. M'Intosh (1823)

The U.S. Supreme Court ruling in *Johnson* laid out the jurisprudential foundation of what is known as Federal Indian Law. The major issue in *Johnson* dealt with whether or not purchases of land by private individuals from American Indians after 1763 were based on good title or whether such private purchases were prohibited by the 1763 Royal Proclamation which held that Britain had the exclusive right to purchase land from Indians. [2] In ruling against the appellants, Marshall held in his majority opinion that private land purchases from Indians after 1763 were not legally valid transactions and any chain of title claims based on these original transactions would not be recognized under the law. Part of Marshall's reasoning was based on the rights of exclusive purchase of Indian land inherited by the United States from Britain. In *Johnson,* Marshall laid out a detailed survey of how land ownership originated in the New World by discovery.[3] Unlike the European Doctrine of Discovery which was used to avoid overlapping land claims by competing European powers, in *Johnson* Marshall's interpretation declared that the aboriginal peoples of America only held a title of *occupancy*, while ownership title resided with the United States.

Marshall's interpretation departed from the European Discovery Doctrine where the latter emphasized land claims in relation to other European powers, rather than the former, which established property ownership in relation to the aboriginal population. Attorney General Wirt, later to represent the Cherokee Nation before the U.S. Supreme Court, in commenting about Marshall's opinion in *Johnson,* wrote that "the Europeans held that the title of the Indians to their lands underwent a change by force of discovery: that is to say, the particular power of Europe which made the first discovery acquired the right to purchase the lands of the Indians, in preference to and in exclusion of all other discoverers" (Norgren 56). Upon discovery, land title still remained with the Native Americans. Marshall differed from this accepted international law by asserting not only the exclusive right to purchase land from Indians on land claimed by Britain, and later the United States, but that such a claim also asserted that the United States and not the Indians held ultimate ownership of the land. Under Marshalls' interpretation of the Doctrine of Discovery, the Indians were acknowledged to have an *occupancy,* rather than full title to their land.

Whether by purchase or conquest, Marshall's legal doctrine dispossessed the Native Americans of their ownership interest in their land. Marshall presented a historical basis to the land claims of the United States wherein he asserted that the United States had inherited the rights of land ownership claimed by Britain. Marshall argued that the European

Doctrine of Discovery was established international law or the "recognized Law of Nations" whereby: (i) discovery of land by one European power would exclude claims by other European Powers and (ii) that such discovery operated against non-Christian lands, or in the case of the New World, that such 'heathens' or 'non-Christian' indigenous people were subsumed within the discovery claims of the Christian European powers. Marshall argued that Britain discovered land in the New World, beginning with John Cabot in 1498:

> So early as the year 1496, her monarch granted a commission to the Cabots to discover countries then unknown to Christian people and to take possession of them in the name of the King of England. Two years afterwards, Cabot proceeded on this voyage and discovered the continent of North America, along which he sailed as far south as Virginia. To this discovery the English trace their title.
>
> (*Johnson v. M'Intosh* 576)

The reference to the charter granted to John Cabot underscores that the charter was to "discover countries then unknown to Christian people." The implication here is that non-Christian peoples could not own land or possess a claim to the land. The literary references that associate Christianity and land ownership can be found in Chapter 4 of this book. Discursive statements referencing this association were made by religious missionaries such as Levi Frisbie and in state court rulings in *Thompson vs. Johnston,* among others.

When England claimed the continent of North America, what of the rights of the indigenous peoples? Were they accorded any rights to their land? In applying legal rhetoric to dispossess Indians of their land ownership, Marshall carefully manipulated his legal opinion to 'impair' the indigenous peoples' 'right to the soil.' Within the confines of a single passage in *Johnson,* Marshall was able to linguistically, under the guise of legal judgment, legally dispossess Native Americans of their land. *Johnson v. M'Intosh* still represents the foundational precedent that limits the extent to which Indian tribes and reservations today can claim jurisdictional sovereignty in relation to the U.S. Federal Government. Marshall's legal dispossession of American Indians was established in *Johnson* because this was the first U.S. Supreme Court ruling that 'impaired' the legal capacity of native tribes in relation to the Federal Government:

> In the establishment of these relations, the rights of the original inhabitants were, in no instance, entirely disregarded; but were necessarily, to a considerable extent, impaired. They were admitted to be the rightful occupants of the soil, with a legal as well as just claim to retain possession of it, and to use it according to their own discretion; but their

> rights to complete sovereignty, as independent nations, were necessarily diminished, and their power to dispose of the soil at their own will, to whomsoever they pleased, was denied by the original fundamental principle, that discovery gave exclusive title to those who made it.
>
> (*Johnson v. M'Intosh* 574)

The operative claim in Marshall's opinion asserts that "their power to dispose of the soil at their own will, to whomsoever they pleased, was denied by the original fundamental principle, that discovery gave exclusive title to those who made it" (574). Commenting on the discovery, Steven Newcomb uses a cognitive approach to interpreting the Doctrine of Discovery cited in *Johnson.* Newcomb's analysis provides a perspective as to how realities can be constructed using metaphorical images. On the use of the Doctrine of Discovery in *Johnson,* Newcomb states:

> Cognitive theory enables us to recognize an underlying claim buried in the *Johnson* ruling: The Europeans mentally gave themselves dominion over and title to the continent by imaginatively conceptualizing themselves as having dominion over and title to the lands of the continent. The concept *discovery* tacitly refers to the ability of the Europeans to imagine the possibility of a particular "reality" and then to act with intensive and sustained human energy on that imagined possibility until the envisioned reality becomes 'manifested' or 'constructed.'
>
> (Newcomb, *Pagans in the Promised Land* 93)

Newcomb's analysis foregrounds the claim by Europeans that discovery did not occur upon the act of setting foot onto the New World, but that discovery was deemed to have been established at the point of 'arriving' upon the New World. The European presumption under this interpretation of discovery is that *no* inhabitants occupied the New World. In Chapter 4 of this book, the state court ruling in *Arnold vs. Mundy* evidences references that uninhabited land was considered to be *terra nullus.* The court in *Arnold* considered the State of New Jersey devoid of inhabitants upon disovery. In Chapter 7 Cotton Mather speaks about the "barren wilderness," a description that provides a literary context to the uninhabited state of the New World upon discovery. In *Johnson,* Marshall considered that Indian occupation of the land left it tantamount to a wilderness:

> But the tribes of Indians inhabiting this country were fierce savages, whose occupation was war, and whose subsistence was drawn chiefly from the forest. To leave them in possession of their country, was to leave the country a wilderness.
>
> (*Johnson v. M'Intosh* 590)

Marshall's statement that "to leave them in possession of their country, was to leave the country a wilderness" appears to build a theory of land ownership based on taming a wild country (590). To tame a country, the inhabitants must be civilized as opposed to Marshall's characterization of the Indians as 'fierce savages.' Chapter 8 reveals several literary sources that formed important literary discourse about the wilderness from Cotton Mather, John Cotton, and John Winthrop to ministers such as Jonathan Edwards. Also, the influence of the early nineteenth-century paintings of the wilderness, by painters such as Thomas Cole of the Hudson River Painting School, expands upon the relationship between civilization and the wilderness. Fenimore Cooper's *The Last of the Mohicans* makes great use of the untamed wilderness as the setting for the novel's Indian protagonists. Therefore, the melding of discursive themes about the wilderness as an untamed and uncivilized place became, over time, prerequisites to dispossessing Indians from owning their land.

Marshall then proceeds to catalog a detailed history of how the Doctrine of Discovery was used by Spain, Portugal, France and England to claim exclusive title to the New World (574). A critical finding of fact in Marshall's depiction of the Discovery Doctrine was that discovery by the European powers conferred upon them the right to make claims on 'heathen' people. The origins of this *religious* Doctrine of Discovery were laid down by Pope Nicholas V 40 years before Columbus 'discovered' the New World. Newcomb explains the history of its concrete religious doctrine:

> To understand the connection between Christendom's principle of discovery and the laws of the United States, we need to begin by examining a papal document issued forty years before Columbus' historic voyage. In 1452, Pope Nicholas V issued to King Alfonso V of Portugal the bull Romanus Pontifex, declaring war against all non-Christians throughout the world, and specifically sanctioning and promoting the conquest, colonization, and exploitation of non-Christian nations and their territories.
>
> (Newcomb, *Five Hundred Years of Injustice: The Legacy of Fifteenth Century Religious Prejudice*)

While Marshall does not expand upon the religious doctrine promulgated by Pope Nicholas V, he does establish a religious finding as to where and upon whom the Doctrine of Discovery could be applied to. Similar to Pope Nicholas' Papal Bull in 1452, Marshall stated:

> The charter granted to Sir Humphrey Gilbert, in 1578, authorizes him to discover and take possession of such remote, heathen, and barbarous lands, as were not actually possessed by any Christian prince or

people. This charter was afterwards renewed to Sir Walter Raleigh, in nearly the same terms.

(Newcomb, *Five Hundred Years of Injustice: The Legacy of Fifteenth Century Religious Prejudice*)

Marshall's description of the New World as a "remote, heathen, and barbarous land" had a strong connection to several literary influences (*Johnson* 577). Writers such as John Heckewelder, in *The Savage in American Literature*, described the barbarous tribes that inhabited North America. Washington Irving, in *Traits of Indian Character*, also describes the Indian as "hordes." In James Fenimore Cooper's *The Last of the Mochians*, bad Indians were portrayed as "savage" and "fiends." Moreover, Pope Nicholas V's Papal Bull of 1452, together with Marshall's integration of Sir Humphrey Gilbert's Grant of 1578, demonstrate a *religious* basis to the Doctrine of Discovery described in *Johnson*.

Cherokee Nation v. Georgia (1831)

After the Cherokee failed to obtain relief from either the President or Congress, they were left with no choice but to stop the State of Georgia from encroaching upon their land by filing a motion for an injunction with the U.S. Supreme Court.[4] In *Cherokee Nation*, the issue was whether or not the Cherokee Nation would be recognized by the U.S. Supreme Court as a "state" or "foreign nation" for the purposes of asserting original jurisdiction to hear claims against the State of Georgia (*Cherokee Nation* 2). Garrison notes:

> The Cherokee maintained that their nation was a foreign state under Article 3, that the Supreme Court could accept jurisdiction over the case, and that the Court could remedy the nation's injuries by striking down the state laws and enjoining enforcement.
>
> (Garrison 129)

The Cherokee, among several claims, also asserted that the Doctrine of Discovery had no standing upon their land since they did not consent to it. Challenging the 1763 Royal Charter, the Cherokee argued the Charter had no standing in relation to the Cherokee people: [5]

> The foundation of this charter, the bill states, is asserted to be the right of discovery to the territory granted; a ship manned by the subjects of the king having, "about two centuries and a half before, sailed along the coast of the western hemisphere, from the fifty-sixth to the thirty-eighth degree of north latitude, and looked upon the face of that coast without even landing on any part of it."

> This right, as affecting the right of the Indian nation, the bill denies, and asserts that the whole length to which the right of discovery is claimed to extend among European nations is to give to the first discoverer the prior and exclusive right to purchase these lands from the Indian proprietors, against all other European sovereigns, to which principle the Indians have never assented, and which they deny to be a principle of the natural law of nations or obligatory on them.
>
> (*Cherokee Nation v. Georgia* 3–4)

Based upon these claims, the Cherokee asked the U.S. Supreme Court to rule that Georgia laws were void within the Cherokee Nation. Georgia, as argued before the Motion in *Georgia v. Tassels* (1830), relied upon a claim of title theory that asserted that the discovery rights of England were inherited by Georgia after the War of Independence and that the Federal Government did not have the exclusive right to "extinguish" Indians' land title. Georgia claimed they had the power to extinguish Cherokee land title *unilaterally* under the 1802 Compact Treaty between the Federal Government and the Cherokee Nation.[6] Georgia's claim to superior land ownership to the Cherokee was asserted despite the fact that the Federal Government and the Cherokee had signed several Treaties, in particular the Treaty of Hopewell (1785), wherein the United States agreed to protect the Cherokee national boundaries against squatters and any other unlawful encroachments upon their territory. As the attorney for the Cherokee William Wirt stated, treaties, not state laws, were the supreme law of the land:

> The bill avers that this Court has, by the Constitution and laws of the United States, original jurisdiction of controversies between a State and a foreign state, without any restriction as to the nature of the controversy; that, by the Constitution, treaties are the supreme law of the land.
>
> (11)

Wirt's argument seeks to make the point that the U.S. Supreme Court had jurisdiction to accept the Cherokee motion since Treaties, not state law, are the "supreme law of the land." On this issue, the Cherokee were attempting to pre-empt any objection by Georgia that state laws concerning Cherokee lands were not subject to judicial review.

If the Cherokee controversy focused on whether Cherokee law was superior to state law in relation to Cherokee land, John Marshall would have no doubt ruled in favor of Cherokee law. Marshall did just that in *Worcester v. Georgia* (1832); however, in this motion, Marshall and the Supreme Court instead looked for other judicial grounds to *avoid* the controversy altogether. Focusing instead on the issue of original jurisdiction or standing, Marshall looked for findings of fact that would establish that the Cherokee were *not* a foreign state, or a state at all, thus precluding the Cherokee from bringing any original action in the State of Georgia to the U.S. Supreme Court. It is on the issue of *standing* that a forensic examination of the court's findings of fact reveals the incorporation of the historical archive of discursive statements that projected the Cherokee as an *inferior race*. Discourses about race and discovery, not legal grounds, were accepted by Marshall as sworn statements to support his legal theory that the Cherokee lacked legal standing to challenge Georgia's encroachment upon Cherokee land:

> A people once numerous, powerful, and truly independent, found by our ancestors in the quiet and uncontrolled possession of an ample domain, gradually sinking beneath our superior policy, our arts and our arms, have yielded their lands by successive treaties, each of which contains a solemn guarantee of the residue, until they retain no more of their formerly extensive territory than is deemed necessary to their comfortable subsistence.
>
> (15)

Marshall refers to the Indians as "a people once numerous, powerful, and truly independent" in the past tense. Marshall was not alone in seeking to project the Indians as a vanishing or even a vanished race. As noted in Chapter 7, Cooper's *The Last of the Mohicans* references a once and powerful Indian race. In the early American Romantic period, between 1778 and through the early 1820s, a new genre of vanishing Indian discourses emerged. These literary discourses are cited in Chapter 6 where the works of Philip Frenbeau, Washington Irving, William Cullen Bryant and missionaries such as John Heckewelder wrote about the Indian as a vanishing race. Marshall was not the first writer to evoke the vanishing Indian theme.

Worcester v. Georgia (1832)

In *Worcester*, John Marshall held that the Cherokee Nation was sovereign in relation to states and that any legislation by the State of Georgia asserting jurisdiction over the Cherokee Nation was void. A key issue in *Worcester* was whether the State of Georgia had violated the Treaty of Hopewell (1785) between the Federal Government and the Cherokee Nation. This issue was also a threshold question in *Worcester* in order to establish jurisdiction by the Supreme Court to hear the matter. As Justice Marshall stated in his majority opinion:

> The indictment and plea in this case draw in question, we think, the validity of the treaties made by the United States with the Cherokee Indians; if not so, their construction is certainly drawn in question; and the decision has been, if not against their validity, "against the right, privilege or exemption, specially set up and claimed under them." They also draw into question the validity of a statute of the State of Georgia, "on the ground of its being repugnant to the Constitution, treaties and laws of the United States, and the decision is in favour of its validity."
>
> (*Worcester v. Georgia* 516)

The Marshall court was reviewing an appeal by the missionary Samuel A. Worcester alleging that the State of Georgia had no right to claim jurisdiction over his person while he was inside Cherokee territory. As a missionary, Worcester helped the Cherokee leadership with their newspaper *The Cherokee Phoenix* and also advised them on their constitutional rights and was acting within the powers granted to him by the Federal Government as a missionary (Norgren 112). Georgia refused to recognize Worcester's missionary status and arrested him on the grounds that he had not obtained a license from the State of Georgia to work and operate inside Cherokee territory (114). Cherokee territory in 1827 included land in what is known today as Georgia, North Carolina and Tennessee.

A vital issue in this case dealt with whether the State of Georgia could pass laws attaching *personal* jurisdiction over persons who were members or residents of the Cherokee Nation. A subsidiary issue was whether the Cherokee Nation was a sovereign nation, such that the State of Georgia had no legal authority to order armed guards to enter upon Cherokee land and arrest individual U.S. citizens under the pretext of Georgia law. Marshall summed up some of these issues by stating:

> The defendant is a state, a member of the union, which has exercised the powers of government over a people who deny its jurisdiction, and are under the protection of the United States. The plaintiff is a citizen of the state of Vermont, condemned to hard labour for four years in the penitentiary of Georgia; under colour of an act which he alleges to be repugnant to the constitution, laws, and treaties of the United States. The legislative power of a state, the controlling power of the constitution and laws of the United States, the rights, if they have any, the political existence of a once numerous and powerful people, the personal liberty of a citizen, are all involved in the subject now to be considered. It behooves this court, in every case, more especially in this, to examine into its jurisdiction with scrutinizing eyes; before it proceeds to the exercise of a power which is controverted.
>
> (*Worcester v. Georgia* 536)

In examining these issues, Marshall examined the historical basis upon which the Native Americans retained their sovereignty. In a departure from his ruling in *Cherokee Nation*, Marshall affirmed the sovereignty and possession of the land by the Cherokee. In a change of how the Doctrine of Discovery operated, Marshall now asserted in *Worcester*:

> They were well understood to convey the title which, according to the common law of European sovereigns respecting America, they might rightfully convey, and no more. This was the exclusive right of purchasing

> such lands as the natives were willing to sell. The crown could not be understood to grant what the crown did not affect to claim; nor was it so understood.
>
> (517)

Marshall now asserted that the British Crown, upon discovery of the New World and after granting charters to private explorers like Sir Walter Raleigh, retained the exclusive right to *purchase* land from the Indians as against all other European powers. In *Johnson*, Marshall asserted that by virtue of the Doctrine of Discovery, Britain not only had an exclusive right to purchase land from the native tribes, but should obtain either by purchase, or *conquest*, the fee simple title to *all lands* it claimed with only a possessory or occupancy right being retained for the Indians. The difference in *Worcester* is that Marshall amended the sovereignty of Indians subject only to the exclusive *purchase* right of the United States:

> The Cherokee Nation, then, is a distinct community, occupying its own territory, with boundaries accurately described, in which the laws of Georgia can have no force, and which the citizens of Georgia have no right to enter, but with the assent of the Cherokees themselves, or in conformity with treaties, and with the acts of congress. The whole intercourse between the United States and this nation is by our constitution and laws, vested in the government of the United States.
>
> (520)

It is illustrative in this opinion, while the Supreme Court amends the sovereignty rights of the Cherokees in relation to Georgia, that such sovereignty is still limited by being "vested in the government of the United States" (520). What of the rights of Indian tribes not cited in *Worcester?* How did Marshall account for their status in relation to all states? What of tribes who had no treaties or treaty rights with the United States? Marshall addressed the issue of Indian sovereignty and land ownership by addressing the predicament of Indian tribes who were not under treaty with the United States. Marshall redefined the Doctrine of Discovery. According to Robertson, he attempts to alter his earlier version of the European Doctrine of Discovery by arguing that discovery gave the United States exclusive right to *regulate* who could buy land from the Indians, that is, individuals or states but that such regulation did limit the pre-discovery ownership claim of the Indians. Marshall's revised Doctrine of Discovery asserts the fee simple title to the United States based on *purchase,* not conquest. According to Robertson:

> Marshall now wrote, echoing Senator Peleg Sprague in the Indian Removal Bill debate, "gave to the nation making discovery, as its inevitable consequence, [only] the sole right of acquiring the soil and of

> making settlements on it"—a pre-emption right. And though it "shut out the right of competition among those who had agreed to it," it could not "annul the previous rights of those who had not agreed to it."
>
> (Robertson 133–4)

Marshall makes it appear as though native sovereignty was restored. Here he drew a line between Georgia and the Cherokee Nation whereby the latter was to have exclusive sovereign rights to govern their land, precluding Georgia jurisdiction over Cherokee territory. One could reasonably assume that Marshall restored exclusive property title back to the Cherokee Nation; however, while Marshall may have invalidated Georgia law over the Cherokee Nation, he reserved the fee simple claim by the Federal Government over the Cherokee Nation. Marshall outlined a long litany of treaties signed between the United States and the Cherokee Nation where the United States, in exchange for land, gave the Cherokee exclusive right to occupy, *but not own*, their land subject to the *protection* of the United States. Marshall highlighted Cherokee sovereignty in relation to Georgia, but his ruling did not acknowledge full land ownership in relation to the Federal Government:

> The Indian nations had always been considered as distinct, independent political communities, retaining their original natural rights as the undisputed possessors of the soil from time immemorial, with the single exception of that imposed by irresistible power, which excluded them from intercourse with any other European potentate than the first discoverer of the coast of the particular region claimed, and this was a restriction which those European potentates imposed on themselves, as well as on the Indians.
>
> (*Worcester v. Georgia* 559)

Marshall establishes Indian sovereignty in the form of "independent political communities" which have "original natural rights," but in language that is unmistakable; these independent natural rights are subject to the imposition of an "irresistible" power. What Marshall means by "irresistible" is not certain, but the implication seems to indicate a power that cannot be defeated or a power that has prevailed in war. The "irresistible" power exception asserts claims of land in relation to other European "potentates" as "well as on the Indians." While Marshall seems to rehabilitate Indian sovereignty he is actually reasserting the "impaired" sovereignty of *Johnson.*

As stated in the introduction to this chapter, these three cases cannot be adequately read as merely settling legal issues raised by (for example) the Cherokee Nation. Rather, whilst purportedly settling a legal dispute arising from the claim of a distinctive community and culture of peoples, Marshall constructed a new colonial subject—the Native American Indian who was to be incapable of holding and cultivating land; however, the ostensible focus of the Trilogy cases is the dominant reading of Marshall's judgment, and my account would be incomplete without providing a summary of these dominant readings.

The Constitutional and political context of the Marshall cases

The debate between states' rights in relation to the U.S. Federal Government came to a boil at the time the U.S. Supreme Court heard *Worcester* in 1832. Norgren writes, "the long-simmering states rights rebellion in South Carolina exploded in the autumn of 1832. Since 1816, tensions had been building between the southern states, which opposed a national tariff policy they felt favored northern economic interests, and the Federal Government" (Norgren 126). In the autumn of 1832 South Carolina passed the Nullification Ordinance in defiance of Federal Tariffs just as Andrew Jackson was about to commence his second term as President. South Carolina's defiance presented a direct challenge to Congress and implicitly to U.S. Federalism. Tensions between the Federal Government and South Carolina were strained enough to inflame neighboring states, such as Georgia and Tennessee, who were already making efforts in the form of state law to remove Cherokee Indians from within their own borders:

> Perhaps a clear pronouncement in favor of Indian sovereignty by a united Court in *Cherokee Nation* would have stalled the fervor for removal. More than likely, though, it would have only pushed Georgia so far toward rebellion that the state might have joined South Carolina in its nullification challenge to the federal government. Instead, Marshall's refusal to grant standing to the Cherokees persuaded Georgia officials to give the federal government more time to arrange an agreement with the tribe to effect its relocation.
>
> (Garrison 151)

President Jackson took a pro-state rights position with regard to the Indian removal issue. Jackson was able to diffuse most Southern anger with the Federal Government on the issue of tariffs; however, South Carolina maintained a firm opposition. While *Worcester* was being heard by the U.S. Supreme Court in 1832, Federal tariffs were being challenged by South Carolina's Nullification Ordinance despite President Jackson's platform to placate southern states by publically supporting the removal of the Cherokee, Choctaws and other eastern Indian Nations. Garrison notes that a misstep by Jackson or by the Worcester litigants could have led to a civil war (196). Acknowledging the tension between the Federal Government and southern states, John Marshall wrote in his letter to fellow Supreme Court Justice Joseph Story of December 25, 1832:

> Should it countenance the obvious design of South Carolina to form a southern confederacy, it may conduce to a southern league—never to a southern government. Our theories are incompatible with a government for more than a single state. We can form no union which shall be closer than an alliance between sovereigns. In this event there is some reason to apprehend internal convulsion. The northern and western section of our state, should a union be maintained north of the Potowmac, will not readily connect itself with the south. At least such is the present belief of their most intelligent men. Any effort on their part to separate from Southern Virginia, and unite with a northern confederacy, may probably be punished as treason. "We have fallen on evil times."
>
> (Marshall and Hobson 826)

John Marshall not only highlights the potential for 'internal convulsion' but similarly indicates the hypocritical position into which President Jackson, elected as a states' rights candidate, would now transform himself. To prevent other states from joining South Carolina, President Jackson supported the Indians Removal Act of 1830 and deliberately failed to enforce or lend political weight to the U.S. Supreme Court's ruling in *Worcester*. It was ironic that Jackson, who ran an anti-Federalist platform, was now compelled to take a firm Federalist stand in order to protect the Union against South Carolina's Nullification Ordinance. John Marshall, noting the irony of President Jackson's transformation from winning the Presidential election in 1828 based on a belief in the protection of the common man against special national interests to defending Federalism, observed to Justice Story: [7]

> to have said he was ready to break down and trample on every other department of the government would not have injured him but to say that he was a Federalist—a convert to the opinions of Washington was a mortal blow under which he is yet staggering.
>
> (825)

Beyond the political crisis brewing between South Carolina and the Federal Government over tariffs, another Constitutional challenge was being presented by state courts who were interpreting the U.S. Constitution in a manner that granted states sovereignty and jurisdiction over Indian land. The focus of the debate centered on several clauses drawn up during the Constitutional Convention of 1789:

> The commitment to a national Indian policy was reaffirmed by the men who met in Philadelphia to the write the U.S. Constitution. Article 1,

> Section 10, barred states from entering into treaties, while the Indian Commerce Clause, Article 1 Section 8, asserted the responsibility of the federal government alone to negotiate with Indian nations.
>
> (Norgren 30)

A strict reading of the Constitutional clauses might lead one to believe that the regulation of Indian land was the province of the Federal Government; however, since states were not interested in surrendering their claim over Indian land they used their own courts to interpret Constitutional clauses, such as the Commerce Clause, to conceal and legitimate their desire for more land under the guise of legal sanction:

> In support of the argument that states had the right to extend criminal jurisdiction over Indians within their boundaries, state courts also argued that the states existed before the United States was formed under the Constitution, and they never surrendered their sovereign power over Indians to the federal government. As the Georgia Supreme Court explained in *State v. Tassels*, "[w]hatever right Great Britain possessed over the Indian tribes, is vested in the State of Georgia, and may be rightfully exercised." No federal statute or treaty could take that away from the state; the federal government did not have the right to make treaties with the Cherokees.
>
> (Rosen 45)

As far as state courts were concerned the claims for state sovereignty over Indian claims of sovereignty were not based upon the issue of "tribal sovereignty" or U.S. treaties, but instead on the issues of State versus Federal jurisdiction:

> The southern courts consequently formulated a states' rights interpretation of the Commerce Clause that attempted to keep the federal government out of almost every aspect of Indian–white relations beyond economic exchange. The framers intended to endow the federal government only with the power to regulate trade with the Indian tribes, the southern courts maintained; the states possessed jurisdiction over every other aspect of Indian affairs.
>
> (Garrison 8)

In *Gibbons v. Ogden* (1824), for example, New York State sought to argue that concurrent jurisdiction prevailed over commercial dealings with Indians between the Federal Government and New York State. New York based its claim on its historic role in managing sales of land between Indian tribes and colonial parties. The lawyer for *Gibbons,* Daniel Webster, argued that:

> because New York had long legislated on issues relating to commerce with Indians (e.g., prohibiting the purchase of land from Indians or the sale of certain kinds of goods to Indians), he said it would cause havoc in state Indian laws if the commerce power were not deemed to be concurrent.
>
> (Rosen 39)

The U.S. Supreme Court disagreed and in *Gibbons* the Supreme Court held that Interstate Commerce was subject only to the Federal Commerce Clause. The U.S. Supreme Court, Chief Justice Marshall writing the opinion, stated in part:

> In argument, it has been contended, that if a law passed by a State, in the exercise of its acknowledged sovereignty, comes into conflict with a law passed by Congress in pursuance of the constitution, they affect the subject, and each other, like equal opposing powers. But the framers of our constitution foresaw this state of things, and provided for it, by declaring the supremacy not only of itself, but of the laws made in pursuance of it. The nullity of any act inconsistent with the Constitution is produced by the declaration that the Constitution is the supreme law. The appropriate application of that part of the clause which confers the same supremacy on laws and treaties, is to such acts of the State Legislatures as do not transcend their powers, but, though enacted in the execution of acknowledged State powers, interfere with, or are contrary to the laws of Congress, made in pursuance of the constitution, or some treaty made under the authority of the United States. In every such case, the act of Congress, or the treaty, is supreme; and the law of the State, though enacted in the exercise of powers not controverted, must yield to it.
>
> (*Gibbons v. Ogden* 210–211)

Commentators such as Deborah Rosen have demonstrated how state courts took advantage of the ambiguities in the U.S. Supreme Court's Trilogy rulings to assert Constitutional grounds to control and regulate Indian tribes within state borders:

> The U.S. Supreme Court cases between 1790 and 1880 that have traditionally been viewed as the major statements of federal authority regarding Indians—*Johnson v. McIntosh, Cherokee Nation v. Georgia,* and *Worcester v. Georgia*—failed to provide clear and consistent constitutionally based rules, and a decision discussing federal authority immediately following the close of the period under study—*United States v. Kagama*—exhibited the continuing ambiguity in the late nineteenth century. The federal government's lack of precision meant that the states were freer to be vague in explaining why they were permitted to

> act as they did. Thus state courts often analyzed constitutional issues of federalism without referring to specific provisions of the Constitution. Furthermore, they often came to conclusions about the meaning of federal statutes without even explicitly naming, much less describing the language of, those statutes. The fact that so many provisions of the federal statutes were ambiguous left the states a fair amount of room for vague interpretation.
>
> (Rosen 30)

In *Removal* Garrison notes:

> the opinions of the southern courts thus filled the legal vacuum created by the federal government's failure to enforce *Worcester*. The southern judiciary held that the Indian tribes were not sovereign nations and that Native Americans were merely the subjects of the state in which they resided. According to southern judges, Native Americans were incapable of cultural cultivation . . . [T]o justify their conclusions, the southern judges intentionally misrepresented the character of Native American social and political culture, distorted the history of U.S.–Indian treaty relations, and ignored relevant and material arguments and precedents that might have led them to different results.
>
> (Garrison 238)

The Trilogy rulings failed to provide clear and consistent guidance and state courts were able to choose which rulings favored their interests. In *Worcester v. Georgia* the Court did not address the original title of the Indians nor the legal fictions that utilized the Doctrine of Discovery in *Johnson*. On the fundamental issue of 'impaired' Indian title, John Marshall could not undo the legal dispossession of Indian land he had pronounced in *Johnson*. *Cherokee Nation* and *Worcester* focused instead on Constitutional and Federal issues, such as legal standing (i.e., whether the Cherokee Nation was a foreign nation to have standing to sue Georgia and whether or not Georgia State laws superseded treaties between the Cherokees and the U.S. Federal Government). Given the inconsistency of Trilogy rulings, state courts were able to challenge the *Worcester* decision on issues turning on Federalism; specifically, whether the U.S. Commerce Clause had concurrent jurisdiction with state law. In contrast, had John Marshall repudiated his judgment in *Johnson* by restoring the 'impaired' title of Indian ownership, state courts would not have been able to challenge *Worcester* on Federalist grounds.

The Virginia–Kentucky militia bounty problem

Between 1792 and 1823 Federal and Constitutional debates served to explain some of the state policies that sought to challenge Indian land ownership. Virginia and Kentucky were seeking to issue land grants to militia veterans in exchange for their service during the war with Britain. During the War of Independence, the American colonies were without the necessary monetary resources to pay their militia. In lieu of wages the colonial governments promised bounty warrants to compensate the militia upon cessation of the war.[8] After the war with England, states such as Virginia and Kentucky were scrambling to expand their western borders to lay claim to unappropriated lands.[9] By making claims upon unappropriated lands, southern states in particular could extend their borders and use the newly acquired land to issue land grants to the militia veterans. "In May 1799, the Virginia legislature had established a land office for the distribution of its 'waste and unappropriated' lands, excepting, inter alia, the lands between the Green and Tennessee Rivers, which were reserved as bounty lands for the officers and soldiers of the Virginia line serving in the Continental Army" (Robertson 83). In 1784 Kentucky discovered that lands west of the Tennessee, which had been set aside for the militia, were in the full possession of the Chickasaw Nation. To complicate matters, the Federal Government interceded and negotiated the Treaty of Hopewell which guaranteed the Chickasaws their rights to the lands west of Tennessee (Robertson 84). Despite the Treaty of Hopewell, Andrew Jackson, prior to his tenure as President and together with former Kentucky governor Isaac Shelby, illegally forced the Chickasaws to concede their title to the lands west of Tennessee in 1818 under the threat of expulsion (85). When the Chickasaws conceded their land claims, Kentucky and Virginia legislators competed over who would obtain land rights west of Tennessee. Virginia sought to lay claim to lands occupied by the Chickasaws because they contended that said grants, operating in similar fashion to pre-emption rights, were conveyable once the Chickasaw abandoned their claim to the land.[10] Robertson notes that "stated differently, where the state had in the past granted Indian lands to its citizens, the grants had always been enforced once the Indians were gone" (86). Subsequent to the controversy between Kentucky and Virginia, the U.S. Supreme Court reviewed the issue of land title in *Johnson*. The subject matter of *Johnson* concerned state claims to land title before and after the establishment of the American Republic. John Marshall, in dicta, selected the issue of Indian land title as an *indirect* way to resolve state land grants by defining the nature of land title under the Doctrine of Discovery.

In *Johnson*, discovery gave the Federal Government ultimate title to all lands. According to John Marshall, Virginia had inherited its claim to unappropriated lands through discovery to pass on to the militia veterans *despite* the Chickasaws' possession. Marshall's opinion in *Johnson* was rooted in the legal argument that only the *discoverer* could purchase or grant land occupied by the Indians:

> British sovereigns and American officials asserted the right to sell Indian land to their citizens before any dealings with the occupying tribe. Purchasers took "subject only to the Indian right of occupancy," but otherwise had a full fee interest. Combined with the exclusive right to purchase Indian lands (or conquer the tribe), discussed in the following section, this created a novel and peculiar "bifurcated title." Ultimate title resided with the European sovereign or its grantee; the Indian occupants retained "Indian title" until they sold (or were otherwise relieved of their lands).
>
> (Kades 75)

The relevance of the above quote highlights the political and constitutional controversies that preceded *Johnson*. John Marshall did not operate in a political vacuum. The political and constitutional debates were major controversies before and during his tenure as Chief Justice of the U.S. Supreme Court. While this examination of the Trilogy cases and their historical context does not attempt to draw a causal relationship between the events outside the Court and John Marshall's opinions in the Trilogy cases, there is enough evidence presented here to argue, as I do, that the early American political discourses between 1789 and 1832 sought to create legal decisions that would be framed as constitutional controversies rather than issues of whether Indians had the legal capacity to *own* their land. Whether the nature of the dispute focused on land grants, the Commerce Clause, or discovery, these legal questions presumed that the United States had already settled the matter of land ownership in relation to the American Indians. Wilkins and Robertson provide an interesting analysis of why John Marshall utilized the Doctrine of Discovery not only to settle the land title dispute between the litigants in *Johnson*, but also to assert full and absolute Federal title to land occupied by Indians. Wilkins asserts that John Marshall was compelled to create a legal fiction based on the Doctrine of Discovery to resolve the land 'disputes' between the litigants and, as Robertson argues, to settle the Kentucky Virginia land warrant controversy. Wilkins quotes John Marshall from his opinion in *Johnson* to evidence the fiction embedded within his judgment:

> However extravagant the pretension of converting the discovery of an inhabited country into conquest may appear; if the principle has been asserted in the first instance, and afterwards, sustained: if a country has been acquired and held under it: if the property of the great mass of the community originates in it, it becomes the law of the land, and cannot be questioned.
>
> (Wilkins 34)

Wilkins argues that:

> [T]he Chief Justice was candidly admitting that the doctrines of discovery and of conquest were nothing more than extravagant pretense without any basis in fact [. . .] the Supreme Court had decided for purely political and economic reason to transform these legal fictions into legal concepts.
>
> (34)

Wilkins' analysis helps to situate the Trilogy cases within the broader constitutional and political colonial context. Certainly, as the conventional interpretation of the Trilogy cases suggests, various writers have sought to link the Trilogy cases to the major Constitutional issues preceding and concurrent with the cases. While I do not argue against such interpretations, I do seek to demonstrate that such interpretations of the Trilogy cases proceed on the basis that the Native American Indian was an extant problem, which Marshall sought to resolve. Such accounts fail to acknowledge the crucial way in which discourses construct the subject, subjects which then become the source of a legal, or other problematic discourse. In the next chapter, I use Foucault's theory of discourse in relation to the Marshall judgment to demonstrate how statements about the capacity of Native Americans were infused into Marshall's judgments in a manner which substituted for the formal testimony of those upon whom the judgments fell.

Federalism

Conventional interpretations of the Trilogy cases *Johnson v. M'Intosh* (1821), *Cherokee Nation v. Georgia* (1831) and *Worcester v. Georgia* (1832) seek to explore how U.S. Supreme Court Chief Justice John Marshall's opinions reflected his attempt to forge a dominant place for Federalism through constitutional interpretations. Burke states that "[m]ost of Marshall's opinion was an elaborate argument for Cherokee independence and most of it was unnecessary to a decision resting on the conflict between federal and Georgia law" (Burke 523). The tension between states' rights and U.S. Federal sovereignty was a significant constitutional point of conflict between 1789 and up to the *Worcester* decision in 1832. To grasp the importance of how Federalism affected the Trilogy judgments and their subsequent narratives, it is important to situate how the conflicts over Federalism affected relations with the American Indians and states' rights. Deborah Rosen and Tim Garrison are two writers who have reviewed how state court decisions and states' rights constructions of the Federal Constitution were manipulated by state courts to promote state policies; in particular, state police powers and control over Indians' lands—lands that were largely occupied by Indians. Rosen, in her examination of state court rulings, writes that: [11]

> in terms of federalism, the states' regulation of Indian land sales, trading, and executor contracts was controversial because Congress covered these subjects in the federal trade and intercourse acts, and the normal rule was that if the federal government had acted on a subject falling within its constitutional power, the states were precluded from legislating on the same topic. In addition, whenever the states negotiated treaties with tribes in order to purchase Indian lands, they arguably came in conflict not only with federal laws asserting exclusive federal control of treaty making with Indians, but also with Section 10 of Article I of the treaty.
>
> (Rosen 29)

Historically, the interesting issue was how the judicial positioning of state courts sought to advance their political objective to control Indians' land, despite apparent Federal jurisdiction over issues of lands and sovereignty. Rosen cites several constitutional paths state courts took to take advantage of any ambiguities in Federal court interpretations regarding Federal jurisdiction over Indian lands. From the status or location of Indian lands within state boundaries to issues of state sovereignty and tenth amendment state *police powers*, state courts found creative methods to take advantage of Federal imprecision in

> linking its exercise of power to its constitutional sources of authority. Indeed, the U.S. Supreme Court cases between 1790 and 1880 have traditionally been viewed as the major statements of federal authority regarding Indians—*Johnson v. McIntosh, Cherokee Nation v. Georgia,* and *Worcester v. Georgia*—failed to provide clear and consistent constitutionally based rules.
>
> (30)

Within this context state courts focused their judicial reasoning to take control of Indian lands. For example, in *Hicks v. Ewhartonah* the Supreme Court of Arkansas held that Federal authority to void contracts between Indians and whites was not applicable. Arkansas argued that such laws were "not applicable to Arkansas Indians who were surrounded by a white population" (Rosen 33). Rosen notes how the Supreme Court of Arkansas introduced the issue of a dominant white population versus a dwindling Indian popoulation as a finding of fact, or reason upon which to construct a legal basis to exempt Arkansas from Federal authority to void contracts between states and Indians.

Rosen's analysis is relevant to this research, which I do not dispute, because it develops a framework that concentrates on political and constitutional issues that turn on Federalism as interpreted by both the U.S. Supreme Court and state courts. Such an approach fails to account for how literary sources and publications during this era constituted a colonial

American construction regarding Indian identity in relation to their legal capacity to hold full title to their lands.

A more clear reflection of the above colonial construction could not have been made other than that by Kermit L. Hall and Melvin I. Urofsky in their Forward to Jill Norgren's *The Cherokee Cases: Two Landmark Federal Decisions in the Fight for Sovereignty*, where they state in describing the thesis of Norgren's book that

> [her] insightful analysis of the famous Cherokee Cases reveals much about the fate of Native Americans in the early nineteenth century. The cases evolved out of attempts by Georgia to assert jurisdiction over Cherokee lands within the state that were protected by a federal treaty. (Norgren vii–viii)

Hall and Urofsky provide further examples of how Federal treaties and Federalism underlie the conventional narratives of Trilogy cases.

Tim A. Garrison, in *The Legal Ideology of Removal*, offers an interpretation of the *Worcester* decision in constitutional terms; however, he also seeks to elucidate a broader explanation for John Marshall's opinion by suggesting a moral rationale. As I will demonstrate below, Garrison adds to the Foucauldian *uniformity of statements* that explain the Trilogy in constitutional terms. Garrison concludes his interpretation with a hint that something more may have been affecting John Marshall's opinion in *Worcester*. "As Marshall wrote the opinion, he must have known at least two things. On the one hand, he perhaps understood that the decision would never be enforced. As such, he could safely and finally clear his conscience regarding his earlier opinions in *Johnson v. McIntosh*, and *Cherokee Nation v. Georgia* and place the Court in a position of high moral authority" (Garrison 197).

Examples of the Federalists' interpretation

While Marshall's opinions have been interpreted as part of the evolving Federalism in the early American Republic, less has been said about how the Marshall judgments can be read against a range of discourses that helped to impose and settle colonial governance. The Marshall judgments were constituted by and constitutive of ways of thinking about the American Indian that were written into a range of texts, such as literary, legal, travel books and journals. A strict reading of the Trilogy cases in the context of their federal ambitions (an ambition which this book does not deny), commonly takes the form of an analysis that seeks to link the Marshall judgments to the political and constitutional challenges between the U.S. Federal Government and southern states to the mid-1830s. The conventional interpretation concentrates on Marshall's supposedly conscious manipulation about the constitutional and political confrontation between the Federal government and states. What the conventional discourses about the Trilogy cases fails to uncover is the equally important but much less consciously evident connection between the content of the Marshall judgments (its propositions, the history it paints, the identities of both native Indians and Americans that it constructs) with ways in which the two protagonists: native Indians and Americans were portrayed in texts that appear at first to bear little relation to the legal judgments, such as literary texts. The structure of legal judgment is such that it is, surprisingly for some, highly susceptible to being influenced in its construction by other forms of literature, including fictional literature. Legal rulings follow findings of fact that are presented as objective and capable of independent verification; however, what I hope to demonstrate is that tropes and images from fictional works are often inserted in legal judgments as if they were *findings of fact*. Furthermore, I argue that these findings of fact influence the outcome (i.e., the ruling) in a judgment as if the judgment was based on objectively verifiable facts and not by fictional images, or tropes. It is important to analyze the structure of legal judgments in order to illustrate how the structure is vulnerable to contamination by other literary sources.

Mathew Fletcher illustrates how pre-Trilogy era images of the American Indian were subsumed as findings of fact in the Trilogy cases:

> The superiority of Euro-American culture was never in question. As Euro-American populations advanced, "that of the Indians necessarily receded." The entire Marshall Court, it appears, was bamboozled by one of the greatest lies ever perpetrated about Indian people—that Indians were hunters and were not (and could not) be farmers. Contemporaneous to the Marshall Trilogy, Henry Schoolcraft, the well-connected Jacksonian charged with surveying the Old Northwest, wrote in 1827 that "[o]ld green fields appeared in spots [on Mackinac Island], which have been formerly cultivated by Indians."[12] A Detroit newspaper editorial gaped in 1831, 'The largest corn I ever saw was raised on these prairies.'[13] And the Cherokee Nation had a surplus of food.[14] According to the Court, however, Euro-American farmers advanced, pushing the Indian 'hunters' away into the 'unbroken forest.'[15] Under this reasoning, Indian lands used for hunting were not owned; in fact, they were "vacant."
>
> (Fletcher 675) [16,17]

Fletcher devotes considerable space in his article to the "notion of federal plenary power over Indians' affairs, canons of Indian treaty construction, the trust relationship between Indians and tribes and the federal government" (630). Fletcher's analysis of the Trilogy also demonstrates the subtle racism underpinning these cases and by extension observes that Marshall and the Supreme Court accepted the "state of things." Fletcher underscores that Marshall incorporated pre-Trilogy images and discourses of Indians as settled fact or sworn statements:

> Chief Justice Marshall's frequent reference to the "actual state of things"[18] was, according to Professor Bob Miller, a reference to the historical "fact" that the reality was . . . "power, war, conquest, give rights, which, after possession, are conceded by the world."
>
> (677)[19]

For the American mind, the question was whether American Indians were weak because they were colonized or they were colonized because they were weak. Marshall's "state of things" perhaps identifies more than any other phrase in his judicial opinions his acceptance of "things" as fact.

Similer to Fletcher, Jill Norgren notes that despite John Marshall's emphatic language in *Worcester* asserting the sovereignty of Indian nations relative to the State of Georgia, President Andrew Jackson and Congress later disregarded Cherokee legal protections. Interestingly Norgren, like Fletcher, identified the *racist* assumption underpinning the Trilogy cases, yet stopped short of explaining how these assumptions were incorporated into Marshall's legal opinions. Norgren writes:

> The *Worcester* doctrine established recognition of Indian sovereignty and confirmed that legal consent was required for the extinguishment of Indian land title. Yet in both the removal and the allotment eras, this legal doctrine was ignored with impunity. In the 1830s the U.S. Supreme Court had neither the will to maintain its opposition to President Jackson and Congress nor the independent means to enforce its pro-Indian doctrine. By the late 1880s, when the legislative and executive branches of the United States had each made a commitment to the new policy of involuntary allotment and assimiliation, the Supreme Court also largely turned its back on the defense of Indian political rights. Indeed, Supreme Court jurisprudence at the end of nineteenth century and in the first years of the new century was marked *more than ever* [my emphasis] by colonialist and racist assumptions.
>
> (Norgren 146)

This book looks behind Marshall's 'actual state of things' to focus on how literature and law were blurred in the Trilogy cases. Fletcher, Norgren and others represent in varied ways how the Trilogy cases are analyzed through political and Constitutional frames. Such frames, however, fail to distinguish between the conjunction of literary discourse and legal judgment.

The examination of the dynamic within legal judgment between literary discourses and John Marshall's *findings of fact* is a non-conventional approach of the Trilogy cases. In taking this approach, I hope to connect this research to a broader body of work usually classified as post-colonial theory, which attempts to uncover colonial practices, conventions and strategies that might appear hidden. The Marshall judgments are clearly linked with a period of colonial acquisition. Recent work has also demonstrated how aesthetic forms were engaged in the colonial enterprise. This research goes one step further in its attempt to show how literary and legal discourses infused each other, blurring the divide between literature and law in the colonial scene. Thus, the literary discourses and the Foucauldian *archives* that were formed therein infused the findings of fact in the Trilogy cases about Indians, suggesting the relative importance of how literature in varied genres informed and limited Marshall's images of Indians. Using Bhabha's theory on colonial discourses, this book also examines how the Trilogy cases overlooked the political, cultural and legal *resistance* by American Indians when contrasted with the conventional interpretations of the Trilogy. [20]

Many of the contemporary narratives of the Trilogy cases presumed that Indians lacked the legal capacity to own their land. When John Marshall, in *Worcester*, sought to limit states' rights it was not in relation to Indians, but in relation to Federal treaties with Indians. Marshall's opinion in *Worcester* centers on the Federal issue, rather than Indian legal capacity. As this chapter has demonstrated, while it may seem that *Worcester* restored national sovereignty to the Cherokee and by implication, the legal capacity of Indians to own their land, Marshall's ultimate Constitutional position was that the Federal Government retained ultimate fee simple title to Indian land. Had Marshall cited Indian land rights as superseding Federal rights, he would have allowed the Cherokee to acquire legal capacity to own their land. This was not possible because Marshall had previously declared the Cherokee a *domestic dependent nation* in *Cherokee*, and in *Johnson* Marshall had already *impaired* the absolute ownership claim of Native Americans. Having foreclosed these avenues of Indian legal capacity, he could only protect the Cherokee against Georgia's attempts to seize their lands within the framework of Federalism.

Notes

1 This quote is part of a course developed by the UAF Interior Aleutians Campus in cooperation with the Tanana Chiefs Conference and the UAF Center for Distance Education. This project has been funded at least in part with Federal funds from the U.S. Department of Education Title III grant and by the U.S. Bureau of Indian Affairs. The content of this publication does not necessarily reflect the views or policies of the U.S. Department of Education or the U.S. Bureau of Indian Affairs nor does by mention of trade names, commercial products, or organizations imply endorsement by the U.S. Government. http://tm112.community.uaf.edu/unit-1/marshall-trilogy-1823-1832/ accessed March 5, 2016.

2 "King George reserved the western lands of the 'several nations or tribes of Indians' that were under his 'protection' as their exclusive 'hunting grounds.' As sovereign of this territory, however, the King claimed ultimate 'Dominion' over the entire region. He further prohibited any private person from directly

buying the interest of native groups in their ancestral soil. This exclusive right of purchase he rather reserved for himself and his heirs alone. As detailed in the Proclamation, he set out a procedure whereby an Indian group, if they freely chose, could sell their land rights to properly authorised representatives of the British monarch. This could only take place at some public meeting called especially for the purpose. It was thus that the constitutional basis was established for the future negotiation of Indian treaties in British North America. The Royal Proclamation thereby established the British Crown as the essential central agent in the transfer of Indian lands to colonial settlers" (Hall).

3 "Not only has the practice of all civilized nations been in conformity with this doctrine, but the whole theory of their titles to lands in America, rests upon the hypothesis, that the Indians had no right of soil as sovereign, independent states. Discovery is the foundation of title, in European nations, and this overlooks all proprietary rights in the natives" (*Johnson v. M'Intosh* 567).

4 The Indian Removal Act of 1830 foreclosed any political opportunities that the Cherokee had to avoid relocation. With Congress and the President refusing to intervene on behalf of the Cherokee to stop Georgia's attempt to eradicate the Cherokee Nation as a political entity, John Ross, the Cherokee leader, resorted to the courts as a last resort in Georgia (Garrison 108).

5 The 1763 Royal Charter was issued by George III and is cited in *Johnson*.

6 In addition to *Georgia v. Tassels* (1830), southern courts produced rulings contrary to John Marshall's judgment in *Cherokee Nation* and *Worcester* claiming that "tribes were not sovereign nations" but that Indians were simply, as individuals, subjects of the states in which they lived. Southern judges held that state authority extended its jurisdiction regardless of Federal Treaties that were signed with Indian tribes within their borders. Southern states in court rulings such as *Caldwell v. Alabama* (1831) and *Tennessee v. Foreman* (1835) held that they could extinguish Indian title if such so-called title fell within their state borders (Garrison 5–6).

7 "He boldly proclaimed himself to be the "CHAMPION OF THE COMMON MAN" and believed that their interests were ignored by the aggressive national economic plans of Clay and Adams" (ushistory.org). http://www.ushistory.org/us/23f.asp accessed March 5, 2016.

8 "The act of the General Assembly passed on June 22, 1779, which established the Virginia Land Office, also provided for the awarding of bounty lands for specified Revolutionary War military service. The purpose of the bounty land system was to encourage longer military service. In order to qualify for bounty land, a soldier or sailor had to serve at least three (3) years continuously in the State or Continental Line or State Navy. Militia service did not count. The process of obtaining bounty lands was lengthy, and, in many cases, land speculators acquired the right to the land from the veteran or his heirs" (*About the Revolutionary War Bounty Warrants*), http://www.lva.virginia.gov/public/guides/opac/bountyabout.htm accessed March 5, 2016.

9 "One of the difficult problems of the new nation was the existence of extensive unoccupied territory between the Thirteen Original Colonies and the Mississippi River. Seven of the Colonies claimed large parts of this territory and some of the claims were conflicting. Recognizing the possibilities for dispute in this situation, the Continental Congress on October 30, 1779, passed a resolution recommending to Virginia and the other interested States that they refrain from granting the unappropriated lands in the western territory during the continuance of the Revolutionary War. The seven States claiming these areas responded favorably to this action and during the period from 1781 to 1802 ceded the lands to the Federal Government" (Van Zandt).

10 The term 'abandoned' is used on par with *alienation* of land. In this context, 'to abandon' a land claim refers to the sale of tribal lands by Indians to the Federal Government.

11 Deborah Rosen, Professor of History, Lafayette College, Easton, Pennsylvania and Tim Garrison, Professor, Department of History, Portland State University, Portland, Oregon.

12 W.B. Hinsdale, *The First People of Michigan* 146 (1930).

13 *Ibid.*

14 David M. Wishart, "Evidence of Surplus Production in the Cherokee Nation Prior to Removal," 55 *J. Econ. Hist.*, 120 (1995) at 76.

15 See *Johnson,* 32 U.S. at 590–91 ("The country in the immediate neighborhood of agriculturalists became unfit for [the Indians]. The game fled into thicker and more unbroken forest, and the Indians followed.")

16 *Ibid* at 596. ("[N]o distinction was taken between vacant lands and lands occupied by the Indians.")

17 *Johnson v. M'Intosh,* 21 U.S. 543 at 590.

18 *Johnson v. M'Intosh,* 21 U.S. 543, 591 (1823); *Worcester v. Georgia,* 31, U.S. 515, 543, 546, 560 (1832).

19 *Worcester v. Georgia,* 31 U.S. at 543.

20 See Chapter 7.

Chapter 3

Colonial knowledge

A unity of discourses

This chapter examines the Marshall judgments to demonstrate how Chief Justice Marshall contributed to a set of discourses that produced a very particular subject—the Native American Indian. According to Marshall, the Native American is of an inferior race, is "war like," "heathen" and "unchristian." Marshall describes the characteristics of this subject with the confidence of someone who is giving, or relying upon, expert evidence concerning the faculties and social habits of the Native Americans under discussion; however, nowhere in the Marshall judgments is any such evidence offered, or considered. From what sources, therefore, did Marshall obtain his understanding of the character and habits of the Native American Indian?

In this chapter, I argue that the conceptualization of the Native American Indian was produced from what Foucault speaks of as a unity of discourses. The idea of the heathen so strongly evident in the Marshall judgment was equally at play in a range of discourses. To deploy Foucault's language, statements about the character and the capacity of the subject that came to be known as the Native American Indian were found in several sources and spanned many discursive traditions. Foucault explains that "groups of statements that have one and the same object form a unity of discourses" (Foucault, *The Archaeology of Knowledge* 35–6). Legal judgments, fictional works, landscapes and portraiture were all united in the object of delimiting the capacity of the Native American. Yet, these sources of various statements that speak of the savage-like qualities of the Native American Indian cannot be conceived, following Foucault, as mere comments upon a subject already produced. Rather those statements produced the very object of the various discourses—the Native American.

As I hope to demonstrate in the ensuing chapter, Chief Justice Marshall deploys knowledge about the Native American, produced through this unity of discourses, as a judge would deploy facts that had been objectively verified, or expert evidence that had been appropriately validated. Such is the strength of discourse that, in a sense, Marshall could not otherwise have engaged the quantity of information produced about the Native American

Indian. Fictional works would not (according to certain discursive traditions) support truth claims, but Marshall makes no distinction between fact and fiction in his ultimately damning assessment of the subject of the Marshall cases.

Whilst Part II of this book examines novels and paintings of this time as part of this unified colonial discourse (a colonial discourse precisely characterized by a certain messiness: by a merging of discursive traditions which in other contexts were distinct, like literature as distinct from law) that produced a marginalized and oppressed colonial subject, this chapter examines how the character of the Native American was inserted into the Marshall cases as factual findings of a legal judgment.

The structure of legal judgment

Given the language used by Marshall in *Johnson* to describe the native Indians, there is little doubt he viewed the indigenous population as "war like," "heathen" and "unchristian" and at least in terms of Marshall's interpretation of the Doctrine of Discovery, Indians were only acknowledged to have an 'occupancy' interest in the lands discovered by Britain. Marshall cited several colonial statutes that underscored the 'inferior race' of the Indians that attached legal and ethnological justification for taking exclusive rights of full land title in the New World, only subject to the occupancy interest of the indigenous peoples. Marshall stated, "Statutes of Virginia, and of all the other colonies, and of the United States, treat them as an inferior race of people, without the privileges of citizens, and under the perpetual protection and pupilage of the government" (*Johnson v. M'Intosh* 569). While Marshall uses the phrase "inferior race" it is notable that he attributes this depiction of the Indians to the "Statutes of Virginia" and "all other colonies" giving the reader the impression that these descriptions of the Indians were settled fact and not his own (569). I argue that while prior state court rulings may have provided Marshall with judicial precedents depicting the Indians as an "inferior race," wider literary discourses also filled in the colonial archive with images of that so-called "inferior race." These wider literary discourses were exemplified by such writers as James Fenimore Cooper with *The Last of the Mohicans*, in addition to the American Romantic depictions of the "vanishing Indian" in the early nineteenth century, portrayed by William Cullen Bryant and Washington Irving.[1]

In *Cherokee Nation v. Georgia*, Marshall's use of terms such as "protection" and "pupilage" adopts findings of fact that depict the Indians as inferior to the "government" by virtue of being "an inferior race of people":

> They occupy a territory to which we assert a title independent of their will, which must take effect in point of possession when their right of possession ceases; meanwhile, they are in a state of pupilage. Their

> relations to the United States resemble that of a ward to his guardian. They look to our Government for protection, rely upon its kindness and its power, appeal to it for relief to their wants, and address the President as their Great Father.
>
> (*Cherokee Nation v. Georgia* 17)

Here Marshall incorporates images of "weakness" and "inferiority" of the Indian in direct relation to the Federal Government. Implicit in these images is the notion that Indian dependence upon the protection of the 'Great Father' acknowledges that one race is superior to the other. The idea of the racial superiority of the European American in comparison to the Indian has several literary components, such as the "hunter state" of Indian culture. James Monroe, among others, wrote about "the *unqualified right* [italics in the original] of a civilized people to claim land used by people in the hunter-state, on the principle that the earth was intended for those who would make it most conducive to the sustenance and increase the human race" (quoted in Jahoda 21–2).[2] Monroe established a racial premise to dispossess Indians from any claim to land ownership, based on their inferior human state to cultivate the land to sustain and promote the collective "human race." By implication, hunter-state peoples fulfil the prerequisite for dependence upon the protection of the "Great Father" in Washington. Indian dispossession is linked to their presumed inability, as Monroe cites, to foster "sustenance and increase the human race." Therefore, while *Johnson* established that the United States, based on the Doctrine of Discovery, could assert exclusive ownership of all the land previously claimed by Britain, in *Cherokee Nation* Marshall incorporated racial depictions to demarcate Indian occupancy from American ownership of Indian land.

Writing in 1823, James Madison wrote, "religion is not in the purview of human government. Religion is essentially distinct from civil government, and exempt from its cognizance; a connection between them is injurious to both" (quoted in Newcomb, *Five Hundred Years of Injustice: The Legacy of Fifteenth Century Religious Prejudice*). Despite Madison's attempt to romanticize the separation of church and state, U.S. Federal Indian Law is grounded on a *religious* doctrine. The United States inherited from Britain the exclusive right not only to purchase any Indian lands, but also to preclude indigenous peoples from selling their land to anyone but the United States Federal Government. What *findings of fact* did Marshall utilize to remove the ownership of interest of the Indians? Indeed, this

> right of discovery given by this commission is confined to countries 'then unknown to all Christian people,' and of these countries Cabot was empowered to take possession in the name of the King of England. Thus asserting a right to take possession.
>
> (*Johnson v. M'Intosh* 576)

Marshall therefore incorporates the phrase "then unknown to all Christian people," implying that places where Christianity did not prevail could not contain people with the legal capacity to own land as compared to Christian nations like England. The genealogy of Marshall's Christian claim to land relates directly back to John Cabot's Charter of 1496. Preceding Cabot's Charter, Pope Nicholas V had asserted an identical claim in 1452. In order to utilize Christianity as a prerequisite to owning land, both the Pope and the King of England asserted that such *non-Christian* lands were occupied by heathens:

> The same principle continued to be recognized. The charter granted to Sir Humphrey Gilbert in 1578 authorizes him to discover and take possession of such remote, heathen, and barbarous lands as were not actually possessed by any Christian prince or people. This charter was afterwards renewed to Sir Walter Raleigh in nearly the same terms.
>
> (577)

Marshall is not only accepting the charter granted to Sir Humphrey Gilbert, but he is also incorporating Sir Humphrey's premise that claims to land are based on occupation by *non-Christian* people. Humphrey's grant is based on the Christian principle, which Marshall is accepting as a sworn statement, that *only* Christians can own land. This illustrates Foucault's *unity of discourses* whereby statements about a subject, over time, come to define a subject. Cotton Mather's *Magnalia* depicts the Christian qualities of the early English settlers on their journey to the dark and unchristian New World. Mather's commentary provided an early American discourse linking Christianity to civilization and land ownership. William Penn writes about the wilderness of the New World in terms of its unplanted darkness; a darkness that could only be made into a Garden by faith in God. Penn was advancing a discursive statement that associated Christianity with light and civilizing the Indians with land title.

Marshall is not only accepting the findings of Gilbert's grant to Cabot, but also adding to the *archive* of the Indians by accepting such findings as the basis for his legal doctrine. Marshall adds to the colonial archive when he portrays Indians as mere heathens and without any Christian basis to acknowledge their ownership of their lands. "The ceded territory was occupied by numerous and warlike tribes of Indians, but the exclusive right of the United States to extinguish their title and to grant the soil has never, we believe, been doubted" (586). Marshall builds on the premise of Gilbert's grant; namely, that his acceptance of Indians as "heathens" and "barbarous" adds to the colonial interpretation that barbarous can mean "warlike tribes of Indians." Marshall is able to transform the Indians into warlike because he incorporates Gilbert's grant work as a finding of fact (577, 590). By incorporating Gilbert's depiction of the Indians as "warlike" Marshall supports his legal claim that:

> It has never been doubted that either the United States or the several states had a clear title to all the lands within the boundary lines described in the treaty, subject only to the Indian right of occupancy, and that the exclusive power to extinguish that right was vested in that government which might constitutionally exercise it.
>
> (584–5)

Never doubted by whom? Indians? Europeans? It is most likely the latter. Therefore, the issue of "doubt" is reinforced by resort to establishing findings that Indians are warlike. DeWitt Clinton, for example, describes the warlike image of the Indian when he states "war was the favorite pursuit of this martial people, and military glory their ruling passion" (Clinton 16).[3] Clinton's depiction of the Indian was built on the literary archive that contained statements that defined the Indians as barbaric, devoid of Christian attributes.[4] These inhuman and barbaric depictions were a staple in many of the captive narratives published between 1682 and 1824. The quote below is from a captive narrative relating to Mary Kinnan's capture *A True Narrative of the sufferings of Mary Kinnan*, written by Shepard Kollock in 1792):

> Instead of that benevolent disposition and warm sensibility to the sufferings of others, which marks their characters in more civilized climes, they quaff with ecstatic pleasure the blood of the innocent prisoner, writhing with agony under the inhuman torments inflicted upon him—whilst his convulsive groans speak music to their souls.
>
> (Quoted in Stodola 112)

In the quote above the uncivilized and inhuman tendencies of Indians underscore their lack of Christianity. As the major European nations competing for land in the New World were basing their claim on Christianity, Marshall accepts as a sworn statement that land ownership is based upon Christianity. Interestingly, while Marshall attempts to support his legal argument on selected findings of fact to disparage the image of the Indians, he is mindful that this argument may be questioned and makes the following statement in *Johnson*:

> However extravagant the pretension of converting the discovery of an inhabited country into conquest may appear; if the principle has been asserted in the first instance, and afterwards sustained; if a country has been acquired and held under it; if the property of the great mass of the community originates in it, it becomes the law of the land, and cannot be questioned. So, too, with respect to the concomitant principle, that the Indian inhabitants are to be considered merely as occupants, to be protected, indeed, while in peace, in the possession of their lands, but to be deemed incapable of transferring the absolute title to others. However this restriction may be opposed to natural right, and to the

> usages of civilized nations, yet, if it be indispensable to that system under which the country has been settled, and be adapted to the actual condition of the two people, it may, perhaps, be supported by reason, and certainly cannot be rejected by Courts of Justice.
>
> (*Johnson v. M'Intosh* 591–2)

Here Marshall formulates his legal opinion not based upon law, or legal precedent, but on *custom.*

> If the principle has been asserted in the first instance, and afterwards sustained; if a country has been acquired and held under it; if the property of the great mass of the community originates in it, it becomes the law of the land, and cannot be questioned.
>
> (591)

Marshall seems to acknowledge that the religious and racial arguments that underpin the Doctrine of Discovery may not have a solid logical footing when he states, "however extravagant the pretension of converting the discovery of an inhabited country into conquest may appear" (591–92). Marshall's incorporation of a legal fiction is not implied or speculative but expressed when he uses the term *pretension.* Questioning the basis of the Doctrine of Discovery, Marshall turns to incorporating a tradition of conquest coded under the phrase "held under it" to establish a legal doctrine built on *tradition* not law. Marshall moves to establish a legal claim to land ownership based on the fact that the "property of the great mass of the community originates in it" (591–2). Marshall justifies the "extravagance" of the Doctrine of Discovery by explaining "to resort to some new and different rule, better adapted to the actual state of things, was unavoidable" (591). Marshall's "actual state of things" is his metaphor for accepting events, such as conquest, as a *fait accompli*—the findings of fact for the legal basis on which to formulate a legal doctrine that asserts American property ownership. Marshall seeks to justify his legal reasoning on the "actual state of things" where the British and the Americans established their claims against Indian lands that were "held under" their conquest; however, this reasoning avoids any judicial connection to findings that were formed by the literary colonial archive. As I argue, numerous genres of literature formed the racial and cultural images that situated the findings of facts, not based on the "actual state of things," but based on the *unity of discourses* that over time formed the colonial archive preceding the Trilogy. Therefore, *Johnson* is a ruling based on accepting findings of fact about the inferior race of Indians and conquest under the Doctrine of Discovery. Marshall's attempt to question his own legal construction by highlighting the "pretense" of such an argument, compared to one based on the "actual state of things," is disingenuous. Marshall's pretense in *Johnson* is not one about the Doctrine of Discovery, but is more about denial of the blurring of law and literature in his judgment.

Marshall inserts findings which, "found by our ancestors in the quiet and uncontrolled possession of an ample domain, gradually sinking beneath our superior policy, our arts and our arms" (*Cherokee Nation v. Georgia* 15). Marshall's incorporation of the *quiet* and *uncontrolled* Indian state implies that the land was merely in possession by an inferior race. Marshall's use of the term "sinking beneath our superior policy, our arts and our arms" diminishes any cultural parity the Cherokee may have alleged in their motion for an injunction (15). Marshall's argument had to presume an unequal state of Cherokee culture in relation to European-American culture because this was a necessary step toward his ultimate legal position that the Cherokee were mere *wards* and a *dependent* nation under the protection of the American Government. In Marshall's master/pupil metaphor, he could legally argue that the Cherokee were anything but a foreign state. Marshall's metaphors were preceded by such writers as William Cullen Bryant who wrote about the "weak" Indian race. Lewis and Clark portrayed the Indians as uncivilized and without any comprehension of land ownership. Similarly, the writings of Adam Smith outlined stages of human development that were used by Britain and southern courts to situate the Indians as a primitive race, which in part cast the Indians as inferior to the European-American culture. I will also argue that Andrew Jackson's speeches portray the Indians as sub-human.[5]

The Cherokee sought to bolster their motion by pointing to the number of treaties signed between the Cherokee Nation and the American Government as evidence that treaties enshrined Cherokee status as a *foreign state.* In their motion, the Cherokee provided a litany of treaties signed with the Federal Government to bolster their claim that they were a foreign nation that did have standing to bring this motion before the U.S. Supreme Court:

> The bill proceeds to refer to the treaty concluded at Hopewell on the 28th November 1785, "between the commissioners of the United States and head men and warriors of all the Cherokees"; the treaty of Holston of the 22nd July 1791, "between the president of the United States by his duly authorized commissioner, William Blount, and the chiefs and warriors of the Cherokee Nation of Indians," and the additional [30 U.S. 1, 5] article of 17th November 1792, made at Philadelphia by Henry Knox, the secretary of war, acting on behalf of the United States; the treaty made at Philadelphia on the 26th June 1794; the treaties between the same parties made at Tellico 2nd October 1790; on the 24th October 1804; on the 25th October 1805, and the 27th October 1805; the treaty at Washington on the 7th January 1806, with the proclamation of that convention by the president, and the elucidation of that convention of 11th September 1807; the treaty between the United States and the Cherokee Nation made at the city of Washington on the 22nd day of

> March 1816; another convention made at the same place, on the same day, by the same parties; a treaty made at the Cherokee agency on the 8th July 1807; and a treaty made at the city of Washington on the 27th February 1819: "all of which treaties and conventions were duly ratified and confirmed by the senate of the United States, and became thenceforth, and still are, a part of the supreme law of the land."
>
> (*Cherokee Nation v. Georgia* 4–5)

These treaties were "duly ratified and confirmed by the Senate"; yet, despite the litany of treaties signed between the Cherokee and Federal Government, Marshall dismissed the motion because the Cherokee lacked standing to bring such an action to the U.S. Supreme Court since the court did not view the Cherokee Nation as a separate state. Since the Cherokee Nation had neither the status of a state, nor of a foreign nation, Marshall asserted that they lacked standing to sue the State of Georgia; therefore, the Supreme Court denied the motion for lack of original jurisdiction. Marshall's legal reasoning was an *ad hominem* argument dismissing the Cherokee motion on grounds that they were not a foreign nation, despite the long history of Federal Treaties with the Cherokee:

> Though the Indians are acknowledged to have an unquestionable, and, heretofore, unquestioned right to the lands they occupy, until that right shall be extinguished by a voluntary cession to our government; yet it may well be doubted whether those tribes which reside within the acknowledged boundaries of the United States can, with strict accuracy, be denominated foreign nations. They may, more correctly, perhaps, be denominated domestic dependent nations. They occupy a territory to which we assert a title independent of their will, which must take effect in point of possession when their right of possession ceases. Meanwhile they are in a state of pupilage. Their relation to the United States resembles that of a ward to his guardian.
>
> (17)

In Marshall's analysis, it is clear that certain findings are incorporated in order to diminish Cherokee sovereignty to one of "pupilage" and "ward to his guardian." Both descriptions depict the Cherokee as unequal partners to be relegated to a "denominated domestic dependent nation." As cited previously, various literary discourses depicted Indians as an inferior race. This literary archive made it appear, by the time Marshall wrote his opinion in *Cherokee Nation*, that the dependent status of the Indian was an unquestioned "actual state of things." Also, while not cited expressly in *Cherokee Nation*, Marshall's depiction is consistent with his findings in *Johnson* where Indians were defined as "heathens" and "non-Christian" to utilize these religious metaphors in order to transform the Cherokee into "wards" and "pupils." Attempting to forge an internal logic to his analysis in *Cherokee Nation,* Marshall asserts that the Cherokee were unable to protect their nation without the paternalistic oversight of the Federal Government; hence, his statement that the Cherokee were a "dependent nation" appears consistent with his *Johnson* ruling. According to Marshall, since the Cherokee had signed treaties yielding land to the Federal Government and since such treaties had asked for the protection of the Federal Government, by implication this protection asserted that the Cherokee were anything but foreign, and were nations dependent upon the Federal Government. Foucault's *discursive archive* theory helps to illustrate how Marshall is able to exclude statements that would also demonstrate that the Cherokee were equal partners when their treaties with the Federal Government were signed.[6] In *Cherokee Nation,* Marshall could not include such statements as they would evidence Cherokee independence rather than dependence. By excluding statements that supported the independence of the Cherokee, Marshall was able to establish findings of fact that supported the *dependent* state of the Cherokee Nation. Therefore, because Marshall asserted that the Cherokee were in a relationship to the United States resembling that of a people under a state of "pupilage," the Cherokee were *de facto* children in relation to the Federal Government; hence, the Cherokee could not claim to be a foreign state. By concluding that the Cherokee were not a foreign state, Marshall was able to dismiss the motion for an injunction and thus side-step the constitutional challenge of whether the laws of Georgia were null and void on Cherokee land.

Given Marshall's opinion, the Cherokee motion was denied because they were (i) not a U.S. state, and (ii) not a foreign nation in the sense of what a foreign nation meant to the court. By virtue of the implicit and underpinning Doctrine of Discovery cited in *Johnson,* the United States' claim to exclusive fee simple ownership of the land upon which the Cherokee were situated denied them the status of a foreign nation. Such is the remarkable interrelationship between *Johnson* and *Cherokee Nation* rulings that even treaties signed between the United States and the Cherokee Nation were linguistically reframed as treaties between the United States and a "foreign dependent nation"; hence, neither a foreign state nor a U.S. state. Therefore, the Supreme Court discovered an interpretive means to deny the motion by the Cherokee Nation against Georgia based on a selective incorporation of findings of fact to support the court's ruling that the Cherokee were *not* a foreign sovereign nation.

An important finding of fact that is accepted as a sworn statement is Marshall's statement that "the Indian nations had always been considered." Marshall's phrase "had always been" denotes, a *tradition,* not *law.* This distinction underscores his blurring of history and law. Tradition rather than judicial precedent is incorporated as a finding of fact by Marshall. Whose tradition is Marshall referring to?

There is another tradition that Marshall discusses in *Worcester,* concerning the various treaties signed between the Federal Government and native tribes. The interesting finding of fact in Marshall's exposition of treaty history is not only the delineation of the Federal treaty preemption over state law, but the revisitation of the dependent and uncivilized state of Indians. In citing the 1819 Congressional Act to protect Indian nations, Marshall wrote:

> This act avowedly contemplates the preservation of the Indian nations as an object sought by the United States, and proposes to effect this object by civilizing and converting them from hunters into agriculturists. Though the Cherokees had already made considerable progress in this improvement, it cannot be doubted that the general words of the act comprehend them. Their advance in the "habits and arts of civilization," rather encouraged perseverance in the laudable exertions still farther to meliorate their condition. This act furnishes strong additional evidence of a settled purpose to fix the Indians in their country by giving them security at home.
>
> (*Worcester v. Georgia* 557)

By incorporating the 1819 Congressional Act, Marshall seamlessly accepts findings of fact about Indian culture, the Indians' mode of existence, their uncivilized state and their unchristian character. What is interesting is the manner by which Marshall accepts his findings. Marshall adopts the 1819 Congressional Act not as a legislative source of law but as a sworn statement about Indian culture and inferiority. While the 1819 Congressional Act provides Marshall with a legal source to underscore the "fact" of Indian inferiority and dependence upon the American Government, Marshall could equally have asserted these findings, as he did in *Cherokee Nation* and *Johnson,* as the "actual state of things" given the colonial archive about Indians.

Marshall also seeks to emphasize that Congressional intent supported Cherokee 'security at home' to underscore Cherokee sovereignty in relation to Georgia law; however, in the same passage Marshall also incorporates findings of fact which underscores the *uncivilized* and deplorable condition of the Cherokee people in relation to European-American culture. Marshall incorporates a tradition of Congressional acts, in particular the Act of 1819, which sought "their advance in the 'habits and arts of civilization' as findings that justify Federal civilizing programs over the Cherokee people" (*Worcester* 588). Similar to his "domestic dependent nation" status in *Cherokee Nation,* in *Worcester* Marshall continues to degrade Cherokee culture while simultaneously, under the guise of protecting Cherokee internal sovereignty, he projects a legal right of internal governance of the Cherokee in relation to Georgia law.

In *Cherokee Nation,* Marshall undermined Cherokee sovereignty as he considered them a 'dependent foreign nation' within the borders of the United States; however, in *Worcester,* Marshall appears to reassert Cherokee sovereignty, but only subject to the Federal Government's exclusive purchase rights. In *Worcester* Marshall did not restore a land ownership claim to the Cherokee in relation to the United States. He did outline legal boundaries with respect to the Cherokee based upon the Doctrine of Discovery and by findings of numerous U.S. treaties, which established a *unique* national sovereignty of the Cherokee in relation to states like Georgia. Marshall stated in *Worcester:*

> It must be admitted, that the Indians sustain a peculiar relation to the United States. They do not constitute, as was decided at the last term, a foreign state, so as to claim the right to sue in the supreme court of the United States: and yet, having the right of self government, they, in some sense, form a state. In the management of their internal concerns, they are dependent on no power. They punish offences under their own laws, and, in doing so, they are responsible to no earthly tribunal. They make war, and form treaties of peace. The exercise of these and other powers, gives to them a distinct character as a people, and constitutes them, in some respects, a state, although they may not be admitted to possess the right of soil.
>
> (581)

The last sentence is most telling because of the phrase "*although they may not be admitted to possess the right of soil.*" By "right of soil," Marshall seeks to ensure that the United States retains the full ownership claim to Indian land asserted under *Johnson;* however, and unlike *Johnson,* Marshall is establishing legal rights and territorial jurisdictional bounds between the Cherokee Nation and the State of Georgia. Marshall's ruling in *Worcester* leaves no doubt that Georgia had no constitutional authority to extend its jurisdiction over Cherokee land, but Cherokee land ownership was still subject to Federal jurisdiction.

Despite Marshall's attempt to protect the national sovereignty of the Cherokee Nation with respect to Georgia, it was too late to halt Indian removal. Soon after this ruling, the composition of the Supreme Court changed as President Andrew Jackson appointed his own justices to the court. John McLean and Henry Baldwin were appointed by Jackson during the 1830 term and John M. Wayne replaced Justice William Johnson (a former member of the Georgia State Supreme Court) who died in 1834. According to Robertson, Wayne was a "vigorous supporter of removal" (Robertson 138). With Justice Marshall dying, 1835 proved to be his last term. As such, the balance of power within the Supreme Court shifted, affording the Jackson appointees the chance to restore the "fee simple" title originally formulated in *Johnson* and restore *state* laws over Indian land. What made the new appointments critical to the jurisprudence of American Federal Indian Law is that Jackson's appointees were placed there, in part, to uphold Marshall's opinion in *Johnson* rather than the majority ruling in *Worcester*. Shortly thereafter Judge Marshall died and further appointments by Jackson insured that *Worcester's* ruling would not usurp the *Johnson* decision.[7]

The Indian Removal Act of 1830 should have been held unconstitutional after *Worcester*, although by the time *Worcester* was decided removal actions were already under way, paving the way for the Federal Government to forcibly dispossess the Cherokee in 1838 from North Carolina and Georgia to Oklahoma. In an event known as the "Trail of Tears" several thousand Cherokee were marched on foot in conditions that can only be described as horrific. Jahoda has written extensively about the *Trail of Tears* and President Andrew Jackson's disregard of the *Worcester* decision. Our aim here was not to review that history, but to examine the major legal issues and to illustrate how the findings of fact in the Trilogy cases blurred any distinction between literature and law.

Notes

1 Other literary genres, including captive narratives, missionary journals and early nineteenth-century histories of the American Republic, together with newspaper accounts, formed a vast archive of discursive images of the Native American.

2 James Monroe (1758–1831), the fifth U.S. president, oversaw major westward expansion of the U.S. and strengthened American foreign policy in 1823 with the Monroe Doctrine, a doctrine established to warn European countries against further colonization and intervention in the Western Hemisphere (Staff).

3 DeWitt Clinton, (born March 2, 1769, Little Britain, N.Y. [U.S.]–died February 11, 1828, Albany, N.Y., U.S.) was an American political leader who promulgated the idea of the Erie Canal, which connects the Hudson River to the Great Lakes (Clinton, *Encyclopaedia Britannica*).

4 The captive narrative genre, such as that of Mary Kinnan, Mary Rowlandson, Hannah Duston, Elizabeth Hanson, Jemima Howe, May Jemison and others, added to the colonial archive about the warlike tendencies of Indians (Stodola ix). DeWitt Clinton was hardly alone in depicting Native Americans as "inhuman."

5 These writers are but some examples of literary influences (i.e., discourses) that formed images of the Native American. Suffice it at this juncture to remind the reader that a vast archive of literary discourses was being developed prior to the Trilogy rulings from 1823–1832. See further examples in Chapters 5, 6 and 7.

6 Quoting Francis Jennings, "the notion of the treaty apparently carried a different connotation for Indians than it did for British and American treaty commissioners. Francis Jennings, the historian and critic of Anglo-American Indian policies, suggested that the British, colonial, and American Governments conceived of treaties as 'arrangements of necessity and convenience, to be dispensed with when circumstance would permit.' Indians, in contrast, regarded treaties as binding 'agreements between sovereign peers'" (quoted in Garrison 49).

7 Robertson reviews the subsequent Supreme Court rulings which sought to undercut the effect of *Worcester*, namely, *Mitchel v. United States (Mitchel I)* (Roberston 138).

Part II

Refining the Native American

Chapter 4

Theory of discourse in a colonial context

Edward Said and the American eighteenth-century literary archive

In Chapter 3 I argued that Chief Justice Marshall failed to distinguish between factual testimony and fictional accounts of the character of the Native American. I argued that this blurring of fact and fiction is a key feature of a colonial discourse and, in the context of the Marshall Trilogy, was a key instrument in the processes in which the Native American Indian was dispossessed of land and other material property. In this part of the book I attempt to substantiate this claim by drawing out the correspondences between Marshall's depiction of the native in the Trilogy cases and their depiction in major literary (including fictional) works of the time and in key works of landscape portraiture. My reading of this body of artistic work is significantly guided by Edward Said's strategy in analyzing the eighteenth-century novel against the novel's colonial backdrop. Said, of course, was heavily influenced by Foucault's theory of discourse; however, Foucault, whilst deploying a number of contexts as a means of elaborating his argument, was largely indifferent to the colonial context. In this regard Edward Said's work—especially in *Culture and Imperialism*—provides an important supplement to Foucault's theory of discourse—one without which this research would be incomplete.

In the first section of this chapter I outline how Said developed Foucault's work in the colonial context. In the second, I provide the reader with an overview of the literary archive as it stood at the time that Chief Justice Marshall pronounced upon the capacity of the Native American Indian. The two remaining sections of this chapter consist of readings of captive narratives, poems, histories, public speeches and landscape paintings in ways that are largely faithful to Said's reading methodology. These various artistic forms contain 'irregular statements' about Indians, which over time have gained purchase far beyond the contexts in which they were originally articulated.

While Michel Foucault provides a theory that accounts for how discursive statements about an object, or subject (i.e. an episteme) can over time form into an archive about a subject, Foucault's theory does not offer a context for precisely how colonial discourses can be formed. Edward Said incorporates Foucault's discourse theory to account for literary discourses, saying that the British novel during the nineteenth century helped to expand the hegemony of British Imperialism. Utilizing Said's research in his *Orientalism* and *Culture and Imperialism,* I argue that varied literary genres produced important discourses about the American Indian that were ultimately incorporated as factual findings by John Marshall in his Trilogy rulings. Said provides an aesthetic context to the formation of discursive images and representations of the American Indians that would normally be deemed a detachment from legal judgment. Said's work helps us to understand how that aesthetic of literary genres can acquire the force of law when literature and law are blurred in legal judgment.

Said offers a theoretical extension of Foucault's discourse theory into the colonial realm. Said helps to situate the claim made in this book that the messiness of the colonial archive preceding the Trilogy rulings becomes understandable when account is taken of the varied literary discourses that were consolidated into an archive about American Indians. The critical role played by Said's work enables an examination of how the aesthetics of literature can become blurred with legal judgment. Where conventional interpretations of the Trilogy cases would claim a separation between law and literature, I argue that John Marshall's opinions in the Trilogy evidence the blurring of the literary, including the aesthetic, with legal findings. This chapter demonstrates how Said's theory of literary discourses accounts for the hegemonic imperial representations of the Other.[1] I also argue that such discursive representations were similarly constituted about the American Indian; yet, I depart from Said in showing how the colonial archive about the Indian assembled both aesthetic and non-aesthetic literary discourses, resulting in a merging of literature and legal judgment.

Today, few would dispute that indigenous people in various parts of the world were dispossessed of land on the grounds that they supposedly lacked the civilized, orderly governance structures that would have enabled them to maintain and develop their lands. According to Chief Justice Marshall, it is the right of the "civilized" to "hold" a "country." What led Marshall to the unequivocal assertion that the American conquerors were "civilized" and the conquered Indian "savage?" What modes of living, cultural practices, and forms of economic activity were, to Marshall and other prominent members of the American judiciary, indicative of a savage as opposed to civilized state of being, such that the "savage" would be rendered vulnerable to loss of land rights through "occupancy," "purchase" or "conquest?" To be more precise, how did the "savage" American Indian appear in Chief Justice Marshall's imagination? What image or set of images came to his senses when he contemplated the issues raised in the case of *McIntosh* and from which sources did these images of the savage Indian come to him?

Without wishing to suggest that there can ever be discovered a precise relation between cause and effect that would allow us to uncover definitive answers to the questions posed, I argue with reference to Edward Said's work on the relation between literary and other aesthetic works and the assertion of colonial power—as exemplified in works like *Orientalism* and *Culture and Imperialism*—that analysis of the practical application of the Doctrine of Discovery, which the Marshall judgments represent, is incomplete without examination of what we might call the "aesthetic context" within which the judgment was produced. I pay particular attention to the influence on Marshall of the nineteenth-century American novel, especially James Fenimore Cooper's *The Last of the Mohicans*, as well as eighteenth-century paintings by Benjamin West and nineteenth-century paintings such as Thomas Cole's *The Oxbow*, among others, who produced popular paintings of the New York wilderness.[2] These aesthetic works created a reservoir of concrete representations of the untamed wilderness and of the supposed savage state which, in part, authorized the Marshall Judgment.

In *Johnson*, Marshall asserted that "[t]he tribes of Indians inhabiting this country were fierce savages, whose occupation was war and whose subsistence was drawn chiefly from the forest" (*Johnson* 590). In *The Last of the Mohicans*, the forest was symbolic of the inevitable location of the savage in a dark wilderness—a source only of evil and danger. The American Indians were therefore overcome by physical force and it was clearly through physical force that their conquest was maintained, but they were also subdued through narrative representations and it is the question of how seemingly innocuous aesthetic forms become powerful weapons in sovereign assertion that is of interest here.

In writing the judgment in *Johnson*, Marshall had recourse to a memory of the subject soon to be colonized. To recover this memory is not a matter of scientific fact-finding but a process of uncovering the sources of historical memory. Literature is one source to which I, following Said, turn to interrogate the historical memory of and about the American Indian. Said is of interest to me not simply because he makes explicit the constitutive link between the production of literary forms and colonial imposition, but also because of what he offers in terms of a practice of literary criticism and analysis—both aspects of Said's work form an important framework for this book.

Culture, imperialism and Edward Said

The writings of Edward Said are still the most influential strands of a post-colonial critique of English culture, especially of the innovations in the nineteenth-century English novel. He argued that such works formed part of a system of intellectual colonialism that was self-perpetuating. They worked to reify European powers' rule of significant areas of the globe.

Said's project has been wrongly understood by some writers as postulating a precise causal relation between the production of literary texts and the practices of colonial governance. Keith Windschuttle is a particular detractor. He chides Said for his failure to account for the "reasons" underscoring imperial conquest. Cause and effect are not concepts that represent the nexus for ascertaining the influence of European culture on a colonized people. Said does not use the example of the English novel to isolate literature as a conditional precedent of colonialization or conquest, but rather to show how novels create images and constructs of the colonized in ways that permit the metropolitan West, not the conquered peoples of the Orient for example, to rationalize and justify their hegemony.

Said distinguishes nineteenth-century British, French and American visions of imperialism from earlier conquests by the Spanish and the Portuguese; however, what was the difference? The difference, according to Said, is that the earlier conquerors based their imperialistic ventures on extracting gold and other resources, unlike their successors who focused on settlement and organization within the conquered territories themselves. This difference facilitated the development of a culture or metropolitan literature that sought to explain or rationalize the conquest and settlement of colonial subjects. It was through this literary power that colonial subjects were defined and portrayed by the metropolitan writer. In order to justify the conquest of nearly three quarters of the globe by the end of the nineteenth century, Britain, France and America had their "best and the brightest of clerks scribbling their limpid excuses" (Leonard 384). Said refers to a cultural discourse that defined the non-European as having secondary cultural, racial and ontological status. This was a conquest not only based on force, but also on *persuasion*. The persuasion was left to the scribes of the metropolitan center.

The conquerors leveraged discourses that incorporated music, literature, art and new science based on anthropology and psychology to create a reality that not only defined the Other but also helped to mirror the metropolitan West in a superior light. Defining the Other helped to project a superior metropolitan image within the European narrative. The amalgamation of these cultural motifs established a broader cultural narrative of the Orient as well as a sense of entitlement for the colonial powers. Like servants in a household, the process was complete; it became background noise or hardly noticed (Leonard 385).

Together with Foucault's discourse theory on discursive formation and archives, Said's theoretical placement of literary texts such as the British novel helps to foreground the role of literature as a discursive statement. Said's literary context in colonial discourse formations provides a valuable theoretical tool against which I will investigate the Marshall Trilogy cases. The literary discourses before and after the American Revolution will reveal that images and representations about the Native American Indian were varied in their sources.

The novel in the late eighteenth- and early nineteenth-century American context, for example, was not the dominant form of literature that helped to shape the discourse or representation of the American Indians. By the early nineteenth century, American eastern intellectuals had virtually no contact with Indians. Most of the north eastern Indian tribes were either exterminated or removed by white colonialists by the late eighteenth century. Eastern intellectuals, who helped recreate the image of the Indian as a nomad rather than as a farmer in the European mode, had their intellectual foundations influenced by early American newspapers such as the Philadelphia *Freeman's Journal*, travel writers such Stephen Long (Kiowas and Cheyennes), Thomas Nuttail (Quapaws) and Henry Marie (Missouri River Basin) as well as reports from the western plains by Lewis and Clark. Hugh Henry Brackenridge, for example, wrote a play on the death of Col. William Crawford that fueled the anti-Indianism of the late 1780s. Brackenridge's writings were spread along the east coast through Francis Baily's *Freeman's Journal*. An examination of Brackenridge's play about Crawford depicts how he compressed time, distorted events and omitted to cite what motives lay behind Crawford's ugly demise (Silver 282).

An important pre-*Johnson* text that was influenced by this literary discourse was James Sullivan's *The History of Land Titles in Massachusetts* (Sullivan). It is argued that literature is not only non-fiction (e.g., the novel), but all text. All text being published between the early 1790s and early 1820s, represents a literary discourse that transformed the image of the American Indian from a farmer to a wandering nomad, as depicted in the Marshall Trilogy cases between 1823 and 1832.

In addition to fiction, plays and historical treatises, eastern intellectuals such as John Marshall were also exposed to missionaries who were reporting on their contact with the Native tribes. Missionaries who were charged with saving Indian souls in the late eighteenth century produced reports depicting Indians as hunters dependent on "game" for their food, who were in need of assistance for learning how to cultivate the earth for sustenance (Banner 154). There are direct references to this image of the Indian as a dependent and roaming "hunter" in the Marshall opinions.

The literary discourse depicting the Indian as a nomad or savage included speeches made to influential societies along the east coast which were published in newspapers. Dewitt Clinton, for instance, spoke in front of the New York Historical Society's annual meeting in 1811, describing the Indians as "hunters." Thomas Jefferson in his instructional letter dated June 20, 1803, to Meriwether Lewis (i.e., of "Lewis and Clark" fame) described the Indians as uncivilized, very similar in his description to Marshall's opinions in the Trilogy cases: "it will be useful to acquire what knowledge you can of the state of morality, religion and information among them, as it may better enable those who endeavour to civilize and instruct them" (Lewis *et al.*, *The Journals of Lewis and Clark* 483).

Said's use of discourse to locate the other

Said was influenced by Michel Foucault's theory that discourse establishes a knowledge–power nexus (Klages 42):

> I have found it useful here to employ Michel Foucault's notion of a discourse, as described by him in *The Archaeology of Knowledge* and in *Discipline and Punish,* to identify Orientalism. My contention is that without examining Orientalism as a discourse one cannot possibly understand the enormously systematic discipline by which European culture was able to manage,—and even produce—the Orient politically, sociologically, militarily, ideologically, scientifically, and imaginatively during the post-Enlightenment period.
>
> (Said, *Orientalism* 3)

Influenced by Foucault, Said argues that discourse works to create "knowledge" about a supposed racial group. "[T]his knowledge wielded power, as it defined and described a culture or racial group, and thus produced the social attitudes, the ideologies and practices, which surrounded and delimited the group or culture being written about" (Klages 154).[3] Said's use of Foucault's discourse theory underscores how imperial writers represented their colonial subject. Said denies that truth can be discovered and instead concentrates on how discourse represents the cultural other. "[H]e also borrowed from Foucault the notion of a 'discourse,' the ideological framework within which scholarship takes place. Within a discourse, all representations are tainted by the language, culture, institutions, and political ambience of the representer" (Windschuttle).

Said's central claim is that the discourses developed by the novel serve not only to perpetuate and reify past cultural conquests of the Other, but in so doing, help to forge the extension of imperialism. Said examines such nineteenth-century English novels as Jane Austen's *Mansfield Park* and its relation to West Indian slavery. What is interesting in Said's examination of this novel is not what is written, but what is silent in the novel about slavery. This is seen when Fanny Price raises a question about slavery, and Sir Thomas answers with silence. There is no common language to connect the question and the answer; yet the silence speaks volumes about the subject of slavery. Said states, "in order to read accurately works like *Mansfield Park,* we have to see them in the main as resisting or avoiding [the colonial setting]" (Said, *Culture and Imperialism* 96). By refusing to answer Fanny's inquiry, Sir Thomas avoids the discussion of slavery in Antigua. Andrew Rubin observed that Said focuses on the silence in texts which brings forth the interdependent realities of the Orient by illustrating a consciousness that would have otherwise remained dormant:

> Making these silences resonate is not merely a question of access to the institutions of public and social authority that help to enable it, but also involves what Said calls a critical consciousness and worldly knowledge of the historical contingencies of material and textual evidence and the authority upon which they depend.
>
> (Rubin, *Techniques of Trouble: Edward Said and the Dialectics of Cultural Philology* 865)

In attempting to develop a consciousness of the colonized in English literature, Said connects the political, historical and non-aesthetic contexts that underscore the fictional narrative. While literature is written by the individual, the text produced by the individual cannot be divorced from the historical and political connections that are either written as thematic backdrops or silent. Said brings the novel's narrative outside the aesthetic for an examination of the cultural relationships that connect the narrative *beyond the author*. The narrative not only produces its own cast of characters and plots but becomes a living subject, affected by the writer's environment and political sphere. "For Said, it is as crucial to read outside Western culture, to become comparative in a new sense: to read Austen without also reading Fanon and Cabral . . . is to disaffiliate modern culture from its engagements and attachments" (Loomba 82). Achieving a contextualized understanding of English literature and other forms of literature permits the reader to develop a consciousness of how narratives aiming either for asthethic or for historical integrity can equally define the colonial subject through the sublimations of the text's authority and discursive traditions. To understand the Marshall Trilogy cases thus requires a contextualized appreciation of the political practicalities (e.g., claims on Indian land) that underlined the literary period between 1780 and 1823.

It is useful to analyze the importance to this project of literary representation because literature, as with other aesthetic forms, provides the *matter* of history. Here Said was also influenced by Giambattista Vico:

> We must take seriously Vico's great observation that men make their own history, that what they can know is what they have made, and extend it to geography: as both geographical and cultural entities—to say nothing of historical entities—such locales, regions, geographical sectors as "Orient" and "Occident" are man-made.
>
> (Said, *Orientalism* 4–5)

Ania Loomba, analyzing several theories, including Lacanian psychoanalysis, writes:

> Language is seen to construct the subject. Perhaps the most radical result of these interconnecting but diverse ways of thinking about

> language was that no human utterance could be seen as innocent. Any set of words could be analysed to reveal not just individual but a historical consciousness at work. Words and images thus become fundamental for an analysis of historical processes such as colonialism.
> (Loomba 36–7)

Juxtaposing Vico and Loomba to Said, one can appreciate Said's 'contraptional criticism' that relates a localized interpretation of a literary text to other places and geographies. The significance of Said's contraptional interpretation turns on the "overlapping experiences and interdependent histories and cultures of conflict" (Said, *Culture and Imperialism* 67). Vico saw that men created history through their writing. Said adopted Vico's *man makes history* framework into the realm of literary discourse. Said, however, took the local (that is, reading text at face value as an aesthetic project) and made it contingent upon time and geography. In unmasking literature's contingency to the wider world beyond the text, Said was able to illuminate a literary consciousness that revealed the discursive tradition depicted by so many genres of literature. In appropriating the culture and languages of the Other within a discursive tradition, the West was able to facilitate its imperialism. This discursive tradition defined the cultural Other within the mind of the West to rationalize the West's cultural status, its cultural identity, and its sense of cultural superiority over the Other. *Orientalism* is a detailed and influential work within the study of Orientalism because, as Talal Asad argued, it is "not only a catalogue of Western prejudices about and misrepresentations of Arabs and Muslims," but even more an investigation and analysis of the "authoritative structure of Orientalist discourse—the closed, self-evident, self-confirming character of that distinctive discourse which is reproduced again and again through scholarly texts, travelogues, literary works of imagination, and the obiter dicta of public men [and women] of affairs" (Asad 648). We will utilize "the closed, self-evident, self-confirming" character described in Said's *Orientalism* to investigate the literary works between 1780 and 1823 that formed the literary archive that preceded Chief Justice John Marshall's majority opinion in *Johnson.*

In looking at discourse as a reflection of knowledge and power, it is also revealing how Foucault dismantles the hierarchical structures of power depicted so forcefully in Marxist analysis, by showing that power is *dispersed.* The dispersion of power through literature is multi-layered, which makes its infiltration into society's cracks so insidious and pervasive. "Power is everywhere; not because it embraces everything, but because it comes from everywhere" (Loomba 40). Whether through eastern colonial newspapers, history books, plays or fiction, the dispersal of power over the American Indian was channelled deeply and widely through such works. This dispersal of power enveloped the Native American between 1780 and 1823 because the post-1780 American literary landscape served to both overtly and unconsciously redraw the image of the Indians from a people who utilized farming and agriculture to support their sustenance to one of roaming nomads whose husbandry was based not on agriculture, but on hunting and barbarous acts of violence against white settlers (i.e., squatters who violated the territorial integrity of prior American and Native American treaties).

For Foucault, power is *produced*; power is not something that is objectively discovered. Said was quite aware of Foucault's ability to see how prisoners or the clinically insane, were defined as abnormal by an administrative bureaucracy that was able to fully represent the Other. While Foucault focused on how individuals were defined by such administrative practices in France during the nineteenth century, Said was able to observe how English literature was able to use its narrative as a way to expand the hegemony of British Imperialism in the nineteenth century:

> We must continue to remember that novels participate in, are part of, contribute to an extremely slow, infinitesimal politics that clarifies, reinforces, and perhaps even occasionally advances perceptions and attitudes about England and the world. It is striking that never, in the novel, is that world beyond seen except as subordinate and dominated, the English presence viewed as regulative and normative.
>
> (Said, *Culture and Imperialism* 75)

What makes Said's analysis unique is how he embraces this discourse in the form of the novel to develop a new perspective on colonial relations, as seen through the literary subject formation of the colonized. By subject formation we identify how works of literature can represent the subject by virtue of how a novel's narrative depicts a certain people. The text of literature can represent a setting and context that defines the character of a race or indigenous population. Said takes the novel and examines how relationships are defined within the novel to satisfy both an aesthetic aim *and* simultaneously develop a fictional world through literary statements about how people live and relate to each other. For Said, it is not so much that a fictional world is created to demonstrate how people relate to each other, but that this fictional world is a form of *rhetorical representation* cementing a constructed reality of how the West sees the Other.

While the novel may be fictional, its mode of operation, the written word, is also a means of rhetoric. "[S]uch texts can create not only knowledge but also the very reality they appear to describe" (Said, *Orientalism* 94). James Fenimore Cooper's Leather Stocking fictional series—e.g., *The Last of the Mohicans* (1826), *The Pathfinder, The Pioneers* (1823) and *The Prairie* (1827) and Lydia Sigourney's 180-page poem (early 1822) *Traits of the Aborigines of America*, helped to create a literary tradition about the American Indian. This literary tradition did not aim to situate the Native Americans as they really were, but as what the authors felt readers wanted to read, or as how they wished their narratives to represent the protagonists of their novels or poems, i.e., what Michel Foucault calls a discourse. "It is the material presence or weight of such a discourse and not the originality of a given author, that is responsible for the texts produced out of it" (94). This is an important point in Said's observation of Foucault's discourse model, which seeks to demonstrate how knowledge is power. It is not enough to simply project this statement as a paradigm of power because one must appreciate the colonial dynamic of this discourse. Said observes that Foucault's discourse theory, specifically bio-power, provides a theoretical framework to understand how discursive statements are integrated and interwoven on individual levels to create a system of power. Foucault's bio-power thus reflects a mass of statements that collectively create the reality, through discourse, of power.

Literary lenses explain metropolitan dominance

An important theme of this research will utilize Said's 'contraptional' approach to reading text (Said, *Culture and Imperialism* 66). An important theoretical tool must investigate what was expressly written by imperial texts and what was silent. While the counter-discursive space may have been absent during the time period when fiction, political theory, paintings and drawings were created, an examination of these discursive sources can still illuminate both the process of imperialism and a resistance to it. In examining Kipling's *Kim* we can investigate the method Said used to understand the process that imperialism incorporated. How we investigate the relationship between text and art and their subjects will say much about the relational aspect that a literary discourse reveals—a discourse that both reflects and creates images of subjected peoples:

> Kipling's India, in *Kim*, has a quality of permanence and inevitability that belongs not just to that wonderful novel, but to British India, its history, administrators, and apologists and, no less important, to the India fought for by Indian nationalists as their country to be won back. By giving an account of this series of pressures and counter-pressures in Kipling's India, we understand the process of imperialism itself as the great work of art engages them, and of later anti-imperialist resistance. In reading a text, one must open it out both to what went into it and to what its author excluded. Each cultural work is a vision of a moment, and we must juxtapose that vision with the various revisions it later provoked—in this case, the nationalist experiences of post-independence India.
>
> (67)

Mikhail Bakhtin, for example, says that:

> fiction, as a subset of rhetoric, has positive qualities. First of all, it is a socially and historically specific form of language use. A novel,

> Bakhtin argues, has more in common at any particular historical moment with other existing forms of rhetoric—with the languages used in journalism, in ethics, in religion, in politics, in economics, for example—than poetry.
>
> (Klages 137)

Bakhtin sees the novel not as the pure aesthetic that has a common feature with poetry, but rather as a source of rhetoric.

Bakhtin's observation that the novel is a form or subset of rhetoric has important implications for the impact that Said sees in the effect that the novel has had on power relations as a branch of imperialism. Said, like Bakhtin, perceives the novel not only in terms of the aesthetic, but of its rhetorical ability to define and represent a reality based on Western domination over the subjugated Other. Said contends that this representation of power relations helps to support imperial systems. Said states:

> I suggested that studying the relationship between the 'West' and its dominated cultural 'Others' is not just a way of understanding an unequal relationship between unequal interlocutors, but also a point of entry into studying the formation and meaning of Western cultural practices themselves. And the persistent disparity in power between the West and non-West must be taken into account if we are accurately to understand cultural forms like that of the novel, of ethnographic and historical discourse . . . where allusions to and structures based on this disparity abound.
>
> (Said, *Culture and Imperialism* 191)

Assessing the role of the novel in Said's framework of imperialism is not an issue of whether the novel or literary discourses led to conquest of the cultural Other, but of understanding that the novel perpetuates and reifies these narrative images and relationships to a wider readership. As the readership expands, the images created by the novel develop over time into a discourse that emerges as the apparent *natural course* of events or history. Like other narratives, legal judgment is influenced by the discursive archive:

> The appropriation of history, the historicization of the past, the narrativization of society, all of which give the novel its force, include the accumulation and differentiation of social space, space to be used for the social purposes . . . the spatial differentiations so apparent in late-nineteenth century novels do not simply and suddenly appear there as a passive reflection of an aggressive 'age of empire,' but are derived in a continuum from earlier social discrimination already authorized in earlier historical and realistic novels.
>
> (Said, *Culture and Imperialism* 78)

As Jane Austen in *Mansfield Park* portrays the "legitimacy of Sir Thomas Bertram's overseas property as a natural extension of the claim, the order, the beauties of Mansfield Park, one central estate validating the economically supportive role of the other" (79), so too John Marshall in *Johnson* viewed the *inevitable* march of history that led to the natural erasure of the American indigenous populations: Frequent and bloody wars, in which the whites were not always the aggressors, *unavoidably ensued* [emphasis added]. European policy, numbers, and skill, prevailed. As the white population advanced, that of the Indians *necessarily receded* [my emphasis added] (*Johnson v. M'Intosh*, 590). Where did the Marshall court discover this historical narrative? While the romanticism of 'Manifest Destiny' appeared after the Marshall Trilogy cases, its progeny was more than evidenced before *Johnson* in 1823. Using the theoretical premises of Said and other writers, I investigate what fictional and non-fictional discourses helped to create the idea of 'inevitability' about the indigenous population's demise in the Marshall Trilogy cases. I examine the literary discourses that focused on the virtue of American Exceptionalism; a creed whose premise lay in promoting the virtuous cause of American expansionism beyond the east coast, by tracing its origins to New England Puritan writings such as Cotton Mather's *Magnalia Christi Americana* of the Massachusetts Bay Colony. American Exceptionalism, together with the myth of the vanishing Indian theme of the American Romantic Movement in the early nineteenth century, was incorporated into the Marshall Trilogy rulings.

My investigation of the Marshall Trilogy cases examines the literary genres before and after the American Revolution of 1776 to examine what images and conceptions about the American Indian preceded the court's ruling in *Johnson* in 1823. My investigation will examine the literary discourse including, but not limited to, works of American fiction and poetry, and also speeches, plays and contemporary newspaper accounts in Massachusetts and Pennsylvania, together with post-1780 treaties and historical texts published in the newly formed United States.

Art and the conquest of the Americas

Said, while mostly known for examining nineteenth-century English fiction, such as Jane Austen's *Mansfield Park* (1814), also includes in his analysis of literary discourse the visual forms of discourse. Visual depictions of Britain's imperial possessions in the New World and the subsequent embrace of this imperial legacy are depicted in paintings and drawings dating back to the late sixteenth century. The water-color sketches of John White right up to Benjamin West's iconoclastic painting of William Penn's treaty in Pennsylvania in the late eighteenth century exemplify varied European discourses about the Native American:

> I refer here not only to 'the invention of tradition' generally, but also to the capacity to produce strangely autonomous intellectual and aesthetic images. Orientalist, Africanist, and Americanist discourse developed, weaving in and out of historical writing, painting, fiction, popular culture. Foucault's ideas about discourse are apt here . . . a coherent classical philology developed during the nineteenth century that purged Attic Greece of Semitic-African roots . . . In time—as Ronald Inden's *Imagining India* tried to show—entire semi-independent metropolitan formations appeared, having to do with imperial possession and their interests.
>
> (Said, *Culture and Imperialism* 110)

With equal eloquence, Said also states: "It is . . . historically inaccurate to ignore those tendencies—whether in narrative, political theory, or pictorial technique—that enabled, encouraged, and otherwise assured the West's readiness to assume and enjoy the experience of empire" (80). Hans-Georg Gadamer, in his *Truth and Method*, provides a similar position on art to Said. Gadamer offers a deeper theoretical basis for viewing art (e.g., paintings), situating art as more than a visual or an aesthetic detachment from the reality that positions the work: Aesthetic experience (Erlebnis) is directed towards what is supposed to be the work proper—what it ignores are the extra-aesthetic elements that cling to it, such as purpose, function, the significance of its content (Gadamer 74). Unlike Emmanuel Kant who measured truth or knowledge only in scientific terms, Gadamer extends the meaning of truth as a hermeneutic, especially as it related to art. Rather than isolate art from history, Gadamer demands that we relate to art as historical fact, as a truth concerning the observer's relationship with the aesthetic form, not for pleasure but for an understanding of the art work in its place in history and time:

> It is necessary to take the concept of experience (Erfahrung) more broadly than Kant did, so that the experience of the work of art can be understood as experience, for this we can appeal to Hegel's admirable lectures on aesthetics. Here the truth that lies in every artistic experience is recognized and at the same time mediated with historical consciousness. Hence aesthetics becomes a history of worldview.
>
> (84)

Using Said and Gadamer, I examine the late eighteenth-century and early nineteenth-century American Romantic painters such as Benjamin West and Thomas Cole. Adopting Gadamer's theoretical connection between the visual and historical consciousness I argue that the political environment at the time of some of the more influential pre-*Johnson* paintings in the later eighteenth century was clearly part of the literary discourse to not only reposition the image of the Native American, but also to ennoble the treaties and the dispossession of Indians by the post-Revolutionary American leadership, mostly notably William Penn.

During the early nineteenth century the new early American Republic, with particular reference to the eastern intellectuals who were driving public and legal discourse, was being influenced by different cross currents of literary text as described above, but unlike earlier periods when England held sway over the colonial landscape, a convergence of practical issues was forming that utilized the various modes of literature to justify the land conquest of Indian territory. The subtle literary changes that were published and painted between the 1790s and 1820s produced cumulative literary discourses that made it seem as if the American Indians were always nomads, *savage, pupils* and perhaps always *wards* of the new American Republic. These terms were cited by Marshall in his Trilogy opinions. While such views would have been mocked by the early eighteenth-century colonial intellectuals, the subsequent political and economic landscape changed dramatically after the American Revolution.

After the Treaty of Paris of 1783 with England, land ownership, especially in the so-called western frontier areas of Pennsylvania, became the nexus upon which literature was being used to recreate the image of the Indian. There were several influences that consciously and unconsciously led the literary representation of native tribes during this time. In terms of how this transformation converged upon the Supreme Court's ruling in *Johnson* we are required to discern the literary currents that were part of the political and legal archive preceding John Marshall's opinions in *Johnson.* A reading of James Sullivan's *The History of Land Titles in Massachusetts* provides a vivid text that created the image used by the Marshall court with respect to land ownership, or the lack thereof, by the native tribes. Sullivan's *History* foreshadowed later speeches and newspaper articles that employed similar legal doctrines and perceptions concerning Indians with respect to whether they were owners (e.g., holders in fee simple) of their land.

The Marshall Trilogy as literature: the insights of law and literature scholarship

Did the Marshall judgments remain free of the literary and other aesthetic influences described in the preceding sections precisely because they are a unique set of legal texts? Are legal texts by their nature insulated from the contexts that inform them? Having analyzed Said's theoretical value in depicting how literature is dispersed and rarefied over the cultural Other within the context of imperialism, it is important also to account for how *legal judgment* is affected by the discourses described by Said in *Culture and Imperialism.* Therefore, how does Said's literary analysis help inform us in an investigation of Marshall's legal judgments? What is the relationship between law and literature? Legal scholars have analyzed the preoccupation with the classical literary canon and the theme of law. They have argued that since legal judgments take the form of written texts in narrative structure, the tools and methodologies for analyzing and critiquing literature can be applied equally to law. Finally, although perhaps more controversially, legal scholars argued that literature can carry the form, the structure and perhaps the force of law.

A central question in the above investigation was posited by Douzinas *et al.*, "In what sense could we say that a work of poetry and literature more generally, inaugurates a law?" (354). Unlike Douzinas *et al.*, we will focus on legal judgment rather than law in general. In another sense, the question assumes that aesthetic texts are dissimilar to legal texts. In terms of legal texts:

> This separation between the legal and the aesthetic had an old and honorable philosophical pedigree. For Plato as much as for most contemporary jurisprudence, law must follow a principle of textual parsimony and persist with an unadorned, unambiguous and clear language, which is considered necessary for its consistent interpretation and application. Clarity of language and certainty of purpose allow the incontestable repetition of the rule and minimize the hazards of interpretation.
>
> (342)

Contrary to Richard Posner's assertion that literature is irrelevant to the law since the former deals with the aesthetic and with universal themes, it is submitted that legal judgment is part of the very literary discourse Posner dismisses (347). While Posner's position attempts to dismiss literature as a discursive influence upon legal judgment, his position does not deny that legal judgment is a force that literature is not. Whether for good or ill, legal judgment is seen as a power that, upon initial inspection, almost appears independent of literary influences. Peter Goodrich, in his *Law in the Court of Love*, presents a view that demonstrates that law is called "positive law" because it consciously or unconsciously incurs an amnesia; namely that the literary world preceding and around law is simply forgotten. Law's ability to discard and avoid its relationship with other genres produces a self-referential legal narrative. In one sense, legal judgment seeks to present itself as a closed logical coherent system, as if it were objectively created, free of external influence, and developed as an independent genre able to establish its own truth, or as Goodrich describes "[l]aw is literature which denies its literary qualities" (Goodrich 112). The difference, some observers cite, is that law is more powerful and thus creates a reality through its very rulings, while literary narratives are seen as merely tangential. Goodrich would argue that law attempts even more than this by discarding aesthetic literature and other genres. Using Goodrich's framework, whereby law attempts to become an independent genre, will be useful in examining how the Marshall opinions attempted to rewrite a history of the Doctrine of Discovery to suit the political practicalities of the early nineteenth century. Despite Marshall's attempt to author a new legal doctrine, it will be shown that the literary genres of fiction, history, and art all seeped into his opinion as *factual findings* akin to sworn statements. The literary archive about Indians preceding the Trilogy cases was influential. Within the context of this study, this archive helped to produce a reification of the literary discourses that dispossessed American Indians from their land, since they established cultural findings of fact to the subject matter of litigation and legal contests leading up the Marshall Trilogy cases.[4]

Read in their legal genre form, observers and readers of the Marshall rulings attempted to discard prior literary discourses of the Doctrine of Discovery. The court and its followers attempted to forget the noble savage and instead, sought to lay claim to a ruling that, by its very creation, was supposed to inform the new American Republic that American Indians were not fee simple owners, but occupants of their land—the very virtue of the nomadic lifestyle. The Marshall court rulings in *Johnson, Cherokee Nation* and *Worcester* make no mention of any prior literary treatment that counters the idea of native tribes as savages, wards, pupils; yet, by declaring as much, the court permitted literary license and by virtue of this "amnesia" law is permitted to instil in its ruling a new legal history of the Indian. Such legal history, incorporated into legal judgment, built on the amnesia both of prior genres and of contemporary literary genres and became evident in contemporary colonial newspapers, plays, paintings and books to create a fictional legal history.

Discourse in the works of Edward Said

Said claims that one should not confine an investigation of the English novel purely to aesthetic terms, but seek to understand the political and social context of the narrative. Connecting a novel's text to a political and social context helps to explain how narratives can represent people by forming images and ideas of the oppressed in the minds of the readers of the metropolitan West. Said reminds us that the text of the novel helps to create a discourse that is dominated by the colonial writers. Such domination is able to represent and portray the colonized, since the latter have no means of self-definition through discourse. Said seeks to raise the level of consciousness of this dynamic within discourse to establish an awareness of how fictional works help to represent a reality that is ultimately derived from text. Ultimately, the dominant discourse contributes to oppression of the colonized by constructing a literary reality that defines the relationship of the colonized to the colonizers. In short, the novel provides an important literary genre to a discursive landscape that represents the relationship between the colonizer and the Other.

The eighteenth-century American literary archive

The literary archive that is observed in this chapter in part describes the legal capacity of the American Indians. The literary images and cultural signs of the Indians provide the findings of fact in the Trilogy that led to the *legal* dispossession of Indians from their land. In Cooper's novel *The Last of the Mohicans*, the images of the Indians, while perhaps more nuanced than John Marshall's opinions, foregrounded the vanishing Indian theme in the minds of early Americans. Cooper's novel contributed to the literary archive by illustrating how the Indians were a doomed race, unable to resist the westward expansion of Western civilization. The combination of Foucault's *archive* and Said's literary Other provide useful theoretical frameworks to understand the influence of the dominant trope of literary discourses about the American Indian.

An examination of the public and legal discourses between 1776 and 1820 will help to situate the literary pathways that formed the findings of fact integrated into the Marshall Trilogy cases. Firstly, it is useful to recall that the idea of a dark and foreboding American wilderness had a strong pedigree in the seventeenth-century writings of New England Puritans. Cotton Mather, a minister and leading Non-Conformist writer, influenced not only the readership of the time, both in New England and old England, but also later writers who regarded him as an inspiration for their own work. Mather claimed that the New England Puritans were sent by God to "plant" civilization in the darkness of the New World:

> 'Tis possible that our Lord Jesus Christ carried some thousands of Reformers into the retirements of an American desert, on purpose that, with an opportunity granted unto many of his faithful servants, to enjoy the precious *liberty* of their Ministry, though in the midst of many temptations all their days, He might there, to them first, and then *by* them, give a *specimen* of many good things, which He would have His Churches elsewhere aspire and arise unto; and *this* being done, he knows not whether there be not *all done*, that New England was planted for; and whether the Plantation may not, soon after this, *come to nothing*. Upon that expression in the sacred Scripture, "Cast the unprofitable servant into outer darkness," He hath been imagined by some, that the *Regiones exter* of America, are the *Tenebra: extenorex*, which the unprofitable are there condemned unto. No doubt, the authors of those Ecclesiastical impositions and severities, which drove the English Christians into the dark regions of America, esteemed those Christians to be a very unprofitable sort of creatures. But behold, ye European Churches, there are golden Candlesticks [more than twice seven times seven!] in the midst of this "outer darkness": unto the upright children of Abraham, here hath arisen *light in darkness*. And, let us humbly speak it, it shall be profitable for you to

> consider the *light* which, from the midst of this "outer darkness," is now to be darted over unto the other side of the Atlantick Ocean. But we must therewithal ask your Prayers, that these "golden Candlesticks" may not quickly be "removed out of their place!"
>
> (Mather, *Magnalia Christi Americana* Vol. 1 25–6)

Mather's description of the "American Desert," "outer darkness," and "dark regions of America" represented literary metaphors of the American landscape; a motif that was conveniently placed to receive "the upright children of Abraham." Mather provides a religious basis for the post-Revolutionary transformation of the American Indian in the public consciousness because it was only the Europeans carrying their "golden candlesticks" who could bring light to the 'dark regions of America.'

American literary sources after 1776

The combination of literary works composed of missionary reports, poems, and historical works helped to forge a European-American discourse on what constituted ownership of land. This discourse played an important role in helping to cement the land speculation that started in earnest after the 1780s in *pre-emption rights* (Banner 151–6). As a practical matter, pre-emption rights were shares that were sold between American speculators to own land in the future, land inhabited by Indians. These shares could then be sold at higher prices when at some future date Indian lands had their land rights extinguished by the Federal Government: in other words, pre-emption rights holders would own the land. According to Banner, there was a confluence of events that resulted in the remaking of the American Indian from agricultural landowners to nomads:

> A major change in American legal thought had taken place during the intervening three decades. In the early 1790s the land not yet purchased from the Indians was thought to be owned by the Indians; by the early 1820s that land was thought to be owned by the state and federal governments. Like many transformations in legal thought, this one was so complete that contemporaries often failed to notice that it had occurred.
>
> (150)

The image of the Indian was transformed, so that any interest in land that the Americans and English might have formally acknowledged Indians to possess somehow vanished to the point "that contemporaries often failed to notice that it had occurred" (Banner 150). Dominant discourses that portrayed Indians as hunters rather than as farmers helped to underline perceptions in the reading public that the land Indians inhabited was not owned by them.

Levi Frisbie was a late eighteenth- and early nineteenth-century missionary who sought to convert American Indians to Christianity. He associated the American aborigine together with other less civilized peoples. Below, Frisbie describes the Indian, among other lesser cultures, as a "wandering savage":

> "Go teach, all nations; go preach the gospel to every creature," still retains its gracious and sacred authority. The declarations, the promises, the benefits of endless life and happiness may be proclaimed with perfect sincerity not only to the learned, the opulent and the polished inhabitants, of civilized countries, but to the swarthy African, the plundering Arab, the roving Tartar, and the wandering Savage who traverses the wilds of America, from the desert plains of Patagonia to the dreary mountains of the frozen pole: and if they will but listen to the joyful sound, embrace its proposals, and comply with its prescriptions, their hearts shall be melted and moulded to a spirit of meekness, piety, and love, and finally blessed with the enjoyment of everlasting peace, purity, and glory in the kingdom of God.
>
> (Frisbie 30)

Given that the Indians were deemed uncivilized, it followed that their land was available for conquest. As James Monroe put it: "The *unqualified right* of a civilised people to claim land used by people in the hunter-state, on the principle that the earth was intended for those who would make it most conducive to the sustenance and increase the human race" (quoted in Jahoda 21–2). Monroe's statement evidences the nature of the discourse that offers a culture's "hunter-state" existence as evidence that such a culture does not utilize the land in a "most conducive" way that is necessary for "sustenance" and to promote the "human race." Monroe's reasoning is built on the presumption that being civilized requires a stable use of land that cannot be attained by a hunter-state race. Indians cannot therefore claim the land as they lack Monroe's required civilized attributes.

John Locke, in his *Second Treatise on Government*, promoted the principle that man in his original state shares a common ownership of untilled, or uncultivated land. If such land is conquered, Locke preserves a possessionary interest for the conquered, and this is exactly how the early American idea of Indian land ownership began to take shape. Locke said:

> the *Inhabitants* of any Country [sic], who are descended, and derive a Title to their Estates from those, who are subdued, and had a Government forced upon them against their free consents, *retain a Right to the Possession of their Ancestors*, though they consent not freely to the Government, whose hard Conditions were by force imposed on the Possessors of that Country.
>
> (Locke, *The Second Treatise on Civil Government* 17)

This "right of possession" can be supplanted by someone else's ownership. Uncultivated land that is not enclosed, tilled, or utilized is not *owned*: when man uses his God-instilled talents and labor to transform the land, he establishes ownership. Locke describes his theory of land entitlement or ownership derived from the use of the land:

> We see in commons, which remain so by compact, that it is the taking any part of what is common, and removing it out of the state nature leaves it in, which begins the property; without which the common is of no use. And the taking of this or that part does not depend on the express consent of all the commoners. Thus the grass my horse has bit; the turfs my servant has cut; and the ore I have digged in any place, where I have a right to them in common with others; become my property, without the assignation or consent of any body. The *labour* that was mine, removing them out of that common state they were in, hath *fixed* my *Property* in them.
>
> (Locke, *Two Treaties of Government* 146)

Christian missionaries to North America added to the literary discourses about how land ownership and aborigines were subject to the International law. The Reverend Jedediah Morse, in communication with the U.S. War Department stated:

> the Indians' independence, their rights, their title to the soil which they occupy are all imperfect in their kind . . . The jurisdiction of the whole country they inhabit, according to the established law of nations, appertains to the Government of the United States, and the right of disposing of the soil attached to the power that holds the jurisdiction.
>
> (Quoted in Jahoda 33)

Morse subjects Indian occupancy of their land to the "established law of nations" asserting that the United States has the "right to disposing the soil."

The concept of the "law of nations" was articulated by the fifteenth-century Spanish legal philosopher Francisco de Vitoria, who is often called the "father of international law." De Vitoria asserted that a people who were prevented from exercising free and peaceable movement by another people were subject to conquest. His reasoning provides a theoretical justification for conquest, not based on the power of the conqueror, but on the prevention of the "free and peaceable" movement of people; however, missing from de Vitoria's theory is whether that same rationale extends to the conquerors once they have claimed ownership of land formally inhabited by another people. He emphasized that the Law of Nations was binding because:

> there exists clearly enough a consensus of the greater part of the whole world and because the principles benefit 'the common good of all.'[5] This distinction seems to rely on the assumption that other principles usually associated with natural law (such as the prohibitions on adultery and idolatry) only affect those who consent to the practices, whereas violations of the Law of Nations (e.g. prohibitions on peaceful travel and trade) have consequences for those who do not consent. Ultimately, de Vitoria's understanding of the Law of Nations led him to defend the practice of Spanish colonialism, even as he emphasized that the Spanish remedy of warfare should be limited to minimal measures required to attain the legitimate objectives of peaceful trade and missionary work. Within de Vitoria's critique of the legality and morality of Spanish colonialism was a rationalization of conquest, albeit a restrictive one.
>
> (*Stanford Encyclopaedia of Philosophy*)[6]

Early thinkers such as de Vitoria provided a legal basis for conquest based on conquering people who sought to prevent "legitimate objectives of peaceful trade and missionary work" (*Stanford Encyclopedia of Philosophy*). Embedded within de Vitoria's legal framework is the presumption that the benefits and goals of "objective trade" and "missionary work" were somehow self-evident.

Missionaries like Frisbie, for example, adopted de Vitoria's rationalization about how the Law of Nations operated to justify, on moral and religious grounds, their sanctimonious need to civilize savages; a people who had yet to attain the stage in human development worthy of respect and recognition were not sufficiently civilized to own land.

This latter rationale was expounded upon by Adam Smith. Adam Smith's writings on the stages of human development proposed a theory for appropriating Indian land by European and American settlers. As discussed above, early American writers attempted to define the Indian as savage. This notion of "civilizing" was well connected to Adam Smith. Smith, one of the founders of the Scottish literary liberal tradition, theorized that human society or evolution consisted of stages from savagery to civilization. The implication of this theory was based on what stage in human development a culture occupied. A culture deemed to be on the savage end of human development was also incapable of owning land. Smith saw human societies as based on four stages of evolution: the hunting, the shepherding, the farming and the commercial epochs. Smith was able to advance a theory of human development through these four stages that later writers could integrate into an economic and social framework with which to later situate the American Indian relative to the English and American settlers (Alvey 3).

Narratives, such as those of the seventeenth- and eighteenth-century captivity genre, cast the Indians as savage because they occupied the pre-farming stage of human development. These narratives were read and distributed throughout the eastern United States. Captive narratives helped to forge post-Revolutionary images of Indian tribes. *A True Narrative of the Sufferings of Mary Kinnan,* for example, depicts a Virginian frontierswoman in the Shenandoah Valley who was taken prisoner by invading savage Indians who killed her young child, scalped her husband, and marched her to the Ohio Valley to work in the Shawnee Indian towns. This 1795 narrative does not so much portray Indians as nomads, but as savages who will kill settler families. Most tellingly, Mary Kinnan's narrative portrays the Indian woman as surprisingly unkind and brutal. In this narrative, Indian women were stripped of their femininity and dehumanized. Mary Kinnan's narrative placed great stress on the savage way of Indian life:

> one of the principle objects of my attention, whilst I lived amongst the Indians, was the humiliating condition of their women. Here the female sex, instead of polishing and improving the rough manners of the men, are equally ferocious, cruel and obdurate. Instead of that benevolent disposition and warm sensibility to the sufferings of others, which marks their characters in more civilized climes, they quaff with ecstatic pleasure the blood of the innocent prisoner, writhing with agony under the inhuman torments inflicted upon him—whilst his convulsive groans speak music to their souls.
>
> (Stodola 112)

Kinnan's narrative is built on images that define the Indian as "ferocious, cruel and obdurate" (112). The Indian is not only cruel, but also a consummate and unrepentant sinner. Enjoying the sight of the "blood of the innocent prisoner" Kinnan portrays the Indians as a ferocious and bloodthirsty race (112).

In *A Genuine and Correct Account of the Captivity, Suffering and Deliverance of Mrs. Jemma Howe,* written by Hunter Gay, Indians were introduced as hideous monsters who could only capture and expose white settlers to the most tortuous treatment upon capture. "The Indians in their savage manner, coming up to Howe, pierced his body with a spear, tore off his scalp, stuck a hatchet in his head, and left him in this forlorn condition" (Stodola 96). Gay's narrative describes the Indians in graphic, barbaric terms which indicate to the reader that Indians are to be feared for their violence. Gay's narrative leaves little room to the reader's imagination where phrases such as "stuck a hatchet in his head" serve to instil terror into the readers. "Almost invariably the Indian captivity narrative concerns the capture of an individual or several family members rather than larger groups, and its plot is most commonly resolved with the captive's escape, ransom, transculturation, or death" (Stodola xi). The silent savagery of the Indian in Stodola's description integrates the need to juxtapose the Other against the fears of civilized settlers. In terms of the Other these narratives could not highlight the superior European-American culture. The role of the captive narrative projects a discourse about barbarous Indians. The transformation of the Indian in the early European-American literary discourses, from noble savage whose sustenance stemmed from both farming and hunting to a nomadic hunter state, served to highlight the uncivilized state of Indians: a state that precluded any right of land ownership.

Early nineteenth-century public discourse

Explorers like Lewis and Clark provided the first reports of Indians west of the Mississippi. These reports were eagerly enjoyed by both east-coast American intellectuals and European readers. Lewis and Clark reported that Indians had no concept of private property. Reports also claimed that Indians roamed the land, hunting for their sustenance. Lewis and Clark provided an important collection of accounts that fit perfectly with the efforts of states seeking to grant land pre-emption rights to former Revolutionary militia. Granting pre-emption rights on land inhabited by Indians was based on the legal premise, although yet to be ruled by any U.S. Court, that Indians were occupants rather than owners of their land, this latter conclusion being based on the nomadic and hunting lifestyles of the American Indian. "Lewis and Clark, along with other explorers, reported finding some tribes who 'have no idea of an exclusive possession of any country,' and others who lacked 'any idea of exclusive rights to the soil'" (Banner 156). Reporting that tribes "had no idea of exclusive rights to the soil" offered yet more evidence that, to American readers, Indians were not only devoid of land ownership, but devoid of an understanding of "right to soil." Other American explorers and travelers made similar depictions of Indians as nomads without any stake in the land, or notion of private property. Stephen Long, in describing the Kiowa and Cheyenne in 1820, found that Indians had "no permanent town, but constantly rove, as necessity urges them in pursuit of the herds of bison" (156). Long offers further discourses describing the nomadic and hunter state of Indians, reflecting on how they "constantly rove" by necessity to pursue "herds of bison." While other travelers into the American West, such as John Bradbury, did report on the agricultural practices of Indians, even these accounts demonstrated that native farming practices were not consistent with the kind of acculturation that supported the idea that Indians truly utilized the land in a way that constituted ownership. For example, Bradbury notes:

> The women, as is the custom with Indians, do all the drudgery, and are excellent cultivators. I have not seen, even in the United States, any crop of Indian corn in finer order, or better managed than the corn

about these villages. They also cultivate squashes, beans, and the small species of tobacco *(Nicotiana rustica).*

(Bradbury, *Travels in the Interior of America, in the Years 1809, 1810, and 1811* 165)

While on the one hand Bradbury states, contrary to explorers like Lewis and Clark, that Indians can farm, it is the women and not the men who are doing the farming. The absence of men in Indian agricultural practices either reinforced the image of the lazy Indian male or supported the notion that men subsisted upon hunting. Bradbury's silence about the role of men worked to reinforce these images of the hunter state even while demonstrating that Indians do cultivate the land. Other writers and explorers from this period, like Thomas Nuttall, reported "[a]s hunters, they are industrious, but pay little attention to agriculture; and pleased by intercourse with the whites, they are not unwilling to engage as boatmen and hunters" (Nuttall 84). Nuttall adds to the discursive depiction that Indians "pay little attention to agriculture" in order to reinforce the image of the Indians as hunters.

In an 1802 speech, future U.S. President John Quincy Adams laid out the rationale for American claims to land based on benevolence, charity and, with seemingly great finesse, a finite place for the American Indians in their own land:

> No European settlement, ever formed upon this continent, has been more distinguished for undeviating kindness and equity towards the savages. There are, indeed, moralists who have questioned the right of the Europeans to intrude upon the possessions of the aboriginals in any case, and under any limitations whatsoever. But have they maturely considered the whole subject? The Indian right of possession itself stands, with regard to the greatest part of the country, upon a questionable foundation. Their cultivated fields; their constructed habitations; a space of ample sufficiency for their subsistence, and whatever they had annexed to themselves by personal labor, was undoubtedly, by the laws of nature, theirs. But what is the right of a huntsman to the forest of a thousand miles over which he has accidentally ranged in quest of prey? Shall the liberal bounties of Providence to the race of man be monopolized by one of ten thousand for whom they were created?
>
> (Williston 185)

Quincy states that European Americans had a divine right to the land of the Americas so long as the conquerors and settlers paid some compensation to the Indians. The compensation was a token of the European-American charity to those who could not fully utilize the land. Here Adams echoes John Locke's utilitarian requirement that in order to possess land, one must utilize it, with the act of labor becoming a means of legitimizing the possession of land . . . otherwise the land would belong in common.

Adams was projecting a viewpoint in 1802 that had taken hold after the American Revolution. When Adams speaks of "equity toward the savage," he is reflecting a broader theme that was taking shape in the public and literary discourses in the early American Republic. Public discourses, like Adams,' were beginning to concentrate on the relationship between ownership of land, American conquest through discovery and so-called savages where the latter, by their innate inhumanity, are incapable of owning land beyond their localized sustenance.

President Thomas Jefferson, the main sponsor of the Lewis and Clark expedition, noted

> if we claim [the Pacific Northwest], it must be on Astor's settlement near the mouth of the Columbia, and the principle of the *jus gentium* [international law] of America that when a civilized nation takes possession of the mouth of a river in new country, that possession is considered as including all its waters.
>
> (Miller and Furse, *Native America, Discovered and Conquered: Thomas Jefferson, Lewis and Clark, and Manifest Destiny* 18)

Perhaps the most telling of Jefferson's inferences is the emphasis on the word "civilized." Indians did not appear in Jefferson's mind as being civilized. Jefferson's subtle but critical point is that discovery upon land occupied by "uncivilized" people conveys to the discoverer the full land title not only against other competing European powers, *but also* against the occupants.

Jefferson seems to acknowledge some form of ownership on the part of the Natives in another context. Jefferson wanted to find ways to appropriate Indian land without war, and to achieve this end he advised his land agents to encourage the Indians and their leaders to trade vigorously with the expanding western republic beyond their financial means. Jefferson promoted a policy to place Indian tribes in debt, which could later be negotiated in exchange for land possessed by Indians. The ability to cede lands by the Indians implies an interest approach to ownership. Establish among the Chickasaws, he wrote,

> a factory for furnishing them all the necessaries and comforts they may wish, spirituous liquors excepted, encouraging them and especially their leading men to run into debt for these beyond their individual means of paying: and whenever in that situation, they will always cede lands to rid themselves of debt.
>
> (Jefferson 374)

Here was a policy of Indian dispossession wrapped within the context of trade. The key was to encourage debt among the Indians "beyond their individual means" and at that point, the United States agents could exact maximum negotiation pressure to force Indians to cede land in exchange for writing off the debt.

Like Adams, DeWitt Clinton of New York, another influential politician and orator, went to great lengths to rationalize American Indian dispossession. Clinton, perhaps evoking Adam Smith's four stages of history, never elevated any of the Indian tribes above a simple state of nomadic peoples who could only reach a primitive state of government. Clinton added to the growing chorus of images about American Indians as savages and unsettled creatures:

> War was the favorite pursuit of this martial people, and military glory their ruling passion. Agriculture and the laborious drudgery of domestic life were left to the women. The education of the savage was solely directed to hunting and war. From his early infancy, he was taught to bend the bow, to point the arrow, to hurl the tomahawk, and to wield the club. He was instructed to pursue the footsteps of his enemies through the pathless and unexplored forest—to mark the most distant indications of danger—to trace his way by the appearances of the trees, and by the stars of heaven, and to endure fatigue, and cold, and famine, and every privation. He commenced his career of blood by hunting the wild beasts of the woods, and after learning the dexterous use of the weapons of destruction, he lifted his sanguinary arm against his fellow creatures. (Clinton 16)

Clinton's words not only portray Indians as a warlike people, but also as a collective culture that is educated in the pursuit of "hunting," the 'tomahawk' and the "club." Clinton's use of the term "career of blood" emphasizes the barbaric nature of Indians' existence. With passages like this, the European American was building a discursive archive about the Indians which cast them as uncivilized and violent. As I will demonstrate, such discourses over time were accepted by both later writers like James Fenimore Cooper and jurists, like John Marshall.

Notes

1 "The Orient is not only adjacent to Europe; it is also the place of Europe's greatest and richest and oldest colonies, the source of its civilizations and languages, its cultural contestant, and one of its deepest and most recurring images of the Other" (Said, *Orientalism* 1). Said's use of the term 'Other' denotes how the discursive production of the Orient translates into the idea of the 'Other.'

2 Benjamin's West produced *The Treaty of Penn with the Indian* and Thomas Cole founded the *Hudson River School*, famed for its American Romantic paintings of

early to mid-nineteenth-century images of New York State. Both painters respectively produced popular images of the American Indian and the back country of the early American Republic.

3 "Most important, such texts can *create* not only knowledge but also the very reality they appear to describe. In time such knowledge and reality produce a tradition, or what Michel Foucault calls a discourse, whose material presence or weight, not the originality of a given author, is really responsible for the texts produced out of it" (Said, *Orientalism* 94).

4 Said is quite aware of how early nineteenth-century American literature was written in the guise of anti-colonialism towards the former mother country, while in reality, this literature helped to forge the reification of a distinctly American imperialism over the Native American. For example, "There is also a dense body of American writing, contemporary with this British and French work, which shows a peculiarly acute imperial cast, even though paradoxically its ferocious anti-colonialism, directed at the Old World, is central to it. One recalls, for example, of the Puritan "errand into the wilderness" and later, of that extraordinarily obsessive concern in Cooper, Twain, Melville, and others with the United States expansion westward, along with the wholesale colonization and destruction of Native American life . . . an imperial motif emerges to rival the European one" (Said, *Culture and Imperialism* 63).

5 Quoting Williams, Robert, 1990. *American Indian in Western Legal Thought*, New York and Oxford: Oxford University Press 391.

6 "Casas and Francisco de Vitoria were two of the most influential critics of Spanish colonial practice. Vitoria gave a series of lectures on Indian rights that applied Thomistic humanism to the practice of Spanish rule. He argued that all human beings share the capacity for rationality and have natural rights that stem from this capacity. From this premise, he deduced that the Papal decision to grant Spain title to the Americas was illegitimate" (*Stanford Encyclopaedia of Philosophy*).

Chapter 5

The discourse of the vanishing Indian in literature

This chapter provides a survey of nineteenth-century American literature, arguing that the depiction of the Native American as a pitiful savage whose disappearance was inevitable was a dominant theme. As stated in the overview to this part, these literary sources appear to assume the value of expert testimony in the Marshall cases—substantiating Marshall's damning judgments about the capacity of the Native American to own and manage his own lands. In the chapter that follows I offer a close reading of Fenimore Cooper's *The Last of the Mohicans.* This novel, while significant in its own right as a literary work in the early nineteenth century, was a key example of the literary works that constructed the Native American and which forms the subject of Chief Justice Marshall's contemplations.

From the moment of English settlement at Plymouth, Massachusetts, to the early nineteenth-century Romantic period, varied images of the American Indian persisted such as "noble children of nature in need of civilization and Christianity or as ferocious, demonic savages in need of extermination" (Arnold). By examining Cooper's *The Last of the Mohicans* we can better understand the nature of the post-colonial American mind that preceded and was contemporary with John Marshall's Trilogy opinions. As Mary Arnold notes "these three romantic idealizations of the Indian (noble warrior, bloodthirsty savage and vanishing Indian) converge in James Fenimore Cooper's *The Last of the Mohicans*" (Arnold). In terms of the theoretical framework that situates our investigation of *The Last of the Mohicans,* I will argue that Cooper's work represents an important literary and intellectual contribution to the *archive* that helped to constitute the findings of fact in Marshall's judicial opinions of the American Indian.

While a major literary theme in early post-colonial America was the vanishing American Indian, its genesis extends back to the early American colonies of the seventeenth century.[1] The Romantic depictions of the vanishing American Indians in the early nineteenth century had an important connection with Christian origins. As Laura Stevens writes "[while much scholarship has pointed out the role that the vanishing Indian played in the assertion of manifest destiny, there is still work to be done on the origins of this image" (Stevens 162). Stevens isolates an important religious theme that laid the discursive foundation for British missionaries to describe the Indians as both "wasted" and in need of "conversion" to Christ (162–3). Foreshowing the American melancholy of the vanishing Indian of later nineteenth-century Romantic writers such as Washington Irving, William Cullen Bryant and Fenimore Cooper, the early British missionaries were able to project the *inevitable* demise of the Indians, whether through disease, or the corrupting influences of European settlement, as God inspired. "In spite of this compassion, some of the greatest signs of God's favor are native deaths. 'Thus farre hathe the good hand of God favoured our beginnings'" (167).

Rather than seeing the deaths of Indians as an ominous sign, for the early European settlers the spreading death among Indians was viewed as a validation of divine approval of their mission, "the colonists take spiritual comfort from indigenous death even as they express their desires to save Indian souls" (167). Colonists were thus able to mourn the death of the Indians as a validation of their divine purpose, a purpose that saw God's plan for the dying Indian.

Some of the seventeenth-century missionary writing narrated a theme that took spiritual inspiration and satisfaction from the very death of Indians as if to cloak the demise of the Indian peoples as a subject for European and later American religious meaning. Death and religion became connected in a fashion that took dynamic rhetorical ownership of the Indian and, by extension, the land. Referring to Experience Mayhew's *Indian Converts*, Stevens notes that:

> The text converts potential enemies into loyal servants and then directs us to watch their religiously sanctioned deaths. Encouraging his readers to gain an intimate, if formulaic, knowledge of these Indians, Mayhew implied that the British (or, more particularly, the Congregationalists of New England) were worthy stewards of America. He preserved images of dead Indians, repeatedly asserting the power of Protestant Christianity over them. He also encouraged his readers to peer inside Indians at the moment of death, glimpsing the state of their souls. In these ways Mayhew taught readers to think of Indian death as a rich repository of spiritual meaning.
>
> (191)

Whether Indians were adopted by British missionaries as subjects to take pity upon as a means to advance their own spiritual justification for conquest over the New World or as a sign of divine providence which underscored an inevitable demise of the Indians, the 'dying Indian' image was a critical element in buttressing the religious righteousness of the New England Separatists and Non-Conformists. Both Separatists and

Non-Conformists saw themselves as models of religious piety in relation to the deviant upheavals of religious dogmas and intolerance in England. Unlike the Romantic period starting in 1780, in post-colonial times, the settlement period incorporated the image of the dying Indian as a vehicle through which to reflect New England piety relative to that of England. In the post-colonial period, the image moved from reflecting the collective piety of New England colonists to a view of the dying Indians as a victim of Western civilization. The 'dying Indian' was not seen as disappearing in a natural setting where civilization and Indians intersected. The Indian demise took on romantic proportions during the post-1812 period once it was established that the rapid onslaught of civilization, not conquest, spelled doom for the Indian race:

> The nostalgia and pity aroused by the dying race produced the best romantic sentiments and gave that sense of fleeting time beloved of romantic sensibilities. The tragedy of the dying Indians, especially as portrayed by the last living member of a tribe, became a staple of American literature, beginning with Philip Freneau's poems in the 1780s. It made its mark on the world literature through James Fenimore Cooper's *The Last of the Mohicans* (1826).
>
> (Berkhofer 88)

John Marshall's majority opinions in the Trilogy cases between 1823 and 1832 were written in the context of this post-colonial Romantic mind set with respect to the American Indian. Fenimore Cooper's *The Last of the Mohicans* typified the "cult of the Vanishing Indians" that exemplified the post-colonial mind which situated John Marshall's legal opinions (Dippie 21). In particular, Fenimore Cooper derived from and helped to constitute a steady stream of literary influences that produced the image of the vanishing American Indian. "Some forty novels published between 1824 and 1834 included Indian episodes, constituting what G. Harrison Orians termed a 'cult of the Vanishing American'" (21). The Vanishing Indian theme is summed up in the title of his solitary masterpiece—*The Last of the Mohicans*—for its appeal was to the awareness of the fleeting quality of time that was so dear to the Romantic temperament (21). The very title evokes a vanishing race, a pitiful demise of a once powerful and noble people. Early American writers such as Philip Frenbeau, Washington Irving and Fenimore Cooper produced uniquely Romantic images of the American Indian receding into the sunset, unable to stop the march of Western civilization. As Berkhofer notes, "[m]ost romantic of all was the impression of the Indian as rapidly passing away before the onslaught of civilization" (Berkhofer 88). Using the American wilderness as the prevalent setting for their work, the American Indian provided early nineteenth-century American Romantic writers with a unique literary subject that distinguished their work from that of similar writers in England.

The myth of the vanishing American Indian was propagated by the Romantic movement in England and America between 1790 and the American civil war in the 1860s. The Romantics evoked images of the rise and fall of nations, heroes and heroines, and social stratification.[2] They sought to challenge the Enlightenment and Neoclassical conventions that frowned upon writers who wrote beyond the narrative rules.[3] In terms of Cooper's oeuvre, his membership and proximity to the New York intellectual and literary elite influenced his literary composition. In contrast, Cooper's work also influenced not only other writers, but painters like Thomas Cole of the New York Hudson River School. Cole used the *The Last of the Mohicans* to construct landscapes of the American wilderness that later evolved into canons of early American Art. As Barker and Sabin note:

> In a quite calculated fashion, therefore, the artists took inspiration from the writers, and vice versa. This is why Cooper's books were so often the subject of paintings in this period. In *Mohicans itself*, it was the landscape and sense of wilderness that was of particular attraction: the great Thomas Cole painted several scenes, which are now considered masterpieces in the history of American art.
>
> (Barker and Sabin 18)

This chapter sets out to examine how Cooper's *The Last of the Mohicans* helped to forge a post-colonial mindset with respect to the vanishing American Indian. Cooper's depiction of the vanishing Indian incorporates a notion that actually depicts the American Indians as having already vanished. Romero captures Cooper's literary sunset of the American Indian, as she notes:

> Cooper would seem to betray his indoctrination in the cult of the vanishing American when he states in the introduction to the 1831 edition of his novel that it was "the seemingly inevitable fate of all [native tribes]" to "disappear before the advances . . . of civilization [just] as the verdure of their native forests falls before the nipping frost."
>
> (Romero 385)

Americans were (and to a certain degree, remain) sensitive to what old Europe thought of them, especially in their dealings with the American Indian. "Sensitivity about the United States' moral stature among the nations of the world made it difficult for Americans to admit to a deep complicity in the Indians' destruction. It was easier to indict the Indians for their own ruin, thereby washing the white man's hands of responsibility"

(Dippie 12). As Dippie stipulates, a "rhetoric of doom" began to manifest itself from poets, novelists and other writes who sought to cast the demise of the American Indian based upon images drawn from nature (13). Dippie draws attention to the Romantic movement's merging of nature and the Indian in order to portray the inevitable disappearance of the Indians as analogous to the seasonal falling of leaves or the morning dew that 'mysteriously disappears' before the noon day sun:

> The Indian was at the sunset of his existence; night was about to swallow a race fated to vanish 'as the snow melts before the sunbeam,'[4] or 'like the morning dew, insensibly and mysteriously to disappear, before the lights of civilization and Christianity.'[5] "Like a promontory of sand, exposed to the ceaseless encroachments off the ocean, they have been gradually wasting away before the current of the white population, which set upon them from every quarter," a Georgia senator observed in 1825.[6] "One by one they perish, like the leaves of the forest that are swept away by the autumn winds; melancholy shrouds them; they die of sadness, and are effaced from the earth by the inexorable destiny," Eliza Lee mourned twenty-two years later.[7] In an address delivered before the Cambridge Phi Beta Kappa Society in 1815, William Tudor, Jr. declared that the Indians were vanishing "like snow before the vernal influence," and their disappearance reminded him of the "sublime allegorical painting of Guido, in which Apollo encircled by the hours, is chasing night and her shadows over the surface of the globe." It could almost represent 'the extinction of our savage precursors before the dawn of science and cultivation'.
>
> (13)[8]

Philip Freneau (1752–1832) appeared as an early American poet lamenting the passing of the American Indian. Many of Freneau's poems were published for mass consumption in popular print; his work initiated the genre of the vanishing Indian that would later influence Irving and Cooper. Freneau's *The Indian Burying Ground* set the tone for the new literary genre:

> In spite of all the learned have said,
> I still my old opinion keep;
> The posture that we give the dead
> Points out the soul's eternal sleep.
> Not so the ancients of these lands;–
> The Indian, when from life released,
> Again is seated with his friends,
> And shares again the joyous feast.
>
> (Freneau)

Freneau, along with Irving, Bryant, Cooper and George Catlin, fashioned a romantic literary vision of the vanishing Indian situated in the sublimeness of the North American wilderness. These writers helped to forge a lasting image of the doomed Indian within the American mind of the early nineteenth century. While these American writers sought to distinguish American literature from that of England, they also based their poems and novels on a doomed race succumbing to the historically inevitable progress of civilization.

American poet, literary critic and slavery abolitionist William Cullen Bryant contributed to vanishing American Indian rhetoric with his 1824 poem *An Indian at the Burying-Place of His Fathers*: [9]

> It is the spot I came to seek—
> My father's ancient burial-place,
> Ere from the vales, ashamed and weak,
> Withdrew our wasted race.
> It is the spot—I know it well—
> Of which our old traditions tell.
> (Bryant, Sturges and Stoddard 58)

Here Bryant portrays American Indians as having *already* disappeared by his use of melancholy to describe the "burial-place" and "wasted race." There is little ambiguity in Bryant's poem where the "wasted race" lies "buried" to be mourned by his sad melancholy. Such portrayals served to promote the figure of the vanishing Indian within the American mind. It is somewhat revealing that Bryant describes the Indian with the word "withdrew," as if to absolve any European-American complicity in their demise. Bryant is not the only early nineteenth-century writer to utilize such rhetoric to portray the disappearing Indian. The vanishing Indian theme added significant literary and cultural legitimacy to the myth of the inevitable demise of the Indian race as a whole, as depicted in James Fenimore Cooper's *The Last of the Mohicans.*

Missionary journals also contributed to popular images of the vanishing Indian in the early nineteenth century. John Heckewelder observed in his *Account of the History, Manners, and Customs of the Indian Nations* (1818):

> Alas! in a few years, perhaps, they will have entirely disappeared from the face of the earth, and all that will be remembered of them will be that they existed and were numbered among the barbarous tribes that once inhabited this vast continent. At least, let it not be said, that among the whole race of white Christian men, not one single individual could be found, who, rising above the cloud of prejudice

> with which the pride of civilization has surrounded the original inhabitants of this land, would undertake the task of doing justice to their many excellent qualities, and raise a small frail monument to their memory.
>
> (Heckewelder XI)

Heckewelder invokes the vanishing image of American Indians, the "barbarous tribes" who "once inhabited this vast continent" (XI). Writing in 1818, Heckewelder depicted the American Indian as having previously *vanished.* Invoking the metaphor of memory, Heckewelder's depiction of the Indians linguistically casts off a "frail monument to their *memory*" [my emphasis] (XI). Depicted by literary sentiments of melancholy, the Indians were relegated to history. Had Heckewelder's vanishing Indians been confined to his missionary journal, perhaps his writing would have yielded less literary influence; however, Fenimore Cooper incorporated Heckewelder's depiction of Indians in his *Leatherstocking* novels, expanding the vanishing Indian mythology to proportions that would otherwise not have been as significant. Cooper's popular reception by readers in Europe and the United States gave the vanishing Indian theme a larger literary following. Keat Murray notes that "it is well-documented that James Fenimore Cooper mined John Heckewelder's Indian ethnographies and histories for information about the Native peoples in his Leatherstocking Tales" (Murray).[10]

Like Bryant, Washington Irving in *Traits of Indian Character* depicts the Indian as a vanished race:

> The eastern tribes have long since disappeared; the forests that sheltered them have been laid low, and scarce any traces remain of them in the thickly-settled States of New England, excepting here and there the Indian name of a village or a stream. And such must, sooner or later, be the fate of those other tribes which skirt the frontiers, and have occasionally been inveigled from their forests to mingle in the wars of white men. In a little while, and they will go the way that their brethren have gone before. The few hordes which still linger about the shores of Huron and Superior and the tributary streams of the Mississippi will share the fate of those tribes that once spread over Massachusetts and Connecticut and lorded it along the proud banks of the Hudson, of that gigantic race said to have existed on the borders of the Susquehanna, and of those various nations that flourished about the Potomac and the Rappahannock and that peopled the forests of the vast valley of Shenandoah. They will vanish like a vapor from the face of the earth; their very history will be lost in forgetfulness; and "the places that now know them will know them no more forever."
>
> (Irving)

By the time *The Last of the Mohicans* was published in 1826 the literary theme of the vanishing Indian was well situated in post-colonial America. Irving's lament for the American Indian *Traits of Indian Character* typified a major theme of the colonial mind. Irving's stanza serves to exemplify the inevitable eradication of the Indians when he evokes sorrow and melancholy.

Cooper's novel was built upon a long history of depictions of dying and vanishing Indians from New England missionaries, to the more recent American Romantic writers who transformed the dying Indians, like Cooper, into a race *already vanished.* The post-colonial mind that situated Cooper's novel was well planted and varied in forming pathetic images of the American Indian, images that also foreshadowed the Marshall Trilogy opinions.

Notes

1 While the *post colonial* here denotes the post-American Revolution period starting in 1780, early American literature sought to distinguish itself from English writers after the war of 1812 with England.

2 Romanticism also, and more importantly, evoked images of an idyllic and pristine rural landscape and the destructive advances of the Industrial Revolution that altered them forever. They were very nostalgic for all things 'country' and bemoaned modernity.

3 The Neoclassic period is usually taken to be the hundred-odd years between 1660 and 1770 or to demarcate the period by authors from Dryden's maturity to Johnson's death (1784). Neoclassical writers paid close attention to learning their craft from classical authors and by imitation of their works. Neoclassical writers aimed for "correctness" in prose and subject (Cuddon and Preston 541).

4 "The North American Indians," *Q. Rev.* (London), XXXI (Apr. 1824) 108 (quoted in Dippie 13).

5 [Nathan Hale], "Heckewelder's Indian History," *NAR,* IX (June 1819) 156 (quoted in Dippie 13).

6 John Elliott, Feb. 22, 1825, *Register of Debates in Cong.*, 18th Cong., 2nd sess., 640.

7 Eliza Lee, *Naomi; or, Boston Two Hundred Years Ago* (1847), quoted in G. Harrison Orians, *The Cult of the Vanishing American: A Century View,* 1834–1934 (Toledo, 1934) 6.

8 William Tudor, Jr., "An Address Delivered to the Phi Beta Kappa Society," *NAR,* 11 (Nov. 1815) 19–20.

9 William Cullen Bryant (Nov. 3, 1794 to June 12, 1878) is best remembered as a poet, most notably for "Thanatopsis" and as editor for 50 years at the New York *Evening Post* (*The New Encyclopaedia Britannica* 586).

10 Murray cites several sources that connect John Heckewelder's missionary work to Fenimore Cooper as follows: Cass, Lewis. "Article IX.-[Review of] 1. *The Pioneers, or the Sources of the Susquehanna: A Descriptive Tale . . .* 2. *The Last of the Mohicans: A Narrative of 1757*" *The North American Review* XXIII (July 1826): 150–78; Rawle, William, "A Vindication of the Rev. Mr. Heckewelder's History of the Indian nations." *Memoirs of the Historical Society of Pennsylvania.* Philadelphia: Historical Society of Pennsylvania I.I. (1826): 258–75; Muszynska-Wallace, E. Soteris, "The Sources of *The Prairie.*" *American Literature,* 21.1 (May 1949): 191–200; Wallace, Paul A.W., "Cooper's Indians." *James Fenimore Cooper: A Reappraisal.*

Mary E. Cunningham (ed.). Cooperstown: New York State Historical, 1954: 55–78; Stockton, Edwin L., Jr., *The Influence of The Moravians Upon the Leatherstocking Tales.* Dissertation. Ann Arbor: University Microfilms International, 1960; Vanderbeets, Richard, "Cooper and the 'Semblance of Reality': A Source for *The Deerslayer.*" *American Literature,* 42.4 (Jan. 1971): 544–6; Slotkin, Richard, *Regeneration Through Violence: The Mythology of the American Frontier, 1600–1860.* Middletown: Wesleyan University Press, 1973.

Chapter 6

Fenimore Cooper's *The Last of the Mohicans*

The Last of the Mohicans is situated during the Seven Years' War between the French and English forces in south-east Canada (Montreal and other parts of Quebec) and present day New England.[1] I choose the term 'forces' to describe the English and French since that is a term more in line with Cooper's depiction.

In competing for trade routes and access to valuable beaver and other furs for European markets, the French traders established alliances with several of the eastern Indian tribes (such as the *Iroquois* and others within the Five Nations) to facilitate trade and also to battle British colonial forces.[2] Within Cooper's novel, such alliances provided broad oppositional parties—French vs. British; however, the Indian and French alliances also produced unexpected twists and tragedies in the novel. Cooper writes about British-held Fort William Henry, situated along the "holy lake" or Lake Champlain, which becomes the center of attention for both the French commander General Montcalm and the fort's commander Colonel Munro, as well as his two daughters. The French, with the aid of their Huron Indian allies, work quietly to surround the fort while Colonel Munro's daughters, Cora and Alice, learning of their father's plight from another English commander, decide to reunite with him. The novel takes us through Cora and Alice's journey through Cooper's "wilderness," where the back country is cast as a foreboding and dark menace to all parties with the exception of the Indians. Cooper attaches several characters to Cora and Alice, in particular Hawkeye (also known as "Natty Bumppo"), the "white" frontiersman and woodsman who has grown up among Mohican tribes and learned the ways of the Indian. Cooper uses Hawkeye symbolically as the hybrid character who joins two races—Indian and European.

Unlike many of the published writings preceding *The Last of the Mohicans*, Cooper's use of Hawkeye and other characters demonstrates that Indians are not a homogenous race in America at this time. This is an important point given that the pre-Cooper polemic and fiction writers sought to portray Indians as savages. Typical of this pre-Cooper literary genre, Hugh Henry Brackenridge, the star correspondent of the *Philadelphia Freeman's Journal*, described Indians as:

> so degenerate from the life of man, so devoid of every sentiment of generosity, so prone to every vicious excess of passion, so faithless, and so incapable of all civilization, that it is dangerous to the good order of the world that they should exist in it.
>
> (Silver 284)

Above, Brackenridge describes the Native Indians as "vicious" and "incapable of all civilization"—traits that mirrored the savage and cruel characteristics that European settlers published in captive narrative accounts. Peter Williamson writes: "White settlers' accounts of being taken into captivity by Indians were a popular form of American literature in colonial times. Many of these captivity narratives emphasised the cruel and barbaric nature of the Indian captors" (Williamson 35).[3]

Cooper's novel, in contrast, is filled with significant impressions and nuances of the different types of native tribes. For example, Uncas and Chingachgook, the last two of the Mohican tribe, are portrayed in the novel as wise and noble in comparison to the devious and shrewd Huron Indian tribe. Cooper personifies the cunning Huron in the character of Magua. He is the humiliated and ousted former Indian leader who was repudiated by Colonel Munro for his drunken ways. Unlike many contemporary writers, Cooper discusses the practice by both French and British officials of manipulating tribal leaders through the use of alcohol. Magua seeks revenge for his humiliation by inserting himself as Cora and Alice's 'scout,' promising to lead them back to their father. The novel soon unites Magua and the daughters of Munro with Hawkeye, Chingachgook and Uncas when they meet in the forest. Upon their meeting Major Heyward, the southern American—English soldier who has risen within the ranks and is traveling with Munro's daughters, reveals to Hawkeye that they have become lost. Upon learning that Magua was the scout, Hawkeye expresses astonishment that any Indian could lose their way in the wilderness and when Hawkeye learns of Magua's tribal roots to the Huron, he immediately underscores the untrustworthy nature of these people. The scene is set and Hawkeye exposes Magua's intent to mislead the daughters. Magua is soon chased away by Hawkeye's long rifle until he reappears later in the novel with deadly consequences for the Mohicans.

Ultimately, through further twists and turns, Cora and Alice, together with Hawkeye, Uncas, David Gamut, Chingachgook and Heyward, make their way back to Colonel Munro's Fort Edwards, despite the presence of French soldiers and shooters around the fort. Cooper uses the wilderness in their journey as an ally that provides cover (fog, mist, trees, etc.) to help Hawkeye and his party reach safety.

Cooper develops characters throughout his novel to portray different attitudes towards race. Cora is of mixed races. Her mother was black and her Scottish father (Commander Munro) is white; Alice, Cora's sister, is white

(Commander Munro married his childhood sweetheart after Cora's mother died). Hawkeye, while white, is able to bridge both Indian and European cultures. Uncas, the son of Chingachgook, the last of the Mohicans, represents the friendly Indian in this mix. Cooper also creates a romantic novel in the American wilderness through Uncas' attraction to Cora and Cora's attraction to Uncas. Major Duncan Heyward, a white southern American is attracted to Alice, and later in the novel Magua seeks to kidnap and marry Cora. He is not motivated by love, but for *revenge* against Colonel Munro, because he knows how repulsive the interracial marriage would appear to the white commander. Cooper employs these racial overtones to reinforce stereotypes, i.e., that some Indians are perceived as savage and barbaric; yet Cooper also humanizes other Indians, such as Uncas and Chingachgook, as noble and wise. Cooper moves beyond the stereotypes and perhaps plays on the fears of early Europeans and Americans that a pliant white woman would prefer to join native tribes.[4] Cora's character embraces Uncas in ways that American society in the early nineteenth century would find abhorrent. But because Cooper is writing a romantic novel as well as an adventure story, tragedy must present itself when the novel ends with Uncas and Cora both being killed while the relationship between Alice and Heyward, both white, survives. Cooper also explores racial perspectives of the early nineteenth century by creating narratives that show Heyward seeking marriage with Alice, yet simultaneously being admonished by Colonel Munro for being a racist in not choosing his mixed-race daughter Cora.

Cooper's narrative weaves together many strands of Indian perspectives and many hues of racism. While a reader can pluck out passages from Cooper's novel that are consistent with Chief Justice John Marshall's description of Indians as savages, that would be too simplistic an analysis of the novel. Cooper forces readers to confront the mixing of races and the possibility that white women might actually find American Indians attractive as potential partners. While Cooper does present a cross spectrum of images and perspectives about race and Indians, the novel's very title suggests an ending presented as the historical inevitability of the Native American's demise. The novel's very title presents the finality of the novel's conclusion from the outset. While Cooper's embrace of the historical demise of the Mohicans mirrors Chief Justice John Marshall's view of the lamentable, but inevitable, demise of the Native American, Cooper takes his readers beyond the aesthetic excitement of the American wilderness, the savage raids and the love interests. He describes the sad and tragic demise of Uncas (the Last Mohican). Uncas is killed because of his forbidden love of Cora. Cora is killed because of Magua's ability to exploit her mixed-ethnic background against Cora's father and the sense of repulsion he will endure at his daughter being taken captive by, or worse married to, a savage Indian. Interestingly, Cooper also obliquely exposes various degrees of racism within his own narrative. On the one hand, Colonel Munro happily accepted his own mixed marriage and mixed-race children. Magua's kidnapping of Cora exploits Commander Munro's apparent disdain for Indians. It is Munro's dehumanization of Indians that Cooper uses to draw attention to Cora's capture and eventual death at the hand of Magua.

In the novel, while characters such as Magua and tribes such as the Huron reinforce the racial stereotypes used by John Marshall, unlike Marshall, Cooper also presents a more complex picture of Indians as a distinctly non-homogenous people. *The Last of the Mohicans* builds a narrative based, in part, on the inevitable conquest of native lands. In Chapter 1, Cooper's opening narrative sets the stage with the theme of historical destiny or inevitable conquest by European "colonists" over the American wilderness, and by extension, the native tribes:

> It was a feature peculiar to the colonial wars of North America, that the toils and dangers of the wilderness were to be encountered, before the adverse hosts could meet. A wide, and, apparently, an impervious boundary of forests, severed the obsession of the hostile provinces of France and England. The hardy colonist, and the trained European who fought at his side, frequently expended months in struggling against the rapids of the streams, or in effecting the rugged passes of the mountains, in quest of an opportunity to exhibit their courage in a more martial conflict. But, emulating the patience and self-denial of the practiced native warriors, they learned to overcome every difficulty; and it would seem, that in time, there was no recess of the woods so dark, nor any secret place so lovely, that it might claim exemption from the inroads of those who had pledged their blood to satiate their vengeance, or to uphold the cold and selfish policy of the distant monarchs of Europe.
>
> (Cooper 11)

As a literary setting to Cooper's novel, the above passage sets the tone or historical theme of inevitability. In the above passage, we read "that in time" the English and the French will dominate the wilderness, and the "practiced Native warriors" would *eventually* have to yield to the dominance of the English and French who had "pledged their blood . . . to uphold the cold and selfish policy of the distant monarchs of Europe." Using Said's theoretical framework to analyze how fictional narratives can assist or help to represent colonial domination, the above passage certainly fits within that paradigm. As will be shown, Said's theory is too narrow in scope; even though broad narratives of colonial domination may be expressed in fictional works, such works do not necessarily promote colonialism, but they can help to unearth the hues and multi-layered human dimension within a narrative that portrays a historical inevitability. It will be demonstrated that while Cooper's *The Last of the Mohicans* produces a narrative that is consistent with Said's literary discourse theory of English literature in the nineteenth century, Cooper also provides vivid textures of different attitudes towards race and culture that run counter to the stereotypical images that were being adopted by early American presidential administrations with respect to *civilizing* the natives as a peaceful method of dominating their land through cultural assimilation (Green 20–21).[5] Unlike American policies between the administrations of George Washington and Andrew Jackson, Cooper uses characters such as Uncas and Cora to depict the reversal of civilizing possibilities from Indian to white culture. Presidents Washington and Jefferson, in particular, sought to depict Native American Indians as uncivilized, their salvation lying in their assimilation into European-American culture. In Cooper's novel, Cora's character confronts this dominant theme. Our interrogation of *The Last of the Mohicans* straddles both the colonial motifs produced by dominant literature to represent the Indian as savage and, at the same time, Cooper's narrative revealing the cultural and racial complexity that Said's theory of colonial literature fails to adequately account for in the early American nineteenth-century literary context.

As previously stated, the title of the novel *The Last of the Mohicans* points to the eventual demise of the Mohicans. As if the title's meaning was not self evident, Cooper finally deals with the demise of the Mohicans through the Lenape Indian character Tamenund who laments his long life, one that has seen the gradual and painful eradication of the Mohican tribe. Tamenund states in the final chapter of the novel:

> The pale faces of the earth, and the time of the red-men has not yet come again. My day has been too long. In the morning I saw the sons of Unamis happy and strong; and yet, before the night has come, have I lived to see the last warrior of the wise race of the Mohicans!
>
> (Cooper 350)

Cooper's use of this gradual and prolonged passage of the Mohicans can be related to the historical context at the time of his portrayal. During the early 1820s, public calls for the removal of the Cherokee and other tribes by states such as Georgia, Tennessee, Alabama and North Carolina were in evidence. Georgia, in particular, passed legislation that sought to make life impossible for the Cherokee under the guise of state sovereignty of rights over land which they occupied. It was hoped by southern state governments that public discourses aimed at legally dispossessing Cherokees of any right or claim, would pressure the Cherokee from their land. Through such discursive pressures, southern states sought to induce the Cherokee and other native tribes to sell their remaining land in exchange for being removed to places west of the Mississippi river, e.g., Oklahoma. Cooper could not but notice that the gradual and ultimate demise of the Cherokee was being enacted not only in Congress, but through the American press (Green 22–3).[6]

Race

Race is a central theme in Cooper's narrative. Cast through such characters as Hawkeye, Uncas, Cora, Alice and Magua and several Indian tribes, Cooper displays a wide spectrum of racial positions present in America during the early nineteenth century. Even before isolating the racial characteristics of Cooper's main characters, it is already evident that the issue of race in Cooper's novel is neither presupposed nor silent in comparison, for example, with Edward Said's examination of Jane Austen's *Mansfield Park*. Whether presumed, or expressly utilized, Cooper does use race as an important theme and to this extent it is well worth interrogating the text to note to what extent Cooper's use of race introduces new perspectives and to what extent those perspectives provide similarities or foundations to racial themes used by the Marshall Trilogy cases; in particular, the *Cherokee Nation* and *Worcester* rulings.

Hawkeye, Magua and Chingachgook

Cooper reinforces stereotypes of native tribes prevalent in the early American Republic, but he also writes about characters that run counter to the dominant cultural representations. In particular, Cooper counters the narrowly based impression that Indians were of one race and one people. Cooper dispels this narrow view to reveal through the two Mohicans (Chingachgook and his son Uncas, and Magua, a Huron) that Indian tribes were varied, not homogenous, and often divided. Furthermore, Hawkeye's interracial friendship with Chingachgook develops as a relationship built on mutual respect for each other's culture. Both European and Mohican cultures are closely examined between these two main characters, not in competition with each other, but to further the understanding of the world as seen through both European and Native American perspectives. Such equality of cultural exchange was not seen as possible, especially by New England Puritans and missionaries, as a natural discourse between Europeans and Indians.

The predominant and colonial view had been that English settlers could 'civilize' the natives, or could ennoble them through missionary attempts to further instil Christian beliefs into this hapless and vulnerable race. The very seal of the State of Massachusetts, during the seventeenth century, depicts a virtually naked Indian male standing in a field saying "come over and help us" (Galvin). Given this dominant representation of the Indian, Cooper's development of a more complex cultural landscape while concurrently utilizing the dominant view, seeks to challenge such views with a portrayal of cultural respect or counter-racial dominance; namely, that Europeans and Indians can form friendships and also view each other's culture in a mutually respectful way:

> "Even your traditions make the case in my favour, Chingachgook," [Hawkeye] said speaking in the tongue which was known to all the Natives who formerly inhabited the country between the Hudson and the Potomack . . . Your fathers came from the setting sun, crossed the big river, fought the people of the country, and took the land; and mine came from the red sky of the morning, over the salt lake, and did their work much after the fashion that had been set them by yours; then God judge the matter between us, and friends spare their words!
>
> (Cooper 30)

In Hawkeye, we see a character who, while born European, is also depicted as someone who has been reared with the ways of the Indian. Hawkeye's exposure to Indian culture has also educated him in the ways of the American wilderness. For example, Hawkeye is also known as "long deer rifle" for his exceptional hunting prowess and knowledge of the land and of the wilderness. While the forest is depicted as a dark and frightful place, for Hawkeye the forest is his home. It is a place where his exposure to Indian culture has made him exceptional among the European characters in the novel. Through Hawkeye, Cooper has bridged races and created a hybrid character, not based on blood, but on being European by birth and Indian by upbringing. In this context, Cooper uses Hawkeye to bridge two dominant cultures in this plot—European and Indian.

What is intriguing about Cooper's varied depiction of Hawkeye is how it stands in direct opposition to John Marshall's view on European and Native American cultural integration. In *Johnson,* Marshall describes how the weaker Indian race of people will slowly be absorbed into the dominant culture as the passage of time completes the people's natural end. For Cooper, such a cultural transformation can also occur in the opposite direction, where the dominant European race seeks to be absorbed in the ways and culture of the Indian. As Cooper shows in the novel, Hawkeye's Indian training and exposure to native tribal culture makes him a better hunter and allows him to act as a surrogate father to Uncas, the son of Chingachgook, one of the two last Mohicans in this story. Cooper positions a European hunter and explorer not only as an experienced hunter, but also as a surrogate father to an Indian. Cooper immediately presents us with a unique character in early American literature, a European character who willingly embraces native culture, rather than a character who not only dismisses the value of Indian culture, but who also believes in the complete destruction of Indians themselves.

Hawkeye

Hawkeye bridges European and Indian culture. Below, we will extract passages of Cooper's novel to display this hybrid cultural character.

The following passage portrays Hawkeye as "scout," a European man knowledgeable in the ways of the wilderness and knowledgeable in the manner and reputation of the Huron tribe in particular (Cooper 32). Juxtaposing Hawkeye's familiarity with his place in the wilderness to Major Heyward's lost party initially introduces a dichotomous relationship between the European characters: Heyward and Hawkeye. Having racial and cultural dexterity, Hawkeye quickly emerges in the novel as a man at home in the very setting long seen as dark and savage by early nineteenth-century European settlers. Our first examination takes us to Chapter 4 of Cooper's novel:

> "Who comes?" demanded the scout [Hawkeye], throwing his rifle carelessly across his left arm, and keeping the fore finger of his right hand on the trigger, though he avoided all appearance of menace in the act—"Who comes hither, among the beast and dangers of the wilderness?"
>
> "Believers in religion, and friends to the law and to the king," returned he who rode foremost. "Men who have journeyed since the rising sun, in the shades of the forest, without nourishment, and are sadly tired of their wayfaring."
>
> "You are, then, lost," interrupted the hunter [Hawkeye], "and have found how helpless 'tis not to know whether to take the right hand or the left." (36)

In this initial dialogue, Hawkeye, as the "scout" is seen at ease with his rifle as Cooper presents him "carelessly" holding the weapon, yet the scout speaks to the strangers and introduces them to the reader as emerging from a wilderness. To the reader, the European scout is the one in command in this dangerous wilderness. To amplify the confusion and alien environment for Major Heyward, Cooper uses Hawkeye to reinforce the juxtaposition of European civilization and North American wilderness with his remark "You are, then, lost . . . and have found how helpless 'tis not to know whether to take the right or the left." This is an insightful exchange for setting up the stereotypical images of dangerous wilderness and English alienation from the wilderness; however, unlike some of the more common early nineteenth-century images, Cooper's Hawkeye is a European scout, comfortable in this wilderness. In another sense, Cooper is also presenting a truly American perspective through Hawkeye—a bridging of race and culture straddling the traditional English focus on reason and religion compared to dangerous American wilderness. As a narrative, Cooper does not allow the dialogue to create a simplistic introduction to colonialism. While there is a dangerous wilderness and a bemused English colonial army, it is not the civilized Major Heyward who is dominating the environment between the wilderness and his party, but Hawkeye. Heyward is the epitome of a European scout who is completely at the mercy of indecision. Hawkeye's ease with the wilderness confounds the civilized Heyward not in juxtaposition to Native Americans, but in relation to the wilderness itself.

If we were to use Said's narrative theory to establish dominance by discourse; a discourse that presumes a cultural superiority over the Other, we do not see Cooper representing such a narrow narrative of domination over a *Native Indian* race. Cooper is not Jane Austen in as much as this early narrative depicts the superiority of hybrid character *vis a vis* the environment. Cooper portrays a dominating wilderness challenging Heyward's trust in religion, law and the king. These last are entirely lost and at the mercy of the environment—hardly a narrative that one would establish as a literary basis for cultural domination.

Moving further into the exchange between Hawkeye and Heyward, Cooper introduces Hawkeye's cultural dexterity in demonstrating the distinctions between honest and dishonest Indians. Cooper's juxtaposition counters any stereotypical or homogenous depiction of the Indian depicted by John Marshall in the Trilogy cases. At this point, it is useful to engage the literary text as an opportunity to tease out Said's theory in relation to Cooper's text:

> "It is enough, for the present, that we [Heyward and company] trusted to an Indian guide to take us by a nearer, though blinder path, and that we are deceived in his knowledge. In plain words, we know not where we are."
>
> "An Indian lost in the woods!" said the scout [Hawkeye], shaking his head doubtingly; "When the sun is scorching the tree tops, and the water courses are full; when the moss on every beech he sees, will tell him in which quarter the north star will shine at night! The woods are full of deer paths which turn to the streams and licks, places well known to every body; nor have the geese done their flight to the Canada waters, altogether! 'Tis strange that an Indian should be lost atwixt Horican and the bend in the river! Is he a Mohawk?"
>
> "Not by birth, though adopted in that tribe; I [Heyward] think his birth place was farther north, and he is one of those you call a Huron."
>
> In reply, Hawkeye said "A Huron!" repeated the sturdy scout, once more shaking his head in open distrust; "they are a thievish race, nor do I care by whom they are adopted; you can never make any thing of them but skulks and vagabonds".
>
> (37)

With respect to the Huron, the tribe most allied to the French in Cooper's novel, Cooper uses some of the homogenous and stereotypical images of the Indians depicted by early American writers, in particular John

Marshall. A common image of the native tribes is that they are barbaric and savage. The Hurons depicted in Cooper's novel are skulks and vagabonds, a "thievish" race; hardly the term associated with a civilized race that plays according to rules and honor. Cooper uses Hawkeye, in part, to cement an image of the Huron and of Magua in this manner. Cooper does not strive to portray the Indians as one race, nor of one color or of one people; through his characters, Uncas and Chingachgook (the Mohicans), Cooper seeks to depict Indians who are both wise and honorable.

In Cooper's novel the native tribes are presented as both savage and wise, as honorable and thievish. The passage below demonstrates how Cooper uses the novel as discourse to represent the honorable and wise Indian within a dominant European-American discourse. For example, contrary to norms of interracial conflict, Hawkeye and Chingachgook have developed a friendship that usurps early American beliefs that white and Indian cultures could not bond on equal footing. John Marshall spent a good deal of time in *Johnson* speaking of how the dominant race would *absorb* the subjugated race. In Cooper's novel at least, this inevitable absorption is countered with a mutual respect between cultures rather than the domination of European over Indian:

> "I [Hawkeye] am not a prejudiced man, nor one who vaunts himself on his natural privileges, though the worst enemy I have on earth, and he is an Iroquois, daren't deny that I am genuine white," the scout replied, "and I am willing to own that my people have many ways, of which, as an honest man, I can't approve. It is one of their customs to write in books what they have done and seen, instead of telling them in their villages, where the lie can be given to the face of a cowardly boaster, and the brave soldier can call on his comrades to witness for the truth of his words . . . but every story has its two sides; so I ask you, Chingachgook, what passed, according to the traditions of the red men, when our fathers first met?"
>
> "Listen, Hawkeye, and your ear shall drink no lie. 'Tis what my fathers have said, and what the Mohicans have done . . . does not this stream at our feet, run towards the summer, until its waters grow salt, and the current flows upward!"
>
> "[Hawkeye] It can't be denied, that your traditions tell you true in both these matters," said the white man; "for I have been there, and have seen them; though, why water, which is so sweet in the shade, should become bitter in the sun, is an alteration for which I have never been able to account."
>
> "And the current!" demanded the Indian, who expected his reply with that sort of interest that a man feels in the confirmation of testimony,

> at which he marvels even while he respects it; "the fathers of Chingachgook have not lied."
>
> "The Holy Bible is not more true, and that is the truest thing in nature." (31–2)

The exchange above demonstrates a mutual respect between Hawkeye and Chingachgook; however, in the pre- and post-*Johnson* years of the 1820s Indians were cast as savages who were naturally inclined toward open warfare; hardly the image of a reasonable race. Yet, in this brief passage, Chingachgook not only listens to Hawkeye's questions and commentary, but Cooper also casts Hawkeye's character as a person who is introspective. Such introspection produces some honest assessments of his European brethren's shortcomings; namely, he acknowledges that the "white" man is not always right. Interestingly, Hawkeye admits that stories have two sides and invites Chingachgook to counsel him on his view of the truth. It appears that this exchange may seem innocuous, but in terms of the cultural context of the 1820s Cooper reproduces a cultural exchange that is based on mutual respect and honest introspection rather than cultural dominance.

Said's framework helps to explain the multi-layered mosaic of Cooper's depiction of the Indian and American culture during the 1820s. On the one hand, some of Cooper's characters show human traits contrary to the dominant view held by European writers of native tribes during the early nineteenth century. Yet, Cooper does not completely depart from the stereotypical representation of Indians. This larger view of the interrelationships between native tribes and the dominant European-American culture, however, produced racial relationships that would be taboo in colonial America, where such taboos as love interest between an Indian man and a European woman are foregrounded in *The Last of the Mohicans.* The love interests we explored between Cora and Magua, and later Uncas and Cora, do have an "historical pedigree." For instance, during the French and Indian wars of the early eighteenth century, although many Indians raided English villages or outposts (e.g., Deerfield, Massachusetts), not only were many colonists killed in such raids, but groups of women and children were notably adopted by various Indian tribes. The horror was not so much in the kidnapping and violence, but in the *voluntary* embrace of Indian life, culture and Indian men by English women (Demos).[7] Cooper plays upon these historical events, perhaps because history was being written by New England Puritan intellectuals in early America who attempted to dismiss the narratives of captured colonial English women who embraced Indian men and their culture. If one were to follow John Marshall's depiction of tribal culture in relation to the dominant march of America, Indians would inevitably be subsumed into the domain of white culture until their collective race and culture were extinguished (*Johnson v. M'Intosh* 543).

Cooper draws out the dominant culture's fear that European women would be subjected to rape and servitude rather than voluntarily embracing a savage over 'white' men or rejecting European culture. Cooper weaves narratives that not only acknowledge the dualism in Puritan culture in relation to Indians, but also develops a romantic narrative that transcends the European–Indian divide. Cora and Uncas for instance, develop a romance; however, because of the confrontations around them between Huron and English forces, they find their relationship tragically doomed by the narrative of war and vengeance. In looking at the dominant Puritan themes of racial revulsion and at the horrific depictions of European women being raped by their savage captors, this theme is expressed in the dialogue between Magua and Cora. A later narrative develops between Cora and Uncas that demonstrates Cooper's Americanization of interracial liaisons which, while consistent with French and Spanish colonists, was at odds with the dominant English view.[8] The latter's view was shared by John Marshall's narrative that Indian culture would eventually be absorbed into the dominant American culture, not the other way around:

> "But it may be appeased. If my father [Cora] has done you this injustice, show him how an Indian can forgive an injury, and take back his daughters. You have heard from Major Heyward—Magua shook his head, forbidding the repetition of offers he so much despised.
>
> "What have you," continued Cora, after a most painful pause, while the conviction forced itself on her mind, that the too sanguine and generous Duncan had been cruelly deceived by the cunning of the savage.
>
> "What a Huron loves [Magua]—good for good; bad for bad."
>
> "You would then revenge the injury inflicted by Munro, on his helpless daughters. Would it not be more like a man to go before his face, and take the satisfaction of a warrior?"
>
> "The arms of the pale faces are long, and their knives sharp!" returned the savage, [Magua] with a malignant laugh; "why should Le Renard go among the muskets of his warriors, when he holds the spirit of the gray-head in his hand?"
>
> "Name your intention, Magua," said Cora, struggling with herself to speak with steady calmness. "Is it to lead us prisoners to the woods, or do you contemplate even some greater evil? Is there no reward, no means of palliating the injury, and of softening your heart? At least, release my gentle sister, and pour out all your malice on me. Purchase wealth by her safety, and satisfy your revenge with a single victim. The loss of both his daughters might bring the aged man to his grave, and where would then be the satisfaction of Le Renard?"

> "Listen," said the Indian again. "The light eyes can go back to the Horicon, and tell the old chief what has been done, if the dark-haired woman will swear, by the Great Spirit of her fathers, to tell no lie."
>
> "What must I promise?" demanded Cora, still maintaining a secret ascendancy over the fierce Native, by the collected and feminine dignity of her presence.
>
> "When Magua left his people, his wife was given to another chief; he has now made friends with the Hurons, and will go back to the graves of his tribe, on the shores of the great lake. Let the daughters of the English chief follow, and live in this wigwam forever."
>
> However revolting a proposal of such a character might prove to Cora, she retained, notwithstanding her powerful disgust, sufficient self-command to reply, without betraying the weakness.
>
> "And what pleasure would Magua find in sharing his cabin with a wife he did not love; one who would be of a nation and colour different from his own? It would be better to take the gold to Munro, and buy the heart of some Huron maid with his gifts."
>
> The Indian made no reply for near a minute, but bent his fierce looks on the countenance of Cora, in such wavering glances, that her eyes sunk with shame, under an impression, that, for the first time, they had encountered an expression that no chaste female might endure. While she was shrinking within herself, in dread of having her ears wounded by some proposal still more shocking than the last, the voice of Magua answered, in its tones of deepest malignancy.
>
> "When the blows scorched the back of the Huron, he would know where to find a woman to feel the smart. The daughter of Munro would draw his water, hoe his corn, and cook his venison. The body of the gray-head would sleep among his cannon, but his heart would lie within reach of the knife of Le Subtil."
>
> "Monster! Well dost thou deserve thy treacherous name!" cried Cora, in an ungovernable burst of filial indignation. "None but a fiend could meditate such a vengeance! But thou overratest thy power! You shall find it is, in truth, the heart of Munro you hold, and that it will defy your utmost malice!"
>
> (Cooper 104–5)

The narrative above portrays Magua's sensitivity to the racial prejudice felt by Colonel Munro. Cooper draws out this racial theme by using Magua's attempt to serve revenge upon Munro through the capture of and marriage to his daughter Cora. Magua's revenge centered on Munro's racial prejudice against Indians and he has devised a plan, telling Cora that he will make her his wife. Cora's reaction to this scheme repulses her in two ways. Firstly, she knows this will horrify her father and secondly, she considers Magua to be nothing more than a savage.

Cooper's mosaic of themes and characters is not built on so simple a foundation as the racial prejudice felt by the dominant British characters. Before we proceed to analyze a far more textured and nuanced account of interracial relationships in *The Last of the Mohicans*, it is worth pausing here to assess how Said's depiction of literature as narrative discourse may represent conquest of the Indians by the European Americans.

If Cooper's narrative were focused on the relationship between Cora and Magua, one could argue that literature reinforces the prejudices or images of the colonized or oppressed class. To this extent, Said's assessment of literary representation as an aid to colonialism would exemplify strong parallels with the exchange cited because Cooper moves beyond a simple European and conquered Indian paradigm to utilize themes such as an interracial romance between Cora and Uncas. Said's discourse theory does not account for Cooper's depiction of Indians as wise and capable of attracting English women as romantic partners. This latter image is in contrast to the dominant view held by American intellectuals in the 1820s. Therefore, Cooper's narratives partially project an American literary canon that achieves realism regarding the Indians that both reinforces and counters the false images of the native tribes.

Early modern English: a tool of colonialism?

Cooper's use of Elizabethan English is evident throughout his novels. Using Elizabethan prose, Cooper seems to be aiming, whether consciously or otherwise, to introduce American literature to English and American readers to romanticize the idea that some Indians, who use Elizabethan words, can be civilized. Indians can be absorbed into American culture by "civilizing" them. It is submitted that Indian characters who use Elizabethan prose in *The Last of the Mohicans* are characterized as noble savages, while uncivilized Indians, such as the Huron, are depicted by Cooper as speaking with Creole English. Similar to Said's examination of Jane Austen's *Mansfield Park,* where slavery was embedded within a narrative to establish the economic foundations to the English estates that were supported by distant colonial plantations, Cooper uses language as a literary sign to reinforce conquest or power over the Indians in terms of cultural superiority. Cooper incorporates Elizabethan prose into the dialogue of Uncas and Chingachgook to represent a civilized Indian relative to the "thievish" Hurons. Instilling Cooper's benevolent Indian characters with mock early modern English dialogue within the context of the American frontier in the eighteenth century is historically inaccurate; yet that is not the aim of Cooper's textual style. Cooper is seeking to use Elizabethan English to produce a uniquely American novel that will be read by both British and American readers. Thus, while the use of Elizabethan prose is an attempt to bridge a transient American literary ascent (from England to America), language in Cooper's novel is also used to reinforce the notion that Elizabethan English used by Indians is a *marker* for both cultural assimilation and cultural superiority. In *The Last of the Mohicans,* Cooper uses this important literary representation to exploit cultural stereotypes both in America and England in the late eighteenth and early nineteenth centuries. Characters such as Uncas and Chingachgook communicate using Elizabethan English in similar fashion to Cora and Hawkeye:

> "Monster!" Well dost thou deserve thy treacherous name!" cried Cora, in an ungovernable burst of filial indignation. "None but a fiend could mediate such a vengeance! But thou overratest thy power! You shall find it is, in truth, the heart of Munro you hold, and that it will defy your utmost malice!"
>
> (105)

In the above passage Cora expresses her revulsion at Magua's revelation that he wishes to force a marriage upon her as the ultimate act of revenge upon her father, Colonel Munro. Cora is repelled because British culture did not accept interracial marriages willingly due to cultural perceptions that Indians were savages and sub-human. What is revealing is how frequently Cooper inserts Elizabethan usages like "thy" and "thou" to mark Cora's cultural superiority over the alleged native savage.

> "Why hast thou left us, pride of the Wapanachki?" he said, addressing himself to the dull ears of Uncas, as if the empty clay retained the faculties of the animated man. "Thy time has been like that of the sun when in the trees; thy glory brighter than his light at noonday. Thou art gone, youthful warrior, but a hundred Wyandots are clearing the briars from thy path to the world of spirits. Who that saw thee in battle would believe that thou couldst die? Who before thee has ever shown Uttawa the way into the fight? Thy feet were like the wings of eagles; thine arm heavier than falling branches from the pine; and thy voice like the Manitou when he speaks in the clouds. The tongue of Uttawa is weak," he added, looking about him with a melancholy gaze, "and his heart exceeding heavy. Pride of the Wapanachki, why hast thou left us?"
>
> (344)

In the passage above, Chingachgook, the elder Mohican, laments over the death of his son Uncas. It is important here to note that Chingachgook and Uncas were *The Last of the Mohicans.* The literary characteristic used by

Cooper with respect to Chingachgook was his wise counsel and sage presence. Cooper saw Chingachgook as a noble savage and to depict him as such, instilled in Chingachgook's speech Elizabethan prose designed to represent to the reader that this is a *learned* savage. In this setting, Cooper gives Chingachgook a civilized role relative to the savage Huron; hence, Cooper's negative and monstrous depiction of Magua.

American Indians did not speak in early modern English prose, or verse. Cooper artificially inserts Elizabethan English to demarcate learned Indians from savage Indians; peaceful Indians from fierce Indians. Cooper's utilization of archaic prose serves as a literary representation to *humanize* some Indian characters. To this extent, Cooper's literary setting, through dialogue and language, does mirror Edward Said's view that literature can help solidify colonial or imperial representations over a race of people. At the dawn of American nationalism Cooper's novel reflects American policy towards native tribes; namely, dispossessing Indians not through force, but through the 'civilizing' policies inaugurated by George Washington's Secretary of War, Henry Knox (Perdue and Green 20–21).[9] Official U.S. policy toward the native tribes in the southeast and New England regions of the early American Republic was to avoid war. American policy sought peaceful means (e.g., President Jefferson's trading posts and credit policies were developed to encourage Indians' indebtedness—indebtedness that was only extinguished by ceding land to the American Government) to absorb not only Native American land to feed the speculative hunger of American settlers, but also to culturally dilute Indians through the "civilizing" of their race with the English language, Christian religion and American manufactured goods. It was this peaceful agenda that Henry Knox felt would ultimately dismantle any long term resistance by Native Americans to European culture, simultaneously warding off political tension or warfare with some of the southern states who sought to forcefully seize Native land.

Cooper displays early modern English usage with another Indian character in *The Last of the Mohicans,* Tamenund. Here Cora, the daughter of Munro, pleads for her life as Magua attempts to seize her in the presence of the Delaware Chief. Cora seeks to reason with Tamenund and Cooper creates a dialogue that partly demonstrates the wisdom and humility of the chief's wise counsel. Consistent with Cooper's attachment of Elizabethan prose to the narrative's civilized characters, he adopts a similar pattern with Tamenund, the chief of the Delaware Indians. By incorporating Elizabethan prose in Tamenund's dialogue with Cora, Cooper is representing to the reader that only good men, wise men and civilized men can command such linguistic usage:

> "What are thou?"
>
> "A woman. One of a hated race, if thou wilt—a Yengee. But one who has never harmed thee, and who cannot harm thy people, if she would; who asks for succor."

"Tell me, my children," continued the patriarch, hoarsely, motioning to those around him, though his eyes still dwelt upon the kneeling form of Cora, "where have the Delawares camped?"

"In the mountains of the Iroquois, beyond the clear springs of the Horicon."

"Many parching summers are come and gone," continued the sage, "since I drank of the water of my own rivers. The children of Minquon are the justest white men; but they were thirsty, and they took it to themselves. Do they follow us so far?"

"We follow none; we covet nothing," answered Cora. "Captives against our wills, have we been brought among you; and we ask but permission to depart to our own in peace. Art thou not Tamenund—the father, the judge, I had almost said, the prophet—of this people?"

"I am Tamenund of many days."

"'Tis now some seven years that one of thy people was at the mercy of a white chief on the borders of this province. He claimed to be of the blood of the good and just Tamenund. 'Go,' said the white man, 'for thy parent's sake thou art free.' Dost thou remember the name of that English warrior?"

"I remember, that when a laughing boy," returned the patriarch, with the peculiar recollection of vast age, "I stood upon the sands of the seashore, and saw a big canoe, with wings whiter than the swan's, and wider than many eagles, come from the rising sun."

"Nay, nay; I speak not of a time so very distant, but of favor shown to thy kindred by one of mine, within the memory of thy youngest warrior." (304)

Based on the above and given Said's theory on literature and colonialism, it is argued that Cooper intentionally filled many of his novels with Elizabethan chapter headings (Gates 716).[10] A reasonable assessment would attribute Cooper's use of Elizabethan English as a literary tool to his desire to reinforce the view that European culture and humanistic English education held the key to being civilized (717).

An examination of the main European characters, Cora, Major Heyward, Hawkeye, Gamut and Colonel Munro, demonstrates that they all use Elizabethan words, such as "thou," "thy," and "thine." Collectively, these characters represent the civilized European race in *The Last of the Mohicans.* In terms of the civilizable Indian race, Cooper identified the characters of Chingachgook and his son Uncas, together with Tamenund, as the wise, sage and learned Indians. Therefore, Cooper develops these native characters as benevolent Indians compared with savage Indians such as the Huron. The common literary thread that is woven throughout the novel is the use of Elizabethan English to elucidate the dichotomy between educated-civilized Indians and the savage Huron.

Elizabethan prose in *The Last of the Mohicans* exemplifies an economic and cultural backdrop.[11] Specifically, characters in *The Last of the Mohicans* who are educated are exemplified by their affected Elizabethan speech and lexis and are presented as the civilized and more superior race. This literary dualism between characters such as Hawkeye, Uncas, Chingachgook, Cora, Alice, Major Heyward, Colonel Munro and Tamenund compared to the Huron, presents a social and colonial framework that both mirrored eastern American intellectual representations of the native tribes and served to reinforce images of civilizable vs. savage Indians:

> "Delaware!" resumed the sage. "Little art thou worthy of thy name. My people have not seen a bright sun in many winters; and the warrior who deserts his tribe when hid in clouds is doubly a traitor. The law of the Manitou is just. It is so; while the rivers run and the mountains stand, while the blossoms come and go on the trees, it must be so. He is thine, my children; deal justly by him."
>
> (Cooper 309)

Above Cooper combines Elizabethan verse with the civilized and wise counsel of the benevolent Indian. Tamenund—the sage native warrior of the Lenape—extols his grace and morality in the passage. Note Cooper's use of honor in his description of a traitor and how he identifies the cultural separation between the wise and honorable Indians—especially compared to those who have been cast off from their tribes, namely Magua's banishment from the Huron.

Notes

1 New England is made up of six U.S. States: Massachusetts, Vermont, New Hampshire, Rhode Island, Connecticut and Maine. The Seven Years' War occurred from 1754–1763.

2 A group of Native Americans originally composed of the Oneida, Onondaga, Mohawk, Cayuga and Seneca nations.

3 A vivid account by Peter Williamson (d. 1799) on his capture by Shawnee or Delaware Indians. Captivity accounts such as these fed eastern seaboard communities with savage images of the Indians.

4 During the seventeenth century there were many battles and raids by Indians upon early New England settlements. Often, Indian raiding parties (in conjunction with French forces) would capture important leaders and women. While more often than not, many of these hostages were later traded for French captives, there were white women who were captured, but then of their own accord, chose to live and stay married with their Indian husbands. John Williams, a minister in the 1600s, based in Deerfield, MA, lost his daughter in exactly this fashion.

5 "Henry Knox was the primary architect of the 'civilization' policy, the program that had enabled the cultural transformation of the Cherokee that Sally Reeese

described so proudly . . . Knox believed that 'civilizing' the Indians would both bring and perpetuate peace with them" (Green 20–21), and, by extension, dilute the native culture with European values and Christian teaching.

6 The early American Republic sought to deliver and grant land to the newly formed states as part of the reconciliation towards a new constitution in the late 1780s. The problem with Federal policy is that the United States did not have the money to buy land from the Indians, land that many states tried to claim as their own, based on the victory against the British. The early Americans rationalized the theft of the Indians' lands as being part and parcel of the British defeat since, as the Americans sought to assert, the spoils of war gave them rights over Indian lands. The problem, however, was that none of the Indian tribes considered themselves defeated nations and most had not been invaded during the Revolution. "Except for the Cherokees, most had not been invaded during the Revolution by American armies, and even among the Cherokees, many warriors sided with the colonists. None considered themselves to have been defeated, and they absolutely rejected the right-of-conquest pretentions of Congress and the states" (Green 23).

7 John Demos's book *The Unredeemed Captive* is a well-written book on the capture of Eunice Williams, daughter of John Williams. John Williams was an eminent minister in Deerfield, Massachusetts, during the period of occupation in the early 1700s. Demos provides an excellent account of the killings, kidnappings and hostage exchanges between the French, the Indians and the English. Williams was caught up in this historical period; however, his daughter Eunice was kidnapped at an early age, eventually married her Indian captor and despite repeated attempts by John Williams and other New England traders and representatives to buy her freedom, she refused to return to her family. Even when Eunice eventually visited her family in Longmeadow, MA, and after the death of her father, she never gave up her connection to her Indian family.

8 African-American historian Carter Woodson cites the "long held belief among Americans that Spanish, Portuguese, and French possessed a greater tolerance for marriages between whites and blacks than the English" (Botham 60).

9 "Henry Knox was the primary architect of the 'civilization' policy, the program that had enabled the cultural transformation of the Cherokees that Salley Rose described so proudly. Secretary of war in the governments of both the Articles of Confederation and the first administration of President George Washington, his main concern was the security of the new United States . . . Knox believed that 'civilizing' the Indians would both bring and perpetuate peace with them" (Perdue and Green 20–21).

10 395 out of 939 headings (Gates, 716).

11 This is similar to Edward Said's analysis of Jane Austen's silence in *Mansfield Park* about the use of slave labor in Antigua as a basis for the economic colonialism.

Chapter 7

The wilderness in American art and literature

> But the tribes of Indians inhabiting this country were fierce savages, whose occupation was war, and whose subsistence was drawn chiefly from the forest. To leave them in possession of their country, was to leave the country a wilderness.
>
> Chief Justice John Marshall, *Johnson v. M'Intosh* (1823)

> The whites have been gradually pressing upon them, as they kept receding from the approaches of civilization. We have purchased the greater part of their lands, destroyed their hunting grounds, subdued the wilderness around them, overwhelmed them with our population, and gradually abridged their native independence.
>
> Chief Justice John Marshall, *Cherokee Nation v. Georgia* (1831)

> The humane policy of the government towards these children of the wilderness must afford pleasure to every benevolent feeling, and if the efforts made have not proved as successful as was anticipated, still much has been done.
>
> Chief Justice John Marshall, *Worcester v. Georgia* (1832)

Discourse theory and the American wilderness

An examination of the American wilderness theme in literature and painting during the American Romantic period (1790 to 1830) provides a subject of study that demonstrates the discursive theories outlined by Michel Foucault and Edward Said.[1] This chapter demonstrates how the Foucauldian discursive formations regulated by dominant power relations established an American Romantic archive about the backwoods.[2] The images of the wilderness have a long and important pedigree in the Romantic movement. This chapter will demonstrate how the cultural realm of dominant power relations during America's early colonial period, until the early nineteenth-century Romantic movement, regulated the discursive statements about the wilderness. Rather than examine the power of guns and other Western arms over the American rough country, this chapter will reveal the varied colonial discourses about the American wilderness that were regulated to assemble the Romantic archive that situated the Trilogy cases.

Some of the dominant power relations that regulated the distribution of discourses about the wilderness derived from colonial Puritans such as Cotton Mather, John Cotton and John Winthrop. Ministers such as Jonathan Edwards in the late seventeenth century also influenced early American painters of the wilderness, such as Thomas Cole of the Hudson River Painting School. The Romantic period also foregrounded images of the frontier from writers, most notably Fenimore Cooper's literary depictions of the Adirondack Mountains in New York and his influence on Cole's paintings. The early Romantic period also saw President Jefferson commission the Lewis and Cark expedition to "explore" the uncharted western interior of the American continent. Collectively, these power relations regulated how the discourse statements about the wilderness were ultimately unified into an archive of images, a "unity of discourses" around a subject.

The American wilderness exemplified a critical physical and cultural backdrop to the varied themes of early colonial domination over the American Indians. From the early sixteenth-century metaphors of the threatening American wilderness to the late nineteenth-century sublimity of nature's grace, these discursive formations were regulated into images of the backwoods to promote Euro-American objectives. Such objectives ranged from the divine purpose of the Plymouth Plantation and Massachusetts Bay Colony to taming wild forests en route to finding spiritual salvation, to populating a 'desert' wasteland, to portray the uncivilized place in early nineteenth-century Romantic America. Said's discursive theory within a colonial setting helps to situate this chapter as an example of how the discourses of the North American wilderness were assembled over time to advance the colonial, and after 1776, the imperial efforts of the European-American expansion. Like Said's examination of nineteenth-century English fiction, demonstrating how literature can discursively define the Other, so too were the discursive statements about the American wilderness utilized by European Americans to culturally define the frontier and, by extension, the American Indian.

On the eve of *Johnson v. M'Intosh*, the discursive archive about the American wilderness had become *findings of facts* about the natural state of Indian land. John Marshall's judicial metaphors in the Trilogy about the American forest were part of the discursive archive that both situated the backwoods and regulated its image. Similar to Foucault's "will to truth," Marshall's depictions of the wilderness in the Trilogy cases were constituted by, and in turn contributed to, the discursive archive that defined the perceptions of the wilderness (Foucault, *The Order of Discourse* 54). Therefore, the archive about the wilderness and the Trilogy cases both served to blur cultural and legal statements. This blurring was at the root of the Marshall opinions; namely, where judgment's *finding of fact*, appearing and being accepted like Foucault's 'murmur,' acquired the status of sworn statements.

The wilderness

The image of the wilderness in American history is an important element in analyzing the Marshall Trilogy cases as judgments within a literary tradition. Whilst earlier chapters in this book explored the literary discourses of the American Indian and how those discourses provided a cultural archive to the Marshall Trilogy cases with respect to the Indians, our project in this chapter concentrates on an examination of the wilderness theme and how Indian land was depicted in literature. This chapter examines an important literary theme that builds upon how both the Indian and European as well as later Euro-American frontiersman, were *distinguished from one another* in early Romantic literature with respect to the American wilderness.

An assessment of how Indians and European colonialists were distinguished in relation to the rough country reveals a multi-layered discourse of how the wilderness was portrayed during different periods in early American literary history. Starting with the first wave of immigrant Puritans, the land was portrayed as barren, dark and populated by heathens. At first, this early colonial characterization of the New World sought to use the wilderness as a place where voyagers from England would need to test their inner faith. By the second generation of English settlers, this barren land was transformed into the *sublime,* which incorporated both disorder and darkness. This evolving image of the wilderness was further utilized as a literary metaphor in the late eighteenth century by writers in several genres, such as histories, sermons, captive narratives, speeches, and poems. The image of the wilderness was most vividly reinvented by early nineteenth-century American writers. Examples of this phenomenon include Fenimore Cooper's *Leatherstocking* series of novels and the early paintings of the Hudson River School. The period between the early 1620s to the early 1830s, provides a literary landscape that invents the wilderness based on the practicalities from the European colonial and later American points of view.

The wilderness and Indians were interwoven with respect to how the English settlers viewed themselves in the New World. Specifically, the juxtaposition of the English settlers against the backdrop of the untamed wilderness and the savage Indians was a necessary corollary to the various images settlers found useful throughout the seventeenth century. It should be noted that this contrast is entirely dependent on the implicit viewpoint that the English colonists were more "civilized" than either their new environs or their native neighbors. At first, the New England settlers framed their voyage to the New World in terms of a missionary expedition, with the wilderness as a conceptual mirror to highlight their religious purposes: this religious zeal is exemplified below with the varied statements of the early Puritans in Massachusetts.

> This hostile picture was darkened as the Pilgrims and Puritans of Massachusetts made known their views. These dissenters were lifted by an unquenchable sense of mission. They were God's agents entrusted to create in America a spiritual Eden whence true believers, freed from the taints of Popery and Anglicanism, would go forth to create in the New World a Celestial City, warmed by the sun of God's approval, and blessed by the fertility and beauty that all the world had known when it was youthful and vigorous. [. . .] To William Bradford they were "savage and brutish men who range up and downe, little otherwise than the wild beasts"; to the Puritan Samuel Purchas, they were "more brutish than the beasts they hunt, more wild and unmanly than that unmanned wild Countrey, which they range rather than inhabited."
>
> (Billington 7)

From Puritians like William Bradford to Samuel Purchas, varied statements about the piety of their mission to the New World and about the "brutish" and "unmanned wild Countrey" exemplified an emerging discursive archive about the American Wilderness.

As subsequent generations of Europeans settled in the New World, the wilderness began to be described as an inhospitable desert that needed to be conquered and tamed. Therefore, the theme in respect to the wild changed from a purely religious perspective to one that was more earthly—a place where Americans could seek a westward destiny to plant a "garden" in the wilderness. Our examination of the wilderness theme will introduce these changing images so we can situate the literary relationships of the Marshall cases.

The image of the wilderness as a dark, dangerous and uncivilized locale in the American mind is reflected in the opinions authored by Justice Marshall.[3] In *Johnson* Marshall projected the Indian and the wilderness together: "[t]o leave them in possession of their country, was to leave the country a wilderness" as if to imply that the continued exclusive possession of the land by the Indians by itself constituted a state of "wilderness" (*Johnson v. M'Intosh* 590). In situating the barbaric nature of the backwoods relative to the civilizing push of the European colonialists competing for land with the Indians, Marshall employs the image of subjugation not merely of people, but of the landscape itself. In *Worcester v. Georgia*, Marshall builds on the civilized stature of the European settlers by speaking to the "children" of the wilderness as if to state, as he did in other parts of his opinions, that the Indians were "hapless wards." Their helplessness was derived from their intrinsic connection to the wilderness; that unruly, uncivilized place, by which, but for the benevolence of the American Government, the Native Americans, as "children," would continue to be subjugated lawless frontiersman. Marshall writes in *Worcester* of the "humane policy of the Government towards these children of the wilderness," implying that the American Government must afford mercy and cultural assimilation toward the Indian (*Worcester v. Georgia* 588). The themes depicted by Marshall about the wilderness in the Trilogy cases were consistent with those of Roderick Nash. In his essay entitled *The Cultural Significance of the American Wilderness*, Nash observed that the people of the "New World were not Americans at all, but transplanted Europeans who regarded the land as a spiritual and physical void which had to be conquered and civilized in the name of Christianity and progress" (Nash, *The Cultural Significance of the American Wilderness* 66–73).

The genre of law

In proceeding toward an examination of the literary discoursers that influenced the Trilogy cases, I am also drawn to Peter Goodrich's *Law in the Courts of Love*. Goodrich lays down the proposition that law's *amnesia*, while not a conscious attempt to disassociate legal judgment from literary discourses, does observe how law and legal judgment seem to unconsciously enter a realm where literature becomes part of the fabric of their institutional world, such that no judicial notice is taken of their existence. The genre of law is in essence and practice unconscious, that is to say that literature is reproduced:

> For those who still believe in the unity and universality of law, and trust in its momentary closures, the autopoetic or self-referential quality of the legal idol or ideal rests upon a peculiarly positive form of forgetting . . . In the theory of judgment as amnesia or loss of memory institutes habits as law and intuition as the strongest form of judgment. In doing so it reinstitutes the phantasm of an immemorial or unknowable knowledge as the only proper source of law.
>
> (Goodrich 113–14)[4]

The effect of legal judgment is confined to the logical structure of the legal opinion and its self-referential genealogy of law within legal judgment. In forgetting law's origins as legal rhetoric, and because of the consequential power of legal judgment in the real world, the very text of legal judgment is allowed by its authoritative majesty to simply assert facts and images as if they are self discovered. Legal judgment attracts a mystic of legal theory based on a logical structure of language and rhetoric. Goodrich's theory reveals the law's forgotten literary genesis. The scope of this chapter is to reveal the image and theme of the wilderness as both a literary and religious genre that was inserted into the Marshall opinions by way of *anamnesis*, or to use Foucault's term, by way of the *archive* that preceded the Trilogy cases.

As Nash has written in *Wilderness and the American Mind*, the wilderness provided a backdrop and cultural mirror from which American culture was developed (Nash, *Wilderness and The American Mind* xi). There would be no

Magnalia by Cotton Mather or *The Last of the Mohicans* by Fenimore Cooper to project the light and civilizing purpose of early American Puritans but for the dark and uncivilized American wild. From a cultural standpoint, the frontier exemplified a basic ingredient of American culture. To situate how American culture was influenced by the image and metaphor of the wilderness, one needs to understand that Europe represented the wilderness in such a way as to project European control, order and civilization.

Early American literary discourse and the wilderness theme

In the seventeenth century, the early European-American settlements in North America produced varied writings, but most were confined to either a religious or a historical sub-genre, best seen in diaries. One of the most prolific writers of the early American settlement period was the Puritan preacher Cotton Mather. Cotton was the son of Increase Mather and believed that New England settlers had arrived in the New World on a civilizing mission, not only to present the world with a unique religious experiment—namely seeking to rule and to establish an organization of men based on God's rule—but also to present his mission and that of other New Englanders alike within the context of reaching the desolate and wild shores of the New World as ambassadors of God's will. Mather, for example, projected the early American visions of the wilderness as occupied by savage Indians and devoid of Christian light and civilization. The *Christian light* upon the American wilderness, however, did not speak in one voice. Puritans still adhered to the Church of England, but disagreed with many of the Catholic practices that prevailed in English Protestantism, such as the marriage ring, the sign of the cross in baptisms, showy vestments and receiving communion, while the Separatists desired to break from the Church of England and sought to establish their own church in the New World. The Massachusetts colony was controlled by the Puritans. In Mather's influential book *Magnalia* he sets out the tone for a significant cultural statement about how the wilderness can be "irradiated" by New England's divine mission. Mather wrote:

> I write the *Wonders of the Christian Religion*, flying from the Deprivation of *Europe*, to the *American Strand*: and, assisted by the Holy Author of that *Religion*, I do, with all conscience of *Truth*, required therein by Him, who is the Truth itself, report the *Wonderful Displays* of His Infinite Power, Wisdom, Goodness, and Faithfulness, wherewith His Divine Providence hath *Irradiated an Indian Wilderness.*
>
> (Wendell 49)

It is worth examining this quote because Mather's useful undercurrents and metaphors, later used by Justice Marshall and other American writers, would expand on this literary etymology. It is interesting to note that Mather refers to the New World as the "*American Strand*." Taken that literally, he portrays the New World as a helpless place, as a transitive verb; one definition of a strand means to put or leave somebody in a difficult or helpless position. Toward the end of Mather's quote, he establishes a missionary purpose for why the "Holy Author" had "irradiated an Indian Wilderness." In this instance we witness a significant American cultural genesis of both the Indians and the role of the wilderness. In using the metaphor of an "irradiated" wilderness, Mather signifies the Christian light that shines upon an "Indian Wilderness." The juxtaposition of light and divine mission has its genesis in American literature in Mather's depiction and justification for the English settlement of New England. In 1652 missionary William Steele similarly utilized the metaphor of Christian light to amplify the wilderness as a place of darkness, possessed by an ungodly people; where the "first fruits of a barren Wilderness" were obtained when civilization and Christianity succeeded in "shining . . . a beam of Light into the darkness of another World" (Nash 37). By 1652 the discourses casting the wilderness "as a place of darkness" were dispersing and forming influential discursive statements that credited European civilization and Christianity as the sources of "light" upon a barren wilderness.

In *Magnalia*, Mather highlights New England's Puritanism by setting forth the history and personal characters of the early settlement fathers. In a discourse on *Toile*, one of the founding New England "chosen" according to Calvinist doctrine, cast in the form of Apostle Eliot, Mather describes Toile's ability to learn the Indian language. Mather describes how, once Toile was able to conquer this foreign tongue, he translated the Gospel in writing—"[p]rayers and pains through faith in Christ Jesus will do any thing." Mather wrote "and being by his prayers and pains thus furnished, he set himself in the year 1646 to preach the Gospel of our Lord Jesus Christ, among these desolate outcasts" (Mather 562). Mather interposes imagery of the Indians as "desolate outcasts," thereby casting the Indian as dissolute merely by virtue of where he lived, namely in the "Indian Wilderness." In an effort to define the purpose and righteousness of the New England "chosen" in the New World, Mather creates a discourse in which the wilderness is perceived as "dissolute" and "wild"—such metaphors were essential in his design to support his Puritan missionary purpose to promote God's will.

While Mather had a profound effect in planting a uniquely English discourse about the morally dissolute Indian and the dark wilderness where he dwelled, it would be naïve to think that it was Mather who first saw the wilderness in these terms. The first English settlers in the New World, even before setting sail across the Atlantic, envisaged the wilderness as a proving ground, a place where the divine mission to spread the gospel and their own faith would be tested. "The savage nature of the wilderness was no surprise to these Puritan settlers. They knew exactly where they were, and they were prepared, even before they landed, with the appropriate texts to describe it" (Williams, *Wilderness Lost: The Religious Origins of the American Mind* 52). Puritans preparing to leave for the New World knew their scripture by heart and anticipated a "howling wilderness" awaiting their arrival in New England:

> The howling wilderness into which New England saints were called was a wilderness of fact, of type, of the world, and of the mind. It was a dense and dangerous forest; it was a parallel type of wilderness through which God's Israel of old had to pass before entering Canaan.
>
> (23)

> Biblical origins of the wilderness as a dangerous place where men would be tested before entering Canaan presented a *European theme* of the dark and foreboding forest in America. At its origins, settlers seeking to take the dangerous and difficult voyage across the Atlantic to the New World saw the wilderness not as a place to be civilized per se, but as a place they had to pass through in order to find the paradise God had prepared. The first New England settlers understood the culture and symbolism of the wilderness as a religious testing ground for their salvation.
>
> (25)

William Bradford, in his *History of the Plymouth Plantation*, described the plight of the English settlers as "poore people" cast into a dangerous wilderness, petitioning God to aid them during their time of tribulation in forming the first settlements. It was not because the settlers were poor, but because they were alone in a *foreign* "wilderness" that their plight needed divine consideration. Bradford's invocation of the wilderness had several meanings, propounding a multi-layered agenda. On the one hand, Bradford chose the wilderness as the setting for the trials and tribulations of the first English settlers. Bradford not only employed the sublime in his prose to magnify the internal anxiety felt by the first settlers in relation to the wilderness, but also focused attention on the inner spiritual quest that would lead the stranded settlers to religious salvation. If the wilderness was indeed the setting, the trial was being stranded in a place unknown as well as ill prepared. Salvation was to look within oneself to find God and survive an ordeal on the margins of civilization. Like John Marshall, Bradford used the wilderness as a theme—a theme that required a spiritual reason to magnify the purpose for the first settlers' journey to the New World. Bradford wrote that

> these poore people here in a wilderness should, notwithstanding, be inabled in time to repay all these engagements, and many more unjustly brought upon them through the unfaithfulness of some, and many other great losses which they sustained, which will be made manifest, if ye Lord be pleased to give life and time.
>
> (Bradford 249)

Struggle, deprivation and danger were all symbols that Bradford used to extol the physical and spiritual sacrifices that the first settlements willingly engaged. Bradford established the wilderness as the backdrop to the journey of the first settlers.

> For artful reasons Bradford recurs to the landscape at the climax of his narrative and insists on it in a rhetorical manner. He permits the North American topography onto his stage in the shape of an agonistic weather-beaten marauder—a trope for everything that jeopardizes the legitimacy of the Pilgrims' action—only because he has learned how to use that image to represent the triumph of spirit over all that threatens and opposes it.
>
> (Laurence 57)

The wilderness became an essential discursive image to demonstrate that the New World was primitive, barren and remote compared to the domestic comfort and intellectual advances of England. Bradford writes

> that whereas the great and known end of the first Comers in the year of our Lord, 1620, leaving their dear Native Country, and all the great end of that was dear to them there; transporting of themselves over the vast Ocean, into this remote vast Wilderness, and therein was Liberty to willingly conflicting with Dangers, Losses, Hardships and Distresses.
>
> (Bradford 239)

Bradford's commentary conjured the first American images of the New England settlements and through his writing about the Plymouth Colony, the first European-American portrayals of the North American wilderness as a dangerous and uncivilized place. The American backdrop to the ultimate legal conquest of the Indian can partly be traced back to Bradford's original literary images of the wilderness. Roderick Frazier Nash writes in *Wilderness of the American Mind*, "when William Bradford stepped off the Mayflower into a 'hideous and desolate wilderness' he started a tradition of repugnance" (Nash, *Wilderness and The American Mind* 23–4).

In his in *Decennium Luctuosum* (1699), Mather continued to project the wilderness as a place of danger and disorder relative to the safe and ordered plantations of the settlers, even though such plantations were hardly safe havens, given the frequent Indian raids. This theme was used by authors whose intellectual impact in early America was widespread; hence the relevancy of Mather's depiction regarding the wilderness.

> The Barbarous Indians left her[5] Asleep, and covered with Snow; but at length waking, what Agonies may you imagine she was in, to find

> herself left a prey for Bears and Wolves, and without any Sustenance, in a howling Wilderness many Scores of Leagues from any Plantation?
> (Lincoln 200)

Here Mather describes the wilderness as a backwoods "many Scores of Leagues from any Plantation" and a "howling Wilderness," evoking a biblical theme.[6]

In the eighteenth century, Jonathan Edwards, a Connecticut Valley minister ensconced in rural Northampton, Massachusetts, continued the "theme of wilderness" from the previous century. For Edwards "the land that we have to travel through [to Heaven] is a wilderness; there are many mountains, rocks, and rough places that we must go over in the way (Nash, *Wilderness and The American Mind* 39). What makes Edwards' sermons relevant to our study is that "Edwards has had more influence on subsequent thought than any other American theologian" (Wendell 83). Edwards was also part of the New England ruling class. In the eighteenth century, New England was still governed as a British Colony. Being born within this influential New England ruling class enabled Edwards to expand the influence of his sermons and theological reach. "Edwards belonged to an elite extended family that was part of ruling class clergy, magistrates, judges, military leaders, village squires, and merchants" (Marsden 3).

The changing nature of the wilderness theme from the dark and barren to the sublime

By the close of the eighteenth century two important strands of intellectual thought were becoming popular in American culture. One strand was the puritanical vision of the wilderness as a dissolute and barren place which men had to traverse to seek salvation. The second strand was the more recent European notion of Romanticism and the sublime, which began to imagine the North American wild not with terror, but with awe and appreciation in comparison with the cities of Europe. The latter theme would later take hold with European scholars and visitors to the New World, such as Alexis De Tocqueville.[7]

Concurrent with European intellectuals' Romanticism was the American transformation of the wilderness from a Biblical metaphor to an obstacle preventing the rapid industrialization and economic expansion that now dominated the post-Revolutionary American landscape. The wilderness was no longer a vast barren expanse where salvation could be won, but a virgin territory that was ripe for conquest by English settlers. Whilst this confrontation between European settlers and the wilderness was a major theme in extolling the triumph of American technology and industry, others, like William Byrd in *History of the Dividing Line*, saw the forest as a "great wilderness" that was preferable to the densely crowded towns and cities.

Byrd wrote

> we chose rather to lie in the open field, for fear of growing too tender. A clear sky, spangled with stars, was our canopy, which being the last thing we saw before we fell asleep, gave us magnificent dreams. The truth of it is, we took so much pleasure in that natural kind of lodging, that I think at the foot of the account mankind are great losers by the luxury of feather beds and warm apartments.
>
> (Byrd 17)

While Byrd was writing about the virtues and splendour of the wilderness, his Romantic sentiments concerning the forest's awesomeness would be echoed in the late nineteenth century with the genesis of the landscape and conservation movements inaugurated by Frederick Law Olmsted (1822–1903), Aldo Leopold (1887–1948) and John Muir (1838–1914). Byrd's view of the wilderness as a place of natural beauty was to be overshadowed by the seventeenth- and eighteenth-century literary discourses, which ultimately depicted the wilderness as a place for religious piety, salvation and Protestant reformation.

John Winthrop, the third governor of the Massachusetts Bay Colony, was an early writer who described the wilderness in the early American settlements as the place where voyagers from England sought to test their faith and to build a *city on a hill*.[8] The civilizing mission of the early New England settlers was 'greatly thematic' with respect to the wilderness. The North American wild was seen by Winthrop as uncorrupted land ripe for the Christian reformation that was to be demonstrated in New England (Miller, *The Doctrine of Discovery in American Indian Law* 15). Success by Winthrop and New England's reformed Non-Conformist Christianity would support their aim to reform Anglicanism and the Church of England and also become the beacon that would set the example before all of Europe. This was the broad agenda of Samuel Danforth's election sermon, delivered on May 11, 1670: *A Brief Recognition of New England's Errand into the Wilderness* helps to explain what Winthrop meant: "For wee must Consider that wee shall be as a Citty upon a Hill, the eies of all people are uppon us," (P. Miller, *Errand Into the Wilderness* 11). "T]he eies of all people are uppon us," was a recruiting message to those from Falmouth to Ipswich who were about to embark upon their journey to the New World, a world of ready land and plenty. Situating what the wilderness meant upon the eve of New England's settlement, with respect to Danforth's sermon, is vital to the understanding of why the wilderness was cast as a dark and virgin land. The wilderness in the 1620s was not a place that was designed for subjugation, but a place where Englishmen who voyaged across the Atlantic could find salvation by submitting and testing their Christian faith in a dark land. The land was seen as virgin, ripe for settlement. "Their concept of the American "wilderness," we must conclude, was not, as it were, carried to America on the *Mayflower* or the *Arabella*, but came out of that wilderness itself" (Heimert 361).

For the second generation of New Englanders, Danforth's sermon provided a historical interpretation not only of what he meant in describing the first generation of English settlers and Winthrop's 'errand,' but also showed how that 'errand' attached a special mission to the transformation of the wild into a beacon of Christian success. The Wilderness in the errand had to be dark and bare, for the wild in its virgin state was evidence that, free of the corrupt governments and churches of Europe, man was capable of finding salvation and Christian reformation. This sentiment was expressed by Heimert:

> The situation was such that, for the moment, the model had no chance to be exhibited in England; Puritans could talk about it, theorize upon it, but they could not display it, could not prove that it would actually work. But if they had it set up in America—in a bare land, devoid of already established (and corrupt) institutions, empty of bishops and courtiers, where they could start de novo, and the eyes of the world were upon it, and if then it performed just as the saints had predicted of it, the Calvinist international would know exactly how to go about completing the already begun but temporarily stalled revolution in Europe.
>
> (P. Miller, *Errand Into the Wilderness* 12)

The New England wilderness was the object of religious piety–the land imagined could be transformed 'de novo' by the Non-Conformist Puritans.

The message that Winthrop had developed in the 1630s carried over into the second and third generations of America; however, by 1642 Winthrop began to lament the failures of the first generation in succumbing to disunity, corruption and a basic moral breakdown relative to the original purpose of the Puritan mission as it was defined in 1630. In this time of moral despondency, Winthrop returned to the wilderness not as a testing ground upon which salvation could be attained, but as an image upon which to situate a fallen generation of settlers who failed to aspire to the original purpose of the settlement. The wilderness became a metaphor that expressed both political and social depression as well as religious concern (Fritzell 21). The back country acquired the image of a dark cloud, a cloud to remind contemporaries that disunity and corruption would return such settlers to the wilderness of despair. Winthrop expressed this mood with some candor:

> For such as come together into a wilderness, where are nothing but wild beasts and beastlike men, and there confederate together in civil and church state, whereby they do, implicitly at least, bind themselves to

> support each other, and all of them that society, whether civil or sacred, whereof they are members, how they can break from this without free consent, is hard to find, so as may satisfy a tender or good conscience in time of trial . . . for if one may go, another may, and so the greater part, and so church and commonwealth may be left destitute in a wilderness, exposed to misery and reproach.
>
> (21)

Within a generation of Winthrop's disparaging image of the wilderness, the founder of Pennsylvania, William Penn, would utilize the wild not as a metaphor of despair, but as a place where liberty and morality could join.[9] The wilderness was no longer a place of danger, but a site where Penn's notions of man's progression could be cultivated. By 1681 Penn's example of liberty and justice converged in the rough country of Pennsylvania.

> Writing to Thomas Taylor in April and July, 1683, and to John Alloway on Nov. 29, Penn proclaimed divine providence, the example to the nations, and the making of the wilderness into a garden, of the desert a green field.
>
> (Frost 590)

Penn's uplifting transformation of the wilderness from a place of proverbial darkness into a garden exemplified a new stage in the image of the North American wild. From Penn's "garden," the wild would be transformed yet again in the early to mid-nineteenth century into a place that would need to be tamed by the technology of the expanding American frontier. But in Penn's time, the image of the garden would situate the wilderness as a place where divine providence would facilitate humanity's flourishing on earth.

The wilderness was an essential backdrop to the colony of Pennsylvania that William Penn used to promote his Quaker themes. Penn's religious zeal, founded upon a personal epiphany and a public conversion to Quakerism, was transferred into Pennsylvania. Without Winthrop's ability to extrapolate, Penn still wrote about the uniqueness of place that distinguished Pennsylvania from other North American English colonies. Penn's mission in Pennsylvania was not defined as a Non-Conformist Christian reformation, but as a place where tolerance, progressive morals and hard work would flourish. Steven Crisp and his Dutch wife Gertrud Derick wrote to Penn in 1684, explaining that "the spiritual flowering of the new colony could not be built by the strength of men and women alone; only God could make Pennsylvania's 'wilderness sing'" (Frost 593). Divine purpose was a prerequisite to humanity's effort to radiate the wilderness. Frost comments on Penn's religious justification for planting a new colony in: "In *Some Account* Penn linked colonization schemes with the Hebrews (Moses and Joshua), Greeks (Lycurgus), and Romans (Romulus), and he defended settlements as means of creating new nations, increasing prosperity, and civilizing barbarians" (580). For Penn, the success of the colony could not be revealed by hard work, but in faith that only God would unlock the mysteries of the wilderness. Bringing tolerance and morality into the wilderness, attested to the faith that people who arrived and toiled in Pennsylvania could prosper if they believed in God, which meant hard work and morality among men. While man could and *should* transform the wilderness into a garden, faith in God was the ultimate transformative event that could metamorphose the wilderness.

Winthrop and Penn produced lasting legacies with their wilderness metaphors. Up until the 1750s, similar metaphors were employed by Quakers and German sectaries to re-establish the missionary purpose of their respective colonies and ultimately, the new American Christian Republic.

> Periodically throughout the eighteenth century, especially in times of crisis, metaphors of the wilderness and the garden, the city upon a hill, the example to the nations reappeared. So far as I can tell, the belief in God's special care of Pennsylvania as symbolized by William Penn remained the possession of Quakers and German sectaries.
>
> (Frost 605)

Metaphors of the wilderness were important themes in religious dogmas written by Winthrop and Penn. Both Winthrop and Penn, in New England and Pennsylvania, had a profound impact on how certain literary images, especially that of the wilderness, came to represent a cultural space that was ripe for settlement. The latter, perhaps in a more subtle manner, helped to form the basis of the later conceptualization of *manifest destiny* that would provide the intellectual and divine basis for the later nineteenth-century domination of the American lands west of the Mississippi. With a religious cover, of which the untamed and dark wilderness was an important backdrop to American Indian wars, one can situate how the wilderness emerged from a literary metaphor into a political and legal motif to justify the righteousness and destiny of European American-westward expansion.

In the early nineteenth century, there emerged an American literature to which the writers James Fenimore Cooper, Walt Whitman, Edgar Allan Poe, William Cullen Bryant, Washington Irving and others belonged. These writers commenced the dawn of a uniquely American style literary genre, steeped within the boundaries of the American wilderness. Land and landscape were intertwined. The soil was ripe for cultivation, settlement and ultimately possession by an industrious new nation. The latter was portrayed as a pastoral landscape by poets from Ann Eliza Bleecker's *Wilderness Pastoral: Reading Vergil in Colonial America* to Bryant's *The Embargo* (1808) where his poems described the land settlements of the early nineteenth-century Americans:

> Oh, ye bright pair, the blessing of mankind!
> Whom time has sanction'd, and whom fate has join'd,
> Commerce, that bears the trident of the main,
> And Agriculture, empress of the plain;
> Who, hand in hand, and heav'n-directed, go
> Diffusing gladness through the world below.
>
> (Meyer 200)

Derived from the Puritans in the early seventeenth century, the genesis of the nineteenth-century Romantic expansion of an American wilderness was a critical literary precursor to America's "manifest destiny," continued in the poems and novels of the New-York-Knickerbocker-Group-based literary movement.[10] The transformation of the colonial rhetoric from taming the wilderness to a political justification for westward expansion in the guise of 'manifest destiny' took shape in the early nineteenth century.

> The aesthetic touches the political at this point; Manifest Destiny can be seen not only as a nineteenth-century political and economic program but as a rhetorical one as well. The duality of land and landscape is, in effect, dialectic: untouched scenes of solitude from which the hand of nature has never been lifted had to be repeatedly affirmed in order to generate a continual replay of America's "primal scene" of discovery and possession. It was necessary for American rhetoric, including American poetry, to persist in emphasizing an untouched nature in order to justify continued expansion and appropriation. Although nineteenth-century politicians may have phrased it differently, they were in fact carrying out the Puritan imperative to settle the so-called "vacant" land.
>
> (199)

Bryant exemplified the poet who uses his words to delineate the limitation of mankind in the vast wilderness. Bryant's poems evoked images that, on their surface, displayed man's seeming ability to conquer and fashion his natural surroundings into landscape. Bryant's stanzas portrayed the intrusion of European Americans upon the land and a literary discourse that, by virtue of man's ability to describe and define the land, had the converse effect of framing the expansive land from the view of the writer. The act of being able to frame and describe the land within words is itself a form of discourse that represents the landscape. Bryant's poem *The Prairie* evokes this theme.

> Man hath no power in all this glorious work;
> The hand that built the firmament hath heaved
> And smoothed these verdant swells, and sown their slopes
> With herbage, planted them with island groves
> And hedged them round with forests.
>
> (209)

The ability to frame land within a human landscape has not been lost among writers such as Peter Fritzell. Peter Fritzell, like Bryant, also frames land into a human landscape. Framed paintings of landscapes control a perspective and depict an environment. Such framing was borrowed from Europeans and played an important part in how the later American landscapes were portrayed.

> By "landscape" I mean what is meant by a historian of the fine arts, a descriptive picture with a frame, with clear "visual" limits. But one can convey an idea of the land, or express a feeling about the land without descriptive aids. Approaches and attitudes toward the environment, ideas and images of the land also constitute "landscapes." They are the methods by which the facts of geographical existence are ordered and made systematic.
>
> (Fritzell 16)[11]

Fritzell's quote is revealing for his interpretation of how historians, whether of the fine arts or otherwise, can literally "frame" landscapes to reflect a reality not in terms of what "is" but of how that reality can be "ordered." In terms of Foucault's discursive formations and statements, such 'frames' become statements not about the world but about how the world can be *regulated.*

According to Fritzell Bryant's use of his literary ability to frame and conquer the land, using verbs or human will over nature, is akin to the images a painter would use to frame a landscape. Bryant demonstrates how poets position themselves as a force within the subject of the poem, namely, the conquest of the wilderness. Verbs like "built," "smoothed," "sown," "planted," or "hedged" regulate what is read. Bryant's poem is riddled with verbs that exude the dominance of man over the land, while simultaneously raising the status of the land above that of the individual: "man hath no power." Bryant seems to have been torn. While on the one hand he sought to provide a literary motif for the westward expansion of the American frontier, hidden within his poem are the sublimations of the Puritan mission; that man can tame the wilderness and transform it into his own earthly paradise.

Bryant's use of the wilderness is similar to John Marshall's. Here I wish to consider Marshall's Trilogy opinions in relation to Bryant:

> The whites have been gradually pressing upon them, as they kept receding from the approaches of civilization. We have purchased the greater part of their lands, destroyed their hunting grounds, subdued the wilderness around them, overwhelmed them with our population, and gradually abridged their native independence.
>
> (*Cherokee Nation v. Georgia* 67)

Like Bryant, Marshall in *Cherokee Nation* employs verbs to describe the human conquest of the wilderness: "purchased," "destroyed," "subdued," and "overwhelmed." Unlike Bryant, Marshall is "subduing" the wilderness while also metaphorically describing the inevitable; "kept receding" from the "approaches" of the Native American in the path of the "gradual abridgement" of the "whites." Phrases like "kept receding" evoke the natural or inevitable advance of the "white" settlers in relation to the Native Indians. The similarities between Bryant and Marshall are uncanny—they were relative contemporaries and both wrote about the wilderness and Indians within the confines of different genres.

Irving provides our project with further images of the wilderness, not from the standpoint of a developing literary novel or poem, but rather earnestly, from his attempt to simply record what he saw on a brief journey beyond the boundary lines of what was deemed civilization in the 1830s. Washington Irving wrote *A Tour of the Prairies* upon his return to the United States from Europe. Irving's return also coincided with President Andrew Jackson's political pressure to pass the Indian Removal Act of 1830. Irving wrote about the inevitability of the European-American frontiersman advancing from east to west, and about other images of the Indian which were similar to those in John Marshall's legal opinions. Prefacing his own observation in the introduction to *A Tour of the Prairies*, Irving wrote:

> Since such, however, seems to be the desire of the public, and that they take sufficient interest in my wanderings to deem them worthy of recital, I have hastened, as promptly as possible, to meet, in some degree, the expectation which others have excited. For this purpose, I have, as it were, plucked a few leaves out of my memorandum book, containing a month's foray beyond the outposts of human habitation, into the wilderness of the Far West. It forms, indeed, but a small portion of an extensive tour; but it is an episode, complete as far as it goes. As such, I offer it to the public, with great diffidence. It is a simple narrative of everyday occurrences; such as happen to every one who travels the prairies. I have no wonders to describe, nor any moving accidents by flood or field to narrate; and as to those who look for a marvellous

> or adventurous story at my hands, I can only reply, in the words of the weary knife-grinder: "Story! God bless you, I have none to tell, sir."
>
> (Irving)

The essential point from Irving's *A Tour of the Prairies* is not so much the image of the Indian as a child in need of a paternalistic American father, but rather the role of the frontier—that is, the space between American east coast and the wilderness—as the imagined location where civilization runs against the hostile back country. This remote country extends to the Puritan images of the wilderness expressed by Mather and Winthrop. Irving portrays the advance of the bees upon the wilderness as a metaphor for the march of civilization. Bees represent the civilizing and technological advances of machines and industrialization upon wilderness. The advance is depicted as bringing "unbought luxury" into the wilderness, as if to dramatize the sweetness and richness of the encroaching European settlements. Washington Irving's "fable of the bees" demonstrates the "sweet" advance of civilization upon the "mouldering" wilderness waiting to be transformed:

> Irving writes his own 'fable of the bees' (the link with Mandeville underlines the eighteenth-century roots of his work) by analysing the space where wilderness and civilization overlap. As the bees advance into the forest, they create a model of how wilderness is transformed into settlement: "The Indians with surprise found the mouldering trees of their forests suddenly teeming with ambrosial sweets, and nothing, I am told, can exceed the greedy relish with which they banquet for the first time upon this unbought luxury of the wilderness."
>
> (Reynolds 92)

Reynolds' analysis could conceivably cast the bees as the spring of the civilized world, entering the frontier where wilderness and Western civilization meet. Reynolds also notes similarities between Fenimore Cooper and Irving in that both writers use the wilderness to stage their narratives and in a like manner. Both writers stage battles, kidnappings and other events at different times through the narrative within their wilderness. Using the metaphor of "removes" Irving's prose foregrounds events and conflicts at different times within the wilderness while he, unlike Cooper, omits the "violence and melodrama" as the context of his tour through the prairies. As Reynolds observes, the transformation from "removes" in the early American literature to "tour" parallels the taming of the savage Indian to the passive child, resigned to the inevitable advance of European civilization. One could plausibly substitute the back country for the savage Indians, as an avatar for the wilderness, as the two subjects are so closely interwoven in both Irving's journal and in earlier American literature (Reynolds 98).

John Marshall's opinion in *Johnson* partly depicts the Indian as a conquered race, seemingly engulfed by the wilderness. The untamed and wild space makes the human integration between the American Indian and European Americans dangerous and impossible. The Indian is portrayed as both inhuman and wild in the sense of being untamed and disordered. Marshall writes:

> The title by conquest is acquired and maintained by force. The conqueror prescribes its limits. Humanity, however, acting on public opinion, has established, as a general rule, that the conquered shall not be wantonly oppressed, and that their condition shall remain as eligible as is compatible with the objects of the conquest. Most usually, they are incorporated with the victorious nation, and become subjects or citizens of the government with which they are connected. The new and old members of the society mingle with each other; the distinction between them is gradually lost, and they make one people . . . But the tribes of Indians inhabiting this country were fierce savages, whose occupation was war, and whose subsistence was drawn chiefly from the forest. To leave them in possession of their country, was to leave the country a wilderness; to govern them as a distinct people, was impossible, because they were as brave and as high spirited as they were fierce, and were ready to repel by arms every attempt on their independence.
>
> (*Johnson v. M'Intosh* 589–90)

Just as Irving uses bees as a metaphor to herald the advance of the civilization upon the Indians, Marshall's metaphorical attempt to assimilate the Indians into the dominant society is merged with their possession of Indian land. Here, "their country" is a signifier for the "wilderness." Possession and wilderness are thus joined to evidence the uncivilized state of the Indian. Only upon Indian assimilation into the "victorious nation" will the uncivilized state of the Indian be subdued. In this context, the humane and benevolent conquerors portrayed by Marshall, similar to Irving's bees, are *unable* to tame and assimilate the Indians as a conquered race because the setting and landscape where Indian possession occurs make the indigenous people appear without the necessary humanity to either accept or appreciate civilization.

The sublime in early American literature

Within the context of understanding the literary themes of the wilderness in relation to the Marshall Trilogy cases by early American writers and painters, this research also explores the role of the sublime.[12] The sublime provides a valuable place to explain a literary theme with respect to the wilderness in American literature before and during the Marshall Trilogy cases. The sublime can also be seen as a literal place where Marshall sought legal order in juxtaposition to the wilderness and the Native American. Like the eighteenth-century English writers and painters, Marshall sought order in a sense of beauty; however, this order was clothed within the motif of Marshall's discursive obscurity to project the sublime as law. Marshall created a complex and logical structure in his legal judgment to project an awe of the law. As examined by Edmund Burke in his *A Philosophical Enquiry into the Origin of our Ideas of the Sublime and Beautiful* ("*Enquiry*") together with Daniel Boorstin's *The Mysterious Science of Law*, the sublime is a valuable literary tool in understanding how to read Blackstone's *Commentaries* not only from the viewpoint of the eighteenth-century reader, but also as a literary interpretation of Marshall's legal process in the Trilogy cases.

Edmund Burke's *Enquiry* projects the sublime as a terror built upon ignorance: "Greatness of dimension, is a powerful cause of the sublime" (Burke 66). The very obscurity of a subject was a necessary element for the sublime, according to Burke. Burke also questioned whether an investigation of our passions and our imaginations was possible through some type of theoretical prism: "was it possible through 'a diligent examination of our passions in our own breasts' to find an exact theory of our passions?" (xi). In one sense Burke's *Enquiry* was a discourse on the possibility of offering a theory to explain the passion in human imagination. He cautiously stated

> for if Taste has no fixed principles, if the imagination is not affected according to some invariable and certain laws, our labour is likely to be employed to very little purpose; as it must be judged a useless, if not an absurd undertaking, to lay down rules for caprice, and to set up for a legislator of whims and fairness."
>
> (xii)

Burke seems to imply that our passions cannot be determined or measured; therefore, attempts to quantify human passions are futile. Daniel Boorstin, in *The Mysterious Science of Law*, also explained how the sublime was defined in the early eighteenth century:

> Sublimity was also an easily comprehended idea. Drawing on Longinus, who found the source of elevated language in "the power of forming great conceptions" and "vehement and inspired passion," men attributed to the sublime the power of inspiring awe. When man felt overpowered, and saw an object greater than himself, this was likely to be the sublime.
>
> (Boorstin 90)

In projecting an object greater than oneself, law or legal judgment could inspire "awe" through its mystery. Here whether conscious nor not, Marshall's opinions in the Trilogy cases did attract such "awe" from both contemporaries and subsequent generations, given the complexity and obscurity of his discursive prose.

Interestingly, Burke questioned his own conclusion by observing that even reason can produce obscurity. It is a paradox that reason, a theoretical attempt to explain man and the world over time through principles of logic, can be accused of obscurity. Burke makes an important point when he states that "reason is the antithesis of passion. Reason, despite its pursuit of clarity in science, is always potentially mystifying, since it is written in a medium instinct with obscurity" (Burke xix). Conversely, reason (and I would argue that law is in the same vein), by its logical self-referential language, obfuscates the very clarity it seeks to project. Whether in science or law, reason is perhaps a false pillar of exposition with respect to the sublime. However, as Burke was writing in the eighteenth century, the laws of nature and reason were part of an English cultural and social environment where the disorganized aesthetics of the world were to be explained and ordered by reason. Daniel Boorstin explained this eighteenth-century context: "the search for laws of aesthetics expressed the new-found confidence of the Enlightenment" (Boorstin 98). Reason, not divine or natural law, could now enable man to define and explain the world.

Boorstin demonstrates how Blackstone sought to demonstrate how the rules of law, while limited in their narrow premises of explanation, could be saved by the legal concept of equity. Looking at the concept of equity in Boorstin's essay, *The Mysterious Science of Law,* it seems as if Blackstone sought to find a theory to save the narrow place of the black letter law through recourse to the wider and more justly based doctrine of justice. By considering the harshness of the black letter law, Blackstone may appear to be situating the law as an inadequate tool to explain the sublime inherent within the complexity of the law's need for applicability in the real world.[13] Boorstin observed that "Burke has explained that 'there are reasons in nature why the obscure idea, when properly conveyed, should be more affecting than clear. It is our ignorance of things that causes of admiration, and chiefly excites our passions'" (103). As Boorstin suggests, ignorance then can be overcome through reason when properly explained. Boorstin focuses on the law's power to obscure; yet he seems to invoke Burke's plea for 'reason' to explain law to affect understanding rather than passions.

Boorstin's observation relates this "ignorance of things" and their exciting of our passions to Blackstone's discussion of law's equity as a device to ultimately contain the sublime within law's complexity:

> For Blackstone explained, as we have seen, "the liberality of modern courts of justice is frequently obliged to have recourse to unaccountable fictions and circuities, in order to recover the equitable and substantial justice, which for a long time was buried under the narrow rules and fanciful niceties of metaphysical and Norman jurisprudence."
>
> (102)

Instead of viewing the complexity of English law in terms of the sublime (and by its complexity something to fear), Boorstin demonstrates that the sublime within English Law is something to be embraced rather than feared. "It is our ignorance of things that causes admiration" (103). Boorstin seems to suggest that ignorance, rather than law's complexity, is the root cause of the passions associated with law. Quoting Blackstone, Boorstin asserts "the multifariousness of English Laws was thus a badge of social progress" (102). Social progress, according to Boorstin is derived from the "multifariousness" of law; hence, complexity in law's structure or meaning now becomes a "badge of social progress."

Using Burke as our basis of analysis, the comparison between beauty and the sublime is a useful analysis in seeking to explain the situation of the sublime within legal judgment. For Burke, beauty was small, smooth and something to be enjoyed by its containment. "The next property constantly observable in such objects is *Smoothness.* A quality so essential to beauty, that I do not now recollect any thing beautiful which is not smooth" (Burke 103). The sublime, in contrast, is large, overbearing, limitless, and overwhelms beauty with terror, according to Burke. "Infinity has a tendency to fill the mind with that sort of delightful horror" (67). As Boorstin writes, English writers in the early eighteenth century were focusing on universal principles to explain the internal passions and feelings associated with beauty. It is within this context that Boorstin draws upon Burke's distinction between beauty and the sublime. Boorstin cites Burke's *Enquiry* in this regard:

> Sublime objects are vast in their dimensions; beautiful ones comparatively small: beauty should be smooth and polished; the great, rugged and negligent . . . Beauty should not be obscure; the great ought to be dark and gloomy; beauty should be light and delicate; the great ought to be solid, and even massive.
>
> (Boorstin 88)

Boorstin demarcates the difference between beauty and the sublime to interpret the early literary attempts to "reason" and find universal principles to explain both.

With respect to the process of legal judgment, it is not enough to merely distinguish between beauty and the sublime; we must also be cognizant of distance. Whilst acknowledging the unknown, a sufficient distance from the sublime allows the reader to respect it as awe inspiring without feeling apprehensive. Even though the issue of distance permits the sublime to be respected, the sublime is not close enough to be seen as beauty and in the metaphorically smooth manner depicted by Burke. Burke provides further elucidation on this issue of distance with *acquaintance,* such that the sublime can be embraced not with terror, but with respectful awe.

Before we develop our discussion on acquaintance and the sublime, we should first consider how Burke establishes the notion of distance with darkness; that is, the unknown and how forces bent on keeping their subjects in the dark use darkness to shroud or obfuscate clarity. Burke states that

> these despotic governments, which are founded on the passions of men, and principally upon the passion of fear, keep their chief as much as may be from the public eye. The policy has been the same in many cases of religion. Almost all the heathen temples were dark. Even in the barbarous temples of the Americans at this day, they keep their idol in a dark part of the hut, which is consecrated to his workshop.
>
> (Burke 54–5)

It is not coincidence that those forces who seek to retain power or create myth use darkness as a shroud to hide sources of power. Burke's quote amply demonstrates how power and obscurity are connected.

Next we need to consider how darkness and obscurity affect the relationship between the sublime and beauty. Burke's discussion of acquaintance will help us comprehend the differences between the sublime and beauty. Burke demonstrates in his *Enquiry* how language, specifically poetry, can take an independent and clear description of landscape drawings and transform it with a few choice words into an unfamiliar place where the sublime resides. Using the description of Satan in *Paradise Lost*, Burke demonstrates how words and descriptions are joined together by Milton to create terrifying images, but how when words within the passages are separated the sense of terror is reduced or blunted. From Burke's *Enquiry*, we quote Milton:

> He above the rest
> In shape and gesture proudly eminent
> Stood like a tower; his form had yet not lost
> All her original brightness, nor appeared
> Less than archangel ruin'd, and th' excess
> Of glory obscured: as when the sun new ris'n
> Looks through the horizontal misty air
> Shorn of his beams; or from behind the moon
> In dim eclipse disastrous twilight sheds
> On half the nations; and with fear of change
> Perplexes monarchs.
>
> (57)

Burke writes on Milton's passage above that

> the mind is hurried out of itself, by a crowd of great and confused images; which affect because they are crowded and confused. Separate

> these images and you lose much of their greatness; yet, joining them with certain words and you infallibly lose the clearness. The images raised by poetry are always of this obscure kind.
>
> (57)

What precisely is Burke's point? It is that the sublime can be evoked more articulately with words rather than visually through paintings? By taking what appears to be clear and harmless images and joining them with adjectives, poetry creates obscurity.

The point of Burke's *Enquiry* is exemplified in part by Boorstin's focus on Blackstone's *Commentaries. Commentaries* acts as a prism through which to examine how legal judgment (i.e., rational thought or reason) can lead to obscurity (i.e., by complexity of language and argument) or the sublime. The sublimity that Burke writes about with regard to astonishment and terror in law is also limited with just enough acquaintance by the reader to establish law's respect. In citing Blackstone's *Commentaries*, Boorstin writes,

> still, as our study of the *Commentaries* has amply illustrated, the line between reason and faith is always difficult and sometimes almost impossible to define . . . the vocabulary of natural law and of the rights of man which Blackstone was using to demonstrate the validity of the English Legal System, was, almost before Blackstone's death, to be used for attacking those very values in which he believed.
>
> (Boorstin 188)

Relevant here is not whether Blackstone intended to create confusion through the use of reason, but in taking Boorstin's position, whether the use of the vocabulary of natural law and the rights of man created a complexity of discourse, namely an apparent linguistic apparatus to provide an explanation of the law and, by use of such apparatus, to create the sublime of the law by embedding a language of obscurity. It is in such use of language to either explain law or to conceal it, that the sublime in law is found.

Boorstin elaborated on this discursive obscurity by explaining how eighteenth-century English artists sought to join beauty and the sublime. The former placed rationality upon nature to order gardens and cathedrals throughout eighteenth-century England (89).[14] "Since the works of nature were supposed to embody the qualities both of "sublimity" and of "beauty," it was inevitable that the English legal system, itself derived from the law of nature, should illustrate these qualities" (90). Boorstin interpreted this union as peculiar to the English legal system, "if the English legal system could be shown to be at once "beautiful" and "sublime," this would reinforce the presumption that these institutions were part of Nature's scheme" (91).

Boorstin denotes a critical point: the joining of beauty and the sublime to the point where "these institutions were part of Nature's scheme" presents the appearance that law is beyond question by virtue of its natural qualities.

Art as discourse in the wilderness conception

Like many of the discourses cited in this chapter, art also played a poignant role in defining the image of the wilderness on the eve of the Trilogy cases. Referencing Hans-Georg Gadamer in *Truth and Method*, art can be seen not only as an aesthetic, but also as an historical text; a text where humanity, through art, formulates morality and ideas based on a *fusion of historical horizons*.

> The nature of all art, as Hegel formulated it, is that it 'presents man with himself.' Other natural subjects—not only the human form—can express moral ideas in artistic presentation. All artistic presentation—whether of the landscape, still life, or even an inspiring view of nature achieves this.
>
> (Gadamer 43)

With regard to Hegel's interpretation of Kant, Gadamer writes, "Hegel understood this perfectly in his lectures on aesthetics when he described the expression of the moral as the 'radiance of the spiritual'" (43). Using Gadamer's interpretation of Hegel's "radiance of the spiritual" as a form of literature in early nineteenth-century American art, it will be shown below how painters, in particular Thomas Cole (1801–1848), illustrated the American landscape as a virgin wilderness, with bright hues to illuminate those elements of the wilderness and to invoke the sublime.[15]

The American sublimation of the wilderness was central in showing how civilization could overcome the wilderness. Painting a landscape of the wilderness allowed artists to frame a glow of awe into rivers, forests and mountains, resulting in a spiritual awakening in the American mind about the back country. This emerging identity helped to foster a belief that humanity could not only dominate the wilderness, but also instil a moral purpose and righteousness into a civilizing mission. The sublimation of the American wilderness by painters was not novel. Images of a barren, savage and uncivilized land, as well as the sublime, were all part of what Gadamer would call a *historical horizon*, meaning that he sought to provide a hermeneutical approach to understanding the text, not based on what is before the reader but on what the reader inherited prior to reading the text,

> the horizon of the present cannot be formed without the past. There is no more an isolated horizon of the present in itself than there are

> historical horizons which have to be acquired. *Rather, understanding is always a fusion of horizon supposedly existing by themselves.*
>
> (Gadamer 305)

The fusion of the past and the present creates a hermeneutical approach to understanding how texts are interpreted. The same approach applies to art.

Art assumed a very conscious role in early nineteenth-century America and contemporary artists used the landscape to elevate the moral and civilizing projection of the new American Republic. Similar to Gadamer, artists like Cole painted landscapes of the American wilderness in part as a reflection of what they perceived, but also as an *imagined* landscape of what they wished to fuse together between different *historical horizons.*[16] Such historical horizons included the Puritan theme of the wilderness as a meeting place for individuals to find inner salvation and the sublime of the wilderness which evoked a sense of awe beyond the rational, a place that isolated man in juxtaposition to the frontier. The sublime also projected a horizon of spirituality within man, not because of the wilderness, but as a place where man could behold the inexplicableness and wonder of the wilderness. Taking some of these literary strands further, the early Hudson River School painters, like Thomas Cole, used these horizons in

Figure 7.1 Thomas Cole 1827 from *"The Last of the Mohicans,"* Cora Kneeling at the Feet of Tamenund. (Explore Thomas Cole)

their nationalist-centered works (Burroughs 3). Cole, for example, was inspired by Cooper's *The Last of the Mohicans* to paint romantic images of the American wilderness. Cole's paintings helped to inspire European-American westward expansion under the guise of *Manifest Destiny* in the middle of the nineteenth century.[17]

This artistic moralizing was intended to largely establish a uniquely American identity, in direct contrast to Europe. Like its literary counterpart, art was engaged in order to define a distinctive American creed and character.[18] Significantly, the wilderness was an image that was used to signify America's destiny. These literary themes were also part of the literary discursive tradition that Marshall inherited as his *historical horizon.*

Thomas Cole is considered the founder of the Hudson River School (Felker 60). An English-born American artist, Cole adopted the Hudson River valley of New York as his home and soon settled in the Catskills, where he painted many of his works depicting the New York and New England wildernesses. Cole's painting, reproduced here, displays a vivid image of the developed and inhabited regions and the shaded wilderness of Mount Holyoke and Northampton Massachusetts, bordering the Connecticut River. The painting is interesting because Cole illuminates the developed areas while the darkest section is the wilderness. The Hudson River School was influenced by the nineteenth-century Romantic artists from Europe, such as English painters J. M. Turner and John Constable. In Cole's *The*

Figure 7.2 Thomas Cole 1836 *The Oxbow (View from Mount Holyoke).*[19]

Oxbow, there seems to be an illumination of pastoral peace where the land was "tamed" in contrast to the darkness of the wilderness. If anything, the cultivated fields in the painting tend to hover over the shadowed wilderness. It can be argued that some of the early Hudson River School paintings by Cole seem to illuminate the beauty and untouched nature of the virgin wilderness prior to European settlement. While the virgin state of the wilderness may evoke feelings of greatness and religious awakening, the juxtaposition of the inhabited next to the wilderness also evokes a sense of authority in contrast to the mysterious wilderness. Such images are consistent with the kind of wild and untamed wilderness themes seen in Marshall's Trilogy opinions.

While the analysis above concentrates on the Hudson River School and its founder, Cole, interestingly, there are images of the same location written by visitors to Mount Holyoke just prior to Cole's painting. In 1829, for example, the American author Theodore Dwight, Jr (1796–1866) produced *Sketches of Scenery and Manners in the United States*, sketches which included his visit to Mount Holyoke. Dwight urged "American citizens to experience the New England landscape as a textbook of culture," one capable of imparting "Christian and Republican virtues" as the historian John Sears has described it (Parry 8). Considered in this context, the modern reader cannot miss the degree to which Dwight's description of the view from Mount Holyoke transformed all the significant details of the topography into "patriotic emblems" of American freedom and superiority relative to the Old World. Dwight for example, like Cole and other writers and painters, used the back country as a place to transform the meaning of the wild to suit whatever passions or political agendas suited them at that time. Certainly, one central theme was the use of the wilderness to inspire viewers and readers to juxtapose their New World, the relatively young United States, with the more established Europe, as a place uncorrupted by Old World prejudices. The era of "manifest destiny" had not yet come to fruition, but the genesis of this political and social doctrine had its intellectual roots in the early nineteenth century with such writers as Dwight and such painters as Cole, who projected themes of the wilderness slowly receding before the advance of European-American settlement in North America. The wilderness was a place of menace and disorder, while the pastoral images of the New England farms gave credence to the civilized notions of the European-American settlers. Writers like Dwight were attempting to form a distinction between the United States and Europe, to develop a uniquely American perspective on wilderness; in part, these writers used the wilderness to amplify their "God-inspired" purposes and build on the romantic ideal of the wilderness as a place of inner spiritual inspiration. The agenda to disperse these images was political, social and spiritual. Regardless of what weight one may place on how or why the wilderness was used, its role in early American history left an indelible mark on the literary tradition that preceded and was concurrent with the Trilogy cases.

Conquest: classifying the wilderness

One other source for viewing the American wilderness as part of a civilizing mission, lay with Lewis and Clark's expedition (1804–1806), sanctioned by President Thomas Jefferson. The journals of the Lewis and Clark Expedition exemplify yet another genre of early American literary discourses that formed a backdrop to the Marshall Trilogy cases. Jefferson had long sought to explore the American West beyond the Mississippi. He actively recruited and found financial support from Congress for such an expedition. As to the tactical goals of the expedition, Jefferson directed Lewis and Clark to take stock of animals, plants, terrain and Native Americans during this exploration; however, Jefferson sought to use the expedition strategically as a means to lay claim to lands west of the Columbia River up to the Pacific Northwest, under the pretext of discovery. The American Republic was still young and claims west of the Mississippi, especially west of the Columbia River ranging across to the Pacific coast, were still being contested by Spain and England. The Lewis and Clark Expedition aimed to start the process of conquering the western regions of North America through discovery; yet, the discovery stratagem was not promoted for public consumption at the time. Quite to the contrary, the expedition was advertised as a clandestine operation to "explore" the unknown and wilderness regions of the continent that were recently purchased from France under the Louisiana Purchase of 1803 (Miller and Furse, *Native America, Discovered and Conquered: Thomas Jefferson, Lewis and Clark, and Manifest Destiny* 136). As in past eras, the wilderness was used to service another practical purpose; in this instance, wilderness *exploration* was a cover for establishing control of further land claims by the United States through discovery.[20]

It is useful for our purposes to situate the Lewis and Clark Expeditions and their literary journals within a larger Jeffersonian desire to appropriate the land occupied by the Indians. As part of his broader duplicitous agenda, Jefferson instructed Lewis and Clark to pacify as many of the Native Tribes as they could through their speeches and letters—using messages that sought to placate the Indians. Jefferson desired to make these Indian tribes dependent upon the Great Father in Washington, DC. Meanwhile, Jefferson was working silently with Congress and several state governors to pursue a different policy that diverged from his public discourses with Native Indians. Away from public scrutiny Jefferson actively made efforts to remove Indians from their land by encouraging easy credit for tribes in exchange for trade. Jefferson's intention was that Indians would become overburdened with debt to U.S. Government-owned trading houses. By encouraging the Federal Government to loan credit to Indian tribes,

Jefferson's policy forced Indians to trade their land to extinguish their debts. Another policy pursued by Jefferson was to encourage the dilution of the Native Indian peoples within the European-American population, so as to extinguish their customs and sever attachment to their land. Jefferson's duplicitous policy was exemplified in his private letter to Governor William Harrison of the Indiana Territory when he wrote:

> To promote this disposition to exchange lands, which they have to spare and we want, for necessaries, which we have to spare and they want, we shall push our trading uses, and be glad to see the good and influential individuals among them run in debt, because we observe that when these debts get beyond what the individuals can pay, they become willing to lop them off by a cession of lands.
>
> (Drinnon 87)

Jefferson's communications with eastern Indian tribes conveyed a completely different stance in his overall relationship with Indians, a stance which projected a more humane and benevolent empathy for Indian culture and respect for land ownership. On November 3, 1802, for example, Jefferson wrote to Handsome Lake, the great Seneca prophet, with respect to Lake's concern for his territorial security:

> You remind me, brother, of what I said to you when you visited me the last winter, that the lands you then held would remain yours, and shall never go from you but when you should be disposed to sell. This I now repeat and will ever abide by. We, indeed, are always ready to buy land; but we will never ask but when you wish to sell . . . Go on then, brother, in the great reformation you have undertaken. Persuade our red brethren then to be sober, and to cultivate their lands; and their women to spin and weave for their families.
>
> (86)

It is not our task to reveal Jefferson's hypocritical policy toward the Native Americans, but rather to highlight the political and literary context of the Lewis and Clark Expedition. The wilderness was utilized by Lewis and Clark as part of a literary backdrop to lay claim to the Pacific Northwest region of the American continent by transforming the wilderness from the disordered and dangerous sublime to the ordered and catalogued record-keeping of their journals. What appears at the beginning of the expedition as a journey into the sublime was by the end of the expedition a classified and ordered transformation of the American continent.

By presenting the western regions as both unexplored and sublime, Jefferson was also able to promote, away from eyes of the American public, the Doctrine of Discovery for purposes of land appropriation in relation to Spain and Britain in the Pacific Northwest. Spain and Britain were still contesting ownership of some of these western regions of America, so Jefferson was determined to forge a legal claim upon them through discovery. In terms of the American Indian, while Lewis and Clark came across many native tribes, Jefferson continued to project the American tribes as nomadic hunters when in fact there was ample evidence of their agricultural skills all along the east coast; however, to acknowledge their agricultural prowess would be to acknowledge Indians' ownership of their land. Jefferson "secretly launched a systematic campaign of psychological warfare against the tribes; it deprecated or denied their own agriculture by urging them to abandon hunting" (86). Because of Jefferson's powers as President he was able to regulate the discourse about the lands beyond the Columbia River as a remote interior region ripe for discovery when in fact these lands had been occupied by native tribes for centuries, not as nomadic hunters, but as established communities.

Following in the footsteps of France, Spain, and England, the United States adopted the *terra nullius* element of the Doctrine of Discovery; namely, even though Indians occupied the land, it was nonetheless considered an empty wilderness. This convenient and linguistically creative language facilitated the conquest of North America's land through the implementation of the Doctrine of Discovery (Drinnon 21). Given Jefferson's concern in establishing first discovery claims of the United States, part of his strategy with Lewis and Clark also entailed an ethnographic approach to taming the wilderness. Jefferson's strategy first sought to classify the landscape and environment west of the Columbia River and second, by establishing a strategy to placate the Native Americans, to promote cooperation and acquiescence towards the "Great Father" in Washington, D.C., Lewis, acting on the instructions of Jefferson, brought gifts and other items to impress upon the Native Americans the power of the United States and to attract their help in facilitating the successful completion of the expedition.

Examined through the narrative of the Lewis and Clark expedition the wilderness was *terra nullius*, or devoid of civilized life. Strategies of conquest were developed by Jefferson to define the Other (i.e., classification) and ethnographic approaches were implemented to attract the cooperation of the Native Indians to facilitate discovery claims over the western lands, such that the United States could bolster its claim against the European powers. Like Presidents before him, Jefferson also leveraged the images of the wilderness as *terra nullius* to achieve the practical conquest of the Northwest. (Miller and Furse, *Native America, Discovered and Conquered: Thomas Jefferson, Lewis and Clark, and Manifest Destiny* 81). Part of Jefferson's goal was to identify the natural resources that the United States could exploit to support its expansion. In order to tame the wilderness one had to understand its resources and its dangers and catalogue its potential. In a sense, much like Cole's *The Oxbow* painting, Jefferson was seeking to develop a Middle America that would be pastoral, civilized and distinctly European. In this context then, Jefferson's actions present an institutional discourse about what the wilderness constituted and how its resources could be utilized to promote the westward expansion.

The process of cataloguing and recording the wilderness is similar to what Said (*Orientalism*; *Culture and Imperialism*) wrote about when describing how nineteenth-century English novelists, through their own classifying and recording of the Orient, defined the Other. This classifying was a method with which to define and occupy the intelligible space between the colonizer and the colonized. Said saw Orientalism as an institution; a process of cataloguing information about the Other. Such institutional cataloguing resulted in the domination of the Orient within a Foucauldian "power and knowledge" framework. Said would argue that the ability to control and classify the descriptions of the "dominated other" is a form of imperialism, a discursive method to domination. In reviewing Said's *Orientalism,* Dawn writes,

> Orientalism, according to Said, had its roots in the older Christian relation to Islam but was modified by the secularizing currents of the Enlightenment and took its definitive form in the late eighteenth century and the first three-quarters of the nineteenth. Orientalism was structured by Western science—natural and humanistic—with its comparison and classification and consequent subjugation of the particular to the universal, the individual to the stereotype.
>
> (Dawn 1334)

Viewed from an Orientalist perspective, Lewis and Clark's Expedition was an important means of defining the Other beyond the Mississippi river. The classifications of the wilderness were but a first step toward demystifying the sublime.

At the time, newspaper accounts of the Lewis and Clark Expedition seemed to suggest that man had travelled to the outermost regions of the Americas—a world of unknown danger, potential and possibilities; however, in reality the wilderness was being used by Jefferson, just as it had been by many of the American forefathers, as a place to conjure images to suit the practicalities and political agenda of the time.[21] Like Jefferson and his predecessors, Marshall's opinions are evidence of his using the wilderness to fashion ethnographic motifs that utilized the wilderness as a place to be civilized.[22]

It is ironic that on the initial English settlement of New England in the early 1620s, the barren and dark wilderness was perceived by many colonists as a place of religious salvation and redemption. In addition to the early English settlers' visualizing the wilderness in a religious context, as subsequent generations passed, the image of the wilderness was transformed into that of a place of disorder and the sublime. By the late nineteenth century,

Americans began to see the wilderness as a place for spiritual harmony and refuge from civilization's urban centers after the Native Americans were virtually eradicated.

The Native American Indians, who had revered and regarded the wilderness as a place of spiritual harmony for over 2,000 years, were transformed by European settlers—through literary discourse, art and law—into "uncivilized heathens," living in wilderness. The same Europeans, interestingly, after 250 years of settlement, would come to see the wilderness as the Native Indians had seen it for nearly two millennia.

Notes

1 I use the term wilderness to denote how early American literature depicted this place as a waste land, a desert and virgin space waiting to be tamed, civilized and conquered, first by European settlers, and later by the westward expansion of Euro-American settlement.

2 The term relates to a place that has yet to become modern and remote.

3 I have taken the metaphor "mind" from author Roderick Frazier Nash in "*Wilderness and the American Mind.*"

4 Goodrich is useful to our examination of the wilderness image with respect to the Trilogy cases because he provides a theoretical framework to Marshall's "institutional amnesia" with respect to the literary basis upon which his legal judgments, in part, have non-legal sources concerning the notion of the wilderness in American culture. In terms of time, the early seventeenth century and up until the early nineteenth century, when Marshall wrote the Trilogy opinions, presents a full spectrum of literary images about the American wilderness. The essential point about Goodrich's theory of amnesia is not to assert that Marshall consciously used a slanted notion of the wilderness theme to dehumanize both the Native Americans and their wilderness, but to illustrate that Marshall, like the genre of legal judgment Goodrich examined, institutionally and habitually forgets the sources of legal judgment. Goodrich's theory is also an example of how Foucault's archive can transform itself into a "murmur" or "a priori" about Indian images prior to the Trilogy cases.

5 Sarah Gerish (seven years old), daughter of Captain John Gerish, recovered from Indian captivity in 1690.

6 Deuteronomy 32:10 Geneva Bible 1599. This Bible, rather than the King James edition, was used by early American colonial writers.

7 *Democracy in America* represents De Tocqueville's major work about America in the early nineteenth century.

8 The image of a city on a hill has its genesis in the *Sermon on the Mount*, Matthew 5:14. "Ye are the light of the world, A city that is set on a hill cannot be hid."

9 "King Charles II of England had a large loan with Penn's father, after whose death, King Charles settled by granting Penn a large area west and south of New Jersey on March 4, 1681. Penn called the area Sylvania (Latin for woods), which Charles changed to Pennsylvania in honor of the elder Penn. Perhaps the King was glad to have a place where religious and political outsiders (like the Quakers, or the Whigs, who wanted more influence for the people's representatives) could have their own place, far away from England. One of the first counties of Pennsylvania was called Bucks County, named after Buckinghamshire (Bucks) in England, where the Penn family seat was, and from whence many of the first settlers came" (*A Brief History of William Penn*).

10 The Knickerbocker Group was a New-York-based literary coterie originally formed by Fenimore Cooper, Washington Irving and William Cullen Bryant. These writers and others contributed novels, poems and journalism to early nineteenth-century American literature. The name Knickerbocker was apparently taken from Irving's pen name, Diedrich Knickerbocker.

11 Mr Fritzell is Assistant Professor of English at Lawrence University, Appleton, Wisconsin. The quote cited above was part of his research done for his doctoral dissertation, "*Landscapes of Anglo-America during Exploration and Early Settlement*" (Stanford University 1966).

12 I use the term sublime to denote the mysterious ways that imaginations can be led by passion. These passions are reflected in the fear and uneasiness that arises not only through great events, but also in the obscure way in which legal judgment is written. My goal here is to integrate the idea of the sublime as a way to situate how John Marshall's jurisprudence, through its textual obscurity, can be seen as a way to promote reason over passion, reason over chaos. The sublime is a useful literary tool to further situate how Marshall's *discursive statements*, by their very reasoned appearance, *regulated* how Indians and the wilderness were perceived.

13 Black letter law refers to the "basic principles of law generally accepted by the courts and/or embodied in the statutes of a particular jurisdiction" (Black 170).

14 Boorstin describes how eighteenth-century painters and builders used a neoclassical order to recover the orderliness in nature. Boorstin cites God's plan for the Universe through the works of Christopher Wren's Cathedral and the couplets of Dryden and Pope embodying the rational aspirations of the Enlightenment. The English countryside adopted Pope's sense of order.

15 Thomas Cole (1801–1848) the founder of the Hudson River School. The Hudson River School was a group of American landscape painters of several generations who worked between about 1825 and 1870 (*The Editors of Encyclopædia Britannica*).

16 Gadamer's term '*historical horizon*,' denotes a hermeneutical system of understanding text based on what the reader inherited prior to reading the text.

17 Cole is most famous for such romantic paintings as *Catskill Mountain Landscape* (1826), *Landscape Composition, St. John in the Wilderness* (1827), *Peace at Sunset (Evening in the White Mountains)* (1827), and *The Clove, Catskills* (1827) among others (Cole, Virtual Gallery, *Explore Thomas Cole.* Thomas Cole Historical Site, 2010. Web. 08 Oct. 2015. http://www.explorethomascole.org/gallery accessed March 25, 2016).

18 Artists like William Cole relied upon patrons to support their work. Cole spent much time in cities like New York and Boston searching for financial backers for his work.

19 "Long known as *The Oxbow*, this work is a masterpiece of American landscape painting, laden with possible interpretations. In the midst of painting *The Course of Empire* (New York Historical Society), Cole mentioned, in a letter dated March 2, 1836, to his patron Luman Reed, that he was executing a large version of this subject expressly for exhibition and sale. The picture was shown at the National Academy of Design in 1836 as *View from Mount Holyoke, Northampton, Massachusetts, after a Thunderstorm.* Cole's interest in the subject probably dates from his 1829–1832 trip to Europe, during which he made an exact tracing of the view published in Basil Hall's *Forty Etchings Made with the Camera Lucida in North America in 1827 and 1828.* Hall criticized Americans' inattentiveness to their scenery and Cole responded with a landscape that lauds the uniqueness of America by encompassing "a union of the picturesque, the sublime, and the magnificent." Although often ambivalent about the subjugation of the land,

here the artist juxtaposes untamed wilderness and pastoral settlement to emphasize the possibilities of the national landscape, pointing to the future prospect of the American nation. Cole's unequivocal construction and composition of the scene, charged with moral significance, is reinforced by his depiction of himself in the middle distance, perched on a promontory painting *The Oxbow.* He is an American producing American art, in communion with American scenery. There are both sketchbook drawings with annotations and related oil sketches of this subject. Many other artists copied or imitated the painting" (Cole, *View from Mount Holyoke, Northampton, Massachusetts, after a Thunderstorm—The Oxbow* (08.228)).

20 The Lewis and Clark Expedition (1804) came after the Louisiana Purchase of 1803 from France; therefore, the lands west of the Mississippi River didn't relate to land formally claimed by France.

21 In October 1806, the Frankfort *Palladium* newspaper printed a news extra to announce the successful return of the Lewis and Clark Expedition from the Pacific "Captains Lewis and Clark are just arrived, and in very good health," letter by John Mullanphy published in the *Palladium* (Lewis and Clark, Kentucky Connections).

22 The legacy of the Marshall Trilogy had its progeny cast in the early 1620s in William Bradford's *History of the Plymouth Plantation.* Using Goodrich's examination of how legal judgment can be formed, the amnesia of judgment or law does inherit, unconsciously, the literary discourse that precedes judgment. Our project here was to reveal the discursive tradition which formed the archive preceding the Marshall opinions; namely, how the wilderness themes were projected as the sublime in American literature, painting and public life.

Part III

Resistance to colonial discourse

Chapter 8

Law and literature

Parts I and II of this book examined how the Native American Indian was constructed through the operation of various statements that were all trained toward the objective of delimiting his or her capacity—specifically, his or her capacity to own land as well as other tangible and intangible assets. This limiting of capacity was part of a project of colonial domination. The research focuses on the Marshall Trilogy as a repository for a range of statements. Such statements were formed through the merging of different discursive traditions that *produced* our modern conceptualization of the American Indian. Dominant accounts, by contrast, would see the Marshall Trilogy cases as a commentary on a Native American that could be said to be in empirical existence *independently* of the kind of discourses of which the Trilogy cases are exemplars.

The final part of the book draws upon different theoretical applications of Foucault's theory of discourse in order to examine the discursive transformations that have taken place which allow the Marshall Trilogy cases to be construed as constitutive, having constructed the modern image of the Native American. In the chapter that follows I will argue that one of the conditions of possibility of the analysis I presented in Part I can also be explained by Foucault's theory of discourse. The scholarly movement of law and literature has enabled me to first embark upon and then elaborate the arguments that I made in Part I. This chapter explores this scholarly movement as a necessary, but theoretical, preliminary to this exploration. Here I examine how discourses are formed and dispersed in a manner which transforms an object of study. What allows Peter Goodrich in his *Law in the Courts of Love* to speak of the repressed literary qualities of the law is a discursive transformation of what (according to Foucault) we would call the enunciative system of law.[1] The law and literature movement is a key intellectual tradition that expresses (i.e., gives evidence of) the way discourses can be radically dispersed and circulated. Whilst there are many facets to the law and literature movement, at its most advanced (as represented, for example, in the work of Aristodemou), there is a denial of any separate realm in which literature can be understood as distinct from law.

In the final chapter of the book I will examine the work of one of the leading theorists on colonial domination and the possibilities inherent in the idea of a post-colony: Homi Bhabha. Bhabha's work demonstrates the impossibility of total colonial dominance. I apply Bhabha's concepts of hybridity and mimicry during a final revisit to the Marshall Trilogy cases. I demonstrate how the cases can be read to reveal the ways and strategies in which human subjects resisted the category of Native American Indian and all the degradation and dispossession that this designation entailed.

While this research examines the relationship between literary discourses and the Marshall Trilogy cases, this is not a study that fits within the literature "as" or literature "in" law movements.[2] Our analysis of the Marshall Trilogy cases examines literature as a discursive platform to reveal how the findings of fact and cultural presumptions in Marshall's judgments had their genealogy in a varied literary tradition; a tradition that was masked, albeit by a tenuous and porous history of the Native Americans, the Doctrine of Discovery and European Utilitarianism. The Trilogy cases exemplified legal judgments built on pillars of literary discourses. These discourses were represented as findings of fact and cultural images that were later incorporated into the Trilogy judgments as sworn statements. Our focus is not to offer a construction of how to interpret the written text of the Trilogy cases, but to reveal the literary pathways which informed Marshall's legal judgment. To better situate this study, it will be useful to delineate what the field of law "as" and "in" literature areas broadly represent and then outline the contours of what this study projects in relation to literature that causes it to stand apart from these fields.[3]

I will also seek to differentiate this project from the Law, Aesthetic and Legal Orientalism schools. While I use the term "school," I do not wish to overstate this term to describe a large movement, but the term is sufficient as a signifier for some writers and their approach to analyzing the relationship between law and other genres, whether they be texts as aesthetic sources, or writers who seeks to project law as a source of legal orientalism which defines legal subjects in different regions of the world.

As a preface to reviewing some of the main tenets of the law "as" field cited above, perhaps a general philosophical statement about why theorists and law schools have attempted to reach outside of law to understand law is appropriate at this point. As Baron writes, "[i]n spite of sharp differences among ['Law as'] schools, all concur that the legal world is not to be understood on its own terms, but requires the application of some method or substance provided by other disciplines" (Baron 1059). Herein lies the essential reason why these so-called law "as" or law "in" literature fields have emerged; namely, that we cannot understand law on its "own terms." In other words, we cannot hope to understand what the law means by merely reading cases or statutes. It appears that this premise advances the position that, conceptually, law is incapable of explaining itself. How ironic it is then that law schools have taught thousands of future attorneys and judges using the case method. What is it about this method that now comes into question? How can fiction help students understand the law? The central focus of this research is not to answer these questions, but to provide some pedagogical context to the law and literature fields that will be reviewed below.

This research seeks to contextualize law as influenced by literary discourses, albeit indirectly through other genres. While the literary discourses examined form their own images of the Native American, the American wilderness and the Doctrine of Discovery, these discourses project a context around law (i.e., an archive); yet, as I will seek to show, judges, through legal judgment, also seek to detach the law from such literary discourses in ways that appear to reveal law's insecurity when faced with such contextualization—especially with literary genres. Unlike the law "as" or the law "in" literature fields, this research seeks to reveal the subliminal and indirect pathways achieved by *findings of fact* in legal judgment to highlight the non-naturalism and non-inevitability of presumptions woven into legal judgment. Until legal judgment is contextualized in ways that account for the nature and effect of findings of facts, it will be difficult for law to attract the social authority it pretends to command by limiting its validity to the internal logic of its own judgments. Logic and structure are not enough to command social authority when law is perceived to be disassociated from social, literary and political environments.[4] This research then, in contrast to the law "as" or law "in" literature fields, examines the literary genres that John Marshall absorbed as sworn statements into the Trilogy cases.

While we may ponder some of the questions cited above, let us be mindful that some theorists do not believe that literature can add to our understanding of law. U.S. Court of Appeal (Seventh Circuit) Judge Richard Posner, for example, asserts that "[w]e should be skeptical about any claim that readers can extract from works of imaginative literature practical lessons for living" (Posner 20). He goes on to say, in the same essay, "you don't get reliable practical tips from literature" (20). Other theorists, such as Robin West, not only disagree with Posner's premise, but counter his law and economics brand of jurisprudence by using *literature* to debunk his embrace of *consent* per se as the cornerstone of a wealth maximizing society and individual autonomy. West asserts, "through a series of contrasts, I will argue that Franz Kafka's fictional works on the nature of law dramatize a dark underside of Posner's argument that the fact of consent morally legitimates our legal, social, and personal worlds" (West 384). West reveals the suspect efficacy of "consent" as a moral presupposition to equity in law. Similar to the Trilogy cases, a further examination of consent will strip away the gloss of judicial coherence and reveal discursive genealogies that, at least through fiction, demonstrate situations where consent, while given, in fact originates in situations that are unfair or coercive, depending upon the relative positions of the parties.

Literature in law

The Law in Literature fields seek to extract meaning and utility by using fictional narratives that have as their subject law, lawyers or narratives written by lawyers. Writers such as Franz Kafka, Albert Camus, Herman Melville, Fyodor Dostoevsky, Charles Dickens and, more recently, Richard A. Weisberg, represent a movement of law in literature.[5] According to the theorists in this field, reading works of fiction that speak about ethical dilemmas of lawyers, trials, judges, or the law in general from the fictional perspective, with real characters and plots, permits the law student, the lawyer, or the general reader to better understand the human dimension of the legal world. A legal world that is not understood only by reading cases, statutes or academic studies about the law. In an effort to humanize and offer lawyers, as well as other participants in the legal world, a window through which to see that legal rules and cases alone are not enough to understand the world of law, the law in literature field seeks to add a sense of realism by lifting fictional narratives, even if law and legal participants are their subject, to broaden the mind of the lawyer. The field has been of the view that this literary dimension to the study of law and its legal participants will offer a perspective on and empathy with everyday life that cannot be instilled by relying on the study of legal rules alone:

> law and literature teachers seek: "to explore visions of the law and justice in selected works of literature"; [sic] "to expose students to broad legal themes (Law and Morality, Law and Authority, Law and Freedom, Law and Punishment) as presented in selected poems, plays, short stories, movies and essays"; [sic] "to consider law in society, use of literary works to raise legal issues, the individual and society"; [sic] "to familiarize the students with great literature that has a legal setting"; [sic] the use of literary theory; and "to focus on works of literary merit that are concerned with law and its effect upon individuals and society"[sic].
>
> (Domnarski 109)

Law as literature

As to the law as literature field, it seeks to apply the tools of literary criticism or interpretation—the hermeneutical—to the study of law. Adherents of this school believe that use of the tools of literary criticism to unearth the meaning of text in works of fiction can also be applied to cases and statutes. In another sense, this school seeks to discover interpretation of legal texts beyond the plain meaning by utilizing textual analysis or approaches not formally employed in the legal profession or law school setting. "There is no literary text, any more than there is a legal text, that can be understood solely from the 'plain meaning' of the story's mere words and phrases"

(Weisburg 9). While it may appear that any plain meaning of text, literary or legal, is difficult to discern, there have developed several strands of textual interpretation that, while outside the scope of this research, still invite some digression here only to capture a sense of how the law in literature field differs from the school of law as literature.

The issue is about how different theorists see *interpretation* of the law not only as a method of legal construction but also as a tool to be used by lawyers or law students to decipher the meanings of legal texts, using methods adopted from literary criticism. "Hermeneutics, the study of methodologies of understanding texts, originated after all with Biblical interpretation and has been most honed within various schools of literary theory and criticism" (11). Weisburg's point suggests then that the hermeneutical tradition of legal interpretation can incorporate the interpretative methods used in various schools of literary theory and criticism.

The Law in Literature field evolved into two broad strands: theory and deconstruction. Both strands seek to explain or interpret texts, whether fictional or legal, using different approaches. The so-called theory strand, depicted by Ronald Dworkin and Stanley Fish, seeks to establish that authors of texts, to the extent that their works and their contexts can be engaged, can constrain the limits of textual meanings. Fish asserted that:

> only the 'interpretive community'—the group of authoritative readers in control of a text at any time—could establish constraints on meaning, and that these constraints had nothing whatsoever to do with the signs themselves within the text but rather were brought about by power struggles within that community.
>
> (11)

It is not clear what Fish means by "readers in control of a text at any time"; however, I will venture to state that Fish seems to imply that readers, or critics closely attuned to the genre and the author regulate the meaning of a text (11); that any constraint on meaning falls into alignment along a "community consensus" of the text rather than using the text itself in the work as the signifier or meaning of the work. Whether the "theory strand" of the Law in Literature field can lay claim to providing improved interpretative tools to lawyers and judges by this community of meaning is unclear.

The other strand of textual interpretation in the law in literature field is concerned with the deconstruction of the text. Weisburg asserts that while such theorists as Derrida, Gadamer and other twentieth-century writers may have provided additional nuanced approaches to interpreting legal texts, lawyers are fully cognizant of the fact that any plain meaning of text is not enough to capture the context, or intent of legal texts. Weisburg depicts the deconstructionists as more of a theoretical detour rather than providing a major shift in hermeneutical approaches to legal texts:

> Lawyers, in my view, did not need the deconstructionist or reader-response "turn" during the 1980s and 1990s to realize that texts have an unfathomable and *perhaps* ultimately un-knowable sense, and that the appeal to objective or originalist theories such as intentionalism or plain meaning are no more than rhetorical tools designed to simplify some common forms of legal disputes or to convince judges that they are doing something scientifically right with a text.
>
> (Weisburg 12–13)

Perhaps while Weisburg is writing about how deconstructionists like Derrida attempt to unearth patterns or truths implicit within textual structures or forms, he is also unintentionally mimicking the university graduate who, upon completion of his or her studies, feels that no further learning need be validated given their certification via diploma or degree in law, business or whatever. The process of learning cannot be confined inside a paradigm, especially a deconstruction that seeks to interpret the meaning of texts. Do legal deconstructionalists believe that applying techniques of interpretation from literature will humanize our understanding of the law, accepting that such literary tools of deconstruction will enhance our understanding of law?

Perhaps Weisburg's depiction of deconstructionists within the Law in Literature field, while useful, provides no significant bearing on interpreting legal texts and resembles James Elkins's point that understanding law requires a re-contextualization of reading such texts (Elkins, *Lawyers and Literature, A First Week's Lecture* 3). By re-contextualizing the way we read law and literature, perhaps to a middle ground, occupied by both pleasure and active reading, we will help lift any hermeneutical limitations that confine our perspectives in each genre's text or our understanding thereof. Deconstruction tools adapted from the Law in Literature field, while perhaps helping us to step out of a narrowly based interpretative approach to text, may also limit the reader into yet another interpretative corner. The illusion is that because the new interpretative method was adopted from literary criticism, our understanding of legal texts is significantly more nuanced.

Both approaches to law "as" and law "in" literature seek to advance the understanding of law and its practice by embedding approaches that are external to the legal profession. In the law "as" literature field:

> If there is a traditional canon of Law and Literature—Antigone, *The Book of Job*, Shakespeare and Dickens, *Billy Budd*, Glaspell's *A Jury of Her Peers—many* of us now find ways in Law and Literature to teach beneath and beyond the canon.
>
> In my view the Law and Literature "movement" (and school of jurisprudence) has missed a golden opportunity in not drawing more fully

> upon stories and novels—and poetry—in which we find lawyers. A lawyer protagonist plays a central role in Tolstoy's "The Death of Ivan Ilych," Harper Lee's *To Kill a Mockingbird,* and Pete Dexter's *Paris Trout.* Lawyers are also found in stories and novels in which the narrator/protagonist is a lawyer but the story does not directly focus on the character as a lawyer, e.g., Melville's "Bartleby, the Scrivener," Albert Camus's *The Fall,* and Walker Percy's *The Second Coming.* And there are still other stories like Katherine Anne Porter's novella, "Noon Wine," in which the central characters are not lawyers, but a lawyer makes a brief but memorable appearance in the narrative. Drawing on these works of literary fiction (historical and contemporary) along with the lawyer-focused short stories of writers like Lowell B. Komie and John William Corrington—both Komie and Corrington are lawyer/authors whose fictional work has been largely ignored in Law and Literature circles—we have the possibility for a course of reading that shifts the focus from Law and Literature to what might descriptively and more accurately be called 'Lawyers and Literature.'
>
> (Elkins, *A New Strain of Law and Literature* 6–7)

According to the law "in" field, these titles imparted knowledge: ethical dilemmas, real consequences upon the application of the black letter law—a list of stories that dramatized the effects of how law within the minds of the characters and between characters was experienced in the human world. While a canon of law "in" literature using new techniques of textual interpretation may be suggested by reading Derrida, Gadamer and others, the point is similar to the law "as" field—approaches to meaning and understanding of law are being attempted outside the genre of law.

Departure from the law "as" or law "in" literature movement

While this research attempts to relate a literary discourse occurring during the Marshall Trilogy cases, this attempt should be not judged as seeking to deconstruct or reinterpret the text of the Marshall cases. While the research has reviewed fiction, public speeches, poems, histories and other genres, reading these sources is not designed to impart greater empathy, or appreciation for the Marshall cases, nor does the research seek to deconstruct the Marshall opinion for insightful meaning using tools of literary criticism. At least with respect to the latter, this research is not a hermeneutical attempt to develop a new approach to readings of the Marshall cases. Nevertheless, it *does* develop a novel approach to reflecting upon legal judgment; specifically, using different literary genres to illuminate the finding of facts that would otherwise fade into the background as foundational pillars for historical presumptions in legal judgment. Historical presumptions are not necessarily accurate sworn statements to support the internal logic of legal judgment. Such findings of fact have genealogical literary strands that underpin their existence. Unlike the law "as" or law "in" literature methodologies, this research foregrounds the relational pathways between literary genres and legal judgment that can be found within findings of facts.

Conventional interpretations have already covered the legal significance of the Marshall Trilogy cases and their impact with respect to the legal conquest of the American Indians.[6] Using Baron, the scope of this research can by defined by what it is not: the debate between those who seek the true interpretation by decoding texts (i.e., deconstructionists) and those who seek better understanding or interpretation by finding the intention of the writer (i.e., intentionalists):

> The preeminent issue for hermeneutic law-and-lits has been power: Who or what "controls" the meaning of a text—the author, the reader, the words of the text, conventions of reading? Beyond a tendency to approach this issue by focusing on a single legal text, the U.S. Constitution, the hermeneutic law-and-lits have found little on which to agree. Intentionalists clash with deconstructionists on one side and textualists on the other. Meanwhile, other scholars enter the argument only to assert that nothing at all turns on the outcome, while still others have made the opposite point: that too much turns on the outcome of real legal cases to make the analogy to literary interpretation apt.
> (Baron 1071)

This research uses literature not as a source of literary or textual interpretation, but as a discursive platform to show that the facts and cultural presumptions used by Marshall were embedded over a wide and varied literary discourse that appeared to be settled fact when adopted by John Marshall in the Trilogy cases. As such, this research attempts to demonstrate that what Marshall took as historical evidence was in fact an example of how legal judgment, rather than being a product of legal doctrines and rules, was more the birth child of literary discourses that dominated representations of the Other or the Native American in ways that even Marshall may not have understood. Maria Aristodemou in *Law and Literature: Journeys from Her to Eternity* provides a revealing theoretical framework that offers further elucidation regarding how representations of the real are morphed into a replication that not only distorts the original subject through false representation, but in which such representations are themselves perceived as *real* by their very repetition. Aristodemou writes "[n]ot only is so-called reality a representation, a phantasm, it is a sign, a text so endlessly repeated that its sources, interests, and assumptions are forgotten or go unquestioned" (Aristodemou 20).

In a narrow sense, the legal judgments of the Trilogy cases, in particular the *Johnson v. M'Intosh* ruling, were an attempt to justify the land pre-emption rights of individual states in relation to the Federal Government in the early American Republic. What this research has demonstrated is how legal judgment, as appropriately described by Peter Goodrich, is an example of a kind of legal *amnesia* when it comes to the sources of its history or findings of fact. Goodrich writes,

> in a more generalised expression the same point is made at length by Derrida in his reading of Kafka's *Before the Law*: "to be invested with its categorical authority, the law must be without history, without genesis, without any possible derivation . . . this silence and this discontinuation constitute the phenomenon of law."
>
> (Goodrich 123)

Goodrich introduces a vital point, namely that law creates a type of fiction by its very institutional nature. The nature of law must be built upon findings of fact that, because they are referred to within legal judgment, become self-referential. Law is defined by its very text and its legal history. Legal judgment has the force of consequences in the real world because law effects people. Law takes on the illusion of power; a power derived not by literature preceding law, but power based on the creation of legal doctrines which, when inserted with the judge's quill, provide a seemingly privileged claim on truth. When judges, for example, deploy their depiction of history, whether correct or incorrect, whether fictional or not, the point is that these legal texts have been given the power to self-justify their meaning. This is why the debate between the law "in" and law "as" literature fields seems to have been surpassed by their pedagogical constraints. Essentially, the power to judge in law allows the law to define the internal or external viewpoint of judgment through the "text" of the judgments. One of the aims of this research is to avoid a journey into the linguistic and textual abyss of literary criticism. Instead this research seeks out a literary discourse that is far more telling in its genealogical connection to positive law where the latter seeks to discard its historical and literary identity.

Law chooses to forget its origins, at least the origins which should have been extracted from history as correct depictions of history. In the Marshall Trilogy cases, Justice Marshall outlined the origins of the Doctrine of Discovery based on a narrow set of literary discourses. Neither source is acknowledged, yet both have dramatic relevance to the legal judgment rendered by the U.S. Supreme Court.

Marshall incorporates selected images of the American Indians from a long-standing literary and discursive archive dating back to the sixteenth century within the express body of his judicial opinions. In addition, his own literary discourse on George Washington was virtually lifted from non-judicial works to justify and posit an Americanized Doctrine of Discovery (Robertson 102).[7] Both sources of Marshall's judicial reasoning, in terms of any attribution to the literary discourses that preceded the Trilogy cases, were ignored completely within the Trilogy judgments.

Goodrich would explain, in my view, Marshall's omission to either cite, or refer to the literary sources of his rulings as an attempt to make law self-founding:

> The defining feature of legal modernity lies in the attempt to make law self-founding. Unable or unwilling any longer to justify or found law upon nature, justice, right or contract, jurisprudence was forced to seek the legitimacy of law, the justification of judgment and the criterion of legality, within law itself.
>
> (Goodrich Chap. 7, 1)

Essentially, Goodrich sees law as partly theoretical and an institutional practice with real consequences that attempt to sanctify its efficacy not by attribution to ethics, nature or literary discourse, but by an institutionalized amnesia concerning such sources in order to instil the perception of the objectivity and sagacity of the law.

Seeking to explain law as a rational institution, Judge Richard Posner has attempted to isolate the relationship between law and economics as the essential calculus to explain and predict judicial decisions by dehumanizing humanity's place in the world with the economic theory of the *rational man*.[8] Posner offers the view on how law should be read to underscore that, because law produces real results, it is thus by its nature precluded from being re-contextualized outside its text. The implications of Posner's paradigm help to shape the environmental and "real" world of people and events that influence the findings of fact of any legal judgment. In reviewing Posner's book *Law and Literature: A Matter or Relation*, Helle Porsdam observed:

> It is this loss of "intrinsic authoritativeness" or constraint, which he sees as the inevitable result of a New Critical approach to the interpretation of legal documents, that concerns Posner throughout *Law and Literature*. By treating a legal document as a piece of literature, New Critics and poststructuralist critics (such as Robin West and the legal feminists and Roberto Unger and the Critical Legal Studies Movement) come dangerously close to opening Pandora's Box. For, in transferring to the legal field the tools of the literary trade, New Critics and poststructuralist critics will also transfer the self-referentiality and exaggerated freedom of interpretation that has characterized the postmodern literary arena. And if a judge achieves this kind of "freedom," what will stop him or her from bending the law according to his or her own subjective taste or whim.
>
> (Porsdam 497)

Porsdam describes the challenges to law's monopoly on "legal interpretation" but, in terms of this research, she stops just short of the essential question that drives this project. The issue is not so much that of allowing tools of literary interpretation to unsettle the constraints of legal interpretation. Even more importantly the "New Critics" (e.g., the Law and Literature field) have at least shaken the rigid and mythical objectivity of law. It is not the interpretation of the text that Chief Justice John Marshall uses in the Trilogy judgments that interests us but rather, what makes his opinions relevant are the *findings of fact that* he accepts in his legal judgments. These judgments are a culmination of literary and other public discourses. It is the examination of the relationship between findings of fact and the archive of literary-public discourses that differ from the Law and Literature field.

In examining the literary discourse that relates to the foundations of Marshall's legal judgment in the Trilogy cases, I am not utilizing either the law "as" or law "in" literature approaches to legal interpretation, but instead I am employing the literary discursive approaches of how literary discourses can "represent" the Other, or the dominated Other, as articulated by the discourse theories of Michel Foucault and Edward Said.

Law and aesthetics

This project also differs from theories of the Law and Aesthetics field. This project seeks to dissociate its focus away from viewing literature as a "unique insight into the underpinnings of law and that stories and poems stand as sources of law" (Weisburg 3). Writers such as Patricia Williams and Peter Goodrich, for example, seek to draw upon the text of objectivity, reason and the apparent motifs of the law to identify an aesthetic about law's text and form to promote the self-aggrandisement of power and justice. As Goodrich explains, law "is in many aspects to be taken as a plastic art, of architecture, statuary, dress, heraldry, painting and insignia—gold rings, rods, coifs, seals and rolls—which provide popular consciousness with a Justice which can be seen and remembered" (96).[9] Patricia Williams in *The Alchemy of Race and Rights* writes about how a legal text that dealt with a racially motivated experience she encountered at *Benetton's* was edited from a personal experience to an impersonal objectified text by law students.[10] Williams stated,

> [w]hat was most interesting to me in this experience was how the blind application of principles of neutrality, through the device of omission, acted either to make me look crazy or to make the reader participate in old habits of cultural bias.
>
> (Quoted in Butler)

She writes, "[w]hat is 'impersonal' writing but denial of self? . . . denial of one's authority in authorship is not the same as elimination of oneself; it is a ruse, not reality" (Butler).[11] Williams sees this highly codified and impersonal writing style as an enforcement of an "aesthetic of uniformity."

The language of law, its style, its prose, its form and its method of citation are all attempts to be anti-aesthetic; however, this attempt produces a legal genre that has its main aesthetic and intellectual grounding in *reason.* Weisberg concentrates on the form of legal opinions for interconnectedness to substance. In a manner similar to Benjamin Cardozo, Weisberg observes that "it is the language used in the opinion, and only that language, that perfectly constitutes the "doing"—the holding—of the opinion" (Weisburg 8). Whether one agrees with Weisberg is not the issue here, but citing Weisberg draws attention to the approach that the Law and Aesthetics field seeks to develop to understand legal judgment by deconstructing the form used in legal opinions. The connection between the form and text written by judges is a necessary link to the substantive outcome of judgment. Stated otherwise, it is the *appearance* of legal judgment as a reasoned text based on case law, style of citation and devoid of emotional language to promote the anti-aesthetic aura of law. As Adam Gearey observes, "law is a kind of confidence trick . . . the system manufactures its own *conditions of legitimacy* [my emphasis] and then attempts to legislate them as a priori universals that have a legitimizing effect through their appeal to reason" (32). Gearey's "confidence trick" aims to expose how the aesthetics of legal text seek to promote the illusion of law's self-legitimation; however, Gearey identifies a critical issue for our project; namely, how law attempts to "legislate . . . a priori universals" which are legitimized (i.e., made real or historical) by either legislation or legal judgment or by judges who simply assert as such. While Gearey is fostering a compelling aesthetic framework to critically isolate the myth around law's reasoned text, he enters the realm of our project's focus in considering what a priori pathways or discourses law seeks to use as the foundation for the "manufacture" of reason in building legal judgment.

Brian Butler posits that law attempts to appear as anti-aesthetic as an aesthetic, or as posited above, a legal genre that has its aesthetic attributes grounded in its illusionary anti-aesthetic prose. Butler states:

> but law really offers an "anti-aesthetic" aesthetic. Looking at the aesthetics offered by law raises questions about symbolic ideals of what is neutral, just, and principled or reasoned, and asks whether such an attitude toward aesthetic factors is biased towards certain conclusions. Observing the aesthetic factors operating in an area purportedly purified of such an influence can help widen appreciation of the importance of aesthetics in everyday concepts such as reason.
>
> (Butler)

Pierre Schlag identified a "grid aesthetic" to law whereby the form and manner of segmenting legal principles, cases and facts become neatly compartmentalized. When organized within the context of legal judgment, such aesthetic legal forms lead to a judgment that displays the organized placement of facts and cases. The judgment presents the illusion of a reasoned organization of doctrines and other authorities in relation to facts. Schlag states:

> In the grid aesthetic, law is framed as a field, a territory, a two-dimensional space that can be mapped and charted. This jurisprudential mapping occurs through the subdivision of the territorial space of law into various parts: contracts/torts. Each part is subdivided into subparts: negligence/intentional torts. These are then subdivided into even smaller subparts. This process continues until a mysterious point is reached where law gives out and all that remains are questions of fact.
>
> (Schlag 1055)

Schlag does not speak to an aesthetic in the form or nature of beauty, but simply to the form and textual landscape of law. In describing legal judgment, Schlag is asking the reader to accept that the very nature of examining how the structure and text of legal judgment is organized is an aesthetic project. A consciousness emerges if the reader begins to view legal text in this way and as such, an aesthetic, albeit a legal one, begins to emerge (Schlag 1053).

As interesting and compelling as the Law and Aesthetics examination of legal text is, this project's aim is not to energize legal text for an aesthetic analysis. Our project asserts that certain texts within legal judgment, especially historical facts, play a different role when compared to the Law and Aesthetics emphasis on deconstructing the form used in legal opinions. The latter is deftly captured by Gearey's "confidence trick" assessment of legal judgment, one which this author shares; however, it is important to note that this project seeks to relate how historical facts or texts within legal judgment, which do not cause a hermeneutical dilemma or problem in terms of interpretation or understanding, nonetheless become posited within legal judgment not at the inception of judgment but as part of a literary discourse. According to Said, such literary discourses, the nineteenth-century English novel for example, can play a critical role in defining dominated peoples or colonial subjects. Said's aesthetic examination of English literature encompasses how these aesthetic works of literature are reconstituted, not only for their pleasurable pursuit by readers, but also serving to constitute or represent a reality that forms part of the legal consciousness within judgment. Using Said's literary theory, I argue that the literary and public discourses before and during the Marshall Trilogy cases developed multi-layered discursive pathways which built the factual and historical a priori truths of the U.S. Supreme Court's rulings. Said wrote that:

> Since my exclusive focus here is on the modern Western empire of the nineteenth and twentieth centuries, I have looked especially at cultural forms like the novel, which I believe were immensely important in the formation of imperial references and experiences. I do not mean that only the novel was important, but that I consider it the aesthetic object whose connection to the expanding societies of Britain and France is particularly interesting to study . . . The power to narrate, or to block other narratives from forming and emerging, is very important to culture and imperialisms, and constitutes one of the main connections between them.
>
> (Said, *Culture and Imperialism* xii–xiii)

In light of the above, while this project does not seek to interpret the text as a hermeneutical enterprise with respect to the Marshall Trilogy cases, I argue that certain terms within the Marshall opinions fall outside the need to deploy hermeneutical tools to find meaning. Neither do we need to react, or underscore the aesthetic motifs of the Marshall opinion since our project seeks to relate how literary discourses provide the historical and public a priori discourses incorporated in legal judgment as findings of fact. While we have examined the literary discursive pathways through which the Marshall Trilogy cases incorporated this tradition, it does not necessarily mean that we have also established a discursive relationship with legal judgment through an aesthetic examination of the legal text.

Legal Orientalism

This project differs from Legal Orientalism in several respects. Legal Orientalism seeks to demonstrate how the Other is defined, partly through legal discourse. Legal discourse is collapsed as part of and similar to the post-colonial discourse that Said sees as helping to forge the definition of the colonialized. According to Teemu Ruskola, "[s]tructurally, Orientalism as a discourse entails the projection onto the Oriental Other of various sorts of things that 'we' are not" (209). While Orientalism does certainly entail general representation onto the Orient, this approach attaches independence to the nature of legal discourse as a *source* of that projection. Legal Orientalism looks to establish 'law's' role in representing the Other, in other words, law as the source of the discursive formation of the Other (209).

Where this research departs from Legal Orientalism is with the premise that the nature of legal discourse cannot be separated as a source of representation, given law's genealogy as a porous enterprise. In the spirit of Goodrich and Gearey, this project seeks to establish a consciousness about the analytical and jurisprudential sources of legal judgment. To assess and discuss the jurisprudential genealogy of legal judgment is to also challenge the existence of law as an independent enterprise. The issue is to avoid accepting law as a closed field, but rather to examine legal judgment as an institutional enterprise that exemplifies the culmination of a discourse, rather than as an enterprise that projects that discourse.[12] When legal judgment is written in all its trappings, its rules, its doctrines and other self-referential motifs, we are at the end, not the beginning of a discourse. Like Said's colonial 'Other,' legal judgment itself is ultimately represented by the very literary discourses it accepts as sworn statements. Legal Orientalism seeks to present its field as an independent legal enterprise. Aristodemou elaborates on this point when she writes:

> Legal language tends to abstract and detach itself from everyday experience once it has spoken; literature on the other hand may reveal what law obscures by reopening the gaps and ambiguities that law necessarily distanced itself from in its insistence on speaking univocally, and forever . . . [O]nce such worlds, however, are shown to be not only artificial but also unfair or tyrannical, it is necessary to reveal the ways by which that artificiality is constructed.
>
> (Aristodemou 24–5)

This research departs from Legal Orientalism, as described in commentary on Alexis de Tocqueville's view on the legally ingrained nature of Americans in the early nineteenth century, when Ruskola writes "This is perhaps not very surprising when one considers that America's foundational myths are also peculiarly legal" (Ruskola 209). Like Ruskola, however, this research examines the foundational myths that preceded the Marshall Trilogy cases and these myths are traced in like manner, where they eventually merge into the "peculiarly legal" expositions of John Marshall's opinions. Ruskola's reasoning, however, posits the "peculiarly legal" as the source of Legal Orientalism whereas this research posits that foundational myths, cloaked within legal discourse, should not be accepted as findings of fact that define the Other. While there appears to be an inherent inconsistency between Tukeema's use of Legal Orientalism in terms of separating American Law from Chinese law; namely, that in defining the 'we' (i.e., American law) in comparison to 'them' (i.e., Chinese law), an inherent inconsistency emerges in her analysis which is driven by juxtaposing a comparison built on a contradiction. The contradiction is that the comparison is built upon "foundational myths," wrapped in the guise of an independent legal enterprise. This research differs from Ruskola's analysis by unmasking independent legal enterprises (i.e., legal judgment) as reflecting the literary and public discourses that precede judgment. While Legal Orientalism seeks to examine the pathways whereby law or legal judgment define a legal subject, this research differs by exposing legal judgments as being defined by the dominant literary and public discourses masquerading as legal history *within* legal judgment.

While Said's approach to how literary discourses can define the Other, I also utilize the writings of Michel Foucault, Hans-Georg Gadamer and Peter Goodrich in assessing how literary discourses are able to constitute a history or reality that reflects colonial or imperial interests or assumptions. Within the context of assessing the Marshall Trilogy cases, we are positioning literary discourse outside the Law and Literature genres because the aim of this research is to relate how the literary and public discourses preceding the Marshall cases provided the historical setting and the political–legal discourse, between the 1780s and 1820s, enabling John Marshall to represent a reality, albeit a fictional reality, that was imagined by these discourses. To use a Goodrichian analogy, we are attempting to awaken legal judgment from its amnesia to situate law as part of an open system of many literary discourses rather than as a self-founding genre.

Legal judgment is not a vacuum, but a porous enterprise that attempts to hide its genealogy.[13] Foucault and Goodrich provide rich theories and expose law's open-textured judgments.[14] We have much to learn in examining the Marshall cases, not only for their legal effects upon the Native American, but equally to reveal that literature, through the prism of literary discourses as much as so-called law, created the essential elements used by the Marshall court to dispossess the Native American under the guise of legal rules, doctrines and ultimately, legal judgment.

Notes

1 Foucault accounts for a statement's position in any discourse as being situated by a system of conditions or relations. A statement is not independent; that is, its subject, verbs and other linguistic characteristics do not operate in a vacuum, detached from a conditional system that gives it meaning. For Foucault, the "*enunciative function* is that which, at the very root of the statement-event, and in that which embodies it, defines at the outset the system of enunciability . . . it is that which defines the mode of occurrence of the statement-thing; it is the system of its functioning" (Foucault, *The Archaeology of Knowledge* 146).

2 The Marshall Trilogy cases encompassed the U.S. Supreme Court rulings in *Johnson v. M'Intosh* (1823), *Worcester v. Georgia* (1832) and *Cherokee Nation v. State of Georgia* (1831). All majority court opinions were authored by Chief Justice John Marshall.

3 "Law-in-literature focuses on the depiction of law and jurisprudential questions in works of literature . . . while Law-as-literature examines legal opinions and arguments from a literary lens—as works of literature" (Solove).

4 I am indebted to Dr Piyel Halder, Senior Lecturer in Law and Acting Director of Graduate Studies, Birkbeck College, University of London, for providing useful insights into the perceived danger of contextualizing law by the 'Law as' or 'Law in' literature schools.

5 Franz Kafka (*The Trial*); Albert Camus (*The Stranger*); Herman Melville (*Billy Budd*); Fyodor Dostoevsky (*The Brothers Karamazov*); Richard H. Weisberg (*Poethics and Other Strategies of Law and Literature*).

6 Lindsay G. Robertson's excellent review of the *Johnson v. M'Intosh* (1823) case provides a detailed account of the legal strategies by the Illinois and Wabash Land

Companies that ultimately led to John Marshall's Court opinion (Roberston 2005). Another good source on the Trilogy cases is Matthew L. M. Fletcher's article "*The Iron Cold of The Marshall Trilogy*" (Fletcher 2006).

7 John Marshall authored a multi-volume biography on George Washington.

8 The "rational man" is a basic theoretical assumption used in many economic models to map consumer maximization and macro aggregate models to explain fiscal, monetary policy and inflation. Economics—from Irving Fisher's "Quantity Theory of Money"; John Maynard Keynes "The General Theory of Employment, Interest and Money" (where he explained the 'consumption function') to Milton Friedman's *The Monetary History of the United States* and *The Methodology of Positive Economics*—has always incorporated the 'rational' behavior of the consumer in its models.

9 See Peter Winn "Legal Ritual" in Kevelson (ed.) *Law and Aesthetics* (New York: Peter Lang, 1992) for a discussion of the relation of law and ritual.

10 Benetton Group S.p.A. is a global fashion name with 6,500 stores in over 120 countries (Benetton).

11 Williams is quoted by Brian Butler.

12 I am indebted to Peter Goodrich's book for this line of analysis; namely, that law or legal judgment incorporates an institutional "amnesia" with respect to literary discourses that precede legal judgment.

13 I am indebted to Peter Goodrich's "*Law in the Court of Love*" for providing a useful perspective on how law institutionally forgets or experiences amnesia when it comes to identifying the historical precedents that sometimes make up the legal histories of judgments. This is not an overt amnesia, but over time, as the law and the legal profession reify their profession and precedents, habits formed within the legal institutional framework produce an inability to acknowledge that, like other genres or forms of writing, law is as indebted to literary discourses that precede judgment.

14 I use open textured as a metaphor to denote the porous nature of legal judgment that is influenced by literary discourses. Being open textured, law or legal judgment is not a closed self-referential discourse, even though the law and its judicial institutions (i.e., courts) adopt a style of writing that makes it appear as if legal judgment and textual rigor (i.e., countless footnotes and textual citations) give law the aura of a non-aesthetic discourse.

Chapter 9

Cherokee resistance

Mimicry as deception

Previous chapters in this part have examined how discursive traditions have formed and reformed in a way that has enabled a critique of a colonial discourse. In this chapter, I explore how the colonial subject—precisely the Native American—has sought to resist colonial imposition, which in turn has meant a resistance to the very classifying of the Native American. The question of subaltern resistance has been discussed by a number of post-colonial theorists, most notably Gayatri Chakravorty Spivak in her celebrated essay *Can the Sabaltern Speak?* and Homi K. Bhabha's *The Location of Culture.*[1] Given that this book draws on a theory of discourse, this chapter focuses specifically on Bhabha's idea of *mimicry* as a particular tool used by subaltern communities to undermine, or otherwise disturb, colonial knowledge.

Foucault offers a theoretical explanation for resistance outside of the colonial setting, while Bhabha's theory of *mimicry* places his work at the center of colonialism. Foucault notes:

> We must make allowances for the complex and unstable process whereby discourse can be both an instrument and an effect of power, but also a hindrance, a stumbling block, a point of resistance and a starting point for an opposing strategy. Discourse transmits and produces power; it reinforces it, but also undermines and exposes it, renders it fragile and makes it possible to thwart it.
>
> (Foucault, *The Order of Discourse* 51)

While Foucault provides a theoretical account for *resistance* from discourse, he does not situate his analysis within the context of a colonial archive. For the purposes of this chapter, I combine Foucault's recognition that resistance includes discursive statements and Bhabha's incorporation of Foucault's discursive theory within the context of a colonial relationship. Specifically, Bhabha's theory of *mimicry* explains both the presence of Cherokee resistance and its exclusion by John Marshall. As to *mimicry*, Bhabha acknowledges a Janus-faced resistance to power: "the ambivalence of colonial authority repeatedly turns from mimicry—a difference that is almost nothing but not quite—to menace—a difference that is almost total but not quite" (Bhabha 131). It is the menace felt by the colonizer in realizing that he is being replicated too closely that forms a kind of resistance within the colonial discourse that Bhabha discusses. This chapter posits that Marshall's silence with respect to Cherokee resistance, can be interpreted as a judicial anxiety, an anxiety born from Bhabha's menace.

In contrast, Said's post-colonial approach to explaining how literature was used as a discursive tool to define colonized peoples, unlike Foucault and Bhabha, does not integrate a counter-discourse or resistance theory into his Orientalism. Nevertheless, as this chapter explains, Said's analysis of nineteenth-century British colonialism is relevant since his discourse theory is heavily influenced by Foucault. Said's Orientalism in turn influenced Bhabha's theory of *mimicry*.

> From such a colonial encounter between the white presence and its black semblance, there emerges the question of the ambivalence of mimicry as a problematic of colonial subjection [. . .] then the work of Edward Said will not let us forget that the 'ethnocentric and erratic will to power from which texts can spring' is itself a theatre of war.
>
> (Quoted in 129)[2]

Said's Orientalism became a theoretical link between Foucault and Bhabha by introducing the colonial context. Said helps to situate a literary dimension into the colonial archive within the context of Foucault's discursive theory. While Said's analysis of the colonial discursive formations about the Other produced a tendency to indicate a power nexus from cosmopolitan centers to colonial Others, the limitations of Said's discursive formations are revealed by colonial resistance and by extension, our examination of Cherokee resistance. Bhabha incorporates Said's theory of colonial discourse by extending the discursive relations from being one dimensional, that is power over the colonized, to a more dynamic reciprocal relationship between colonizer and colonized. Foucault's theory accounts for why John Marshall did not incorporate findings of fact that would explain Cherokee resistance, while Bhabha's theory highlights the counter-discourses that situates Cherokee resistance. This chapter also asserts that even Bhabha's theory of *mimicry* does not account for the strategic resistance exemplified by the Cherokee.

Michel Foucault's theory about discursive statements and their regulated distribution helps to explain why John Marshall omitted the very public and fierce resistance by the Cherokee Nation with respect to land encroachments by such U.S. states as Georgia. John Marshall's majority opinions in the Trilogy focused on the legal capacity of American Indians to own their land, rather than acknowledging discourses that promoted 'civilized' statements of Cherokee farming, political organization, and a written language. Collectively, John Marshall's Trilogy opinions are dominated by discourses that incorporate disparaging statements about the American Indians: statements best exemplified by terms like "savages," "hunters" and "domestic dependent nations." These harmful statements were regulated by the colonial *archive* about Native Americans prior to Marshall's judgments. These judgments gradually became part of the trope of literary discourses that framed American Indians as tenants, rather than owners of their land. Foucault notes that in relation to "statements," in this context disparaging statements of Indians,

> it characterizes not what is given in them, but the very fact that they are given, and the way in which they are given. It has this quasi-invisibility of the 'there is,' which is effaced in the very thing of which one can say: 'there is this or that thing.'
>
> (Foucault, *The Archaeology of Knowledge* 124)

Not only was the colonial archive about American Indians formed before the Trilogy, but through Foucault's "return to the origin" we can explain how the Trilogy judgments also contributed to the formation of the legal archive about Indians collectively. Foucault explains how the "return to the origin" serves to transform the subject of the discourse:

> In this way we can understand the inevitable necessity, within these fields of discursivity, for a 'return to the origin.' This return, which is part of the discursive field itself, never stops modifying it . . . it constitutes an effective and necessary task of transforming the discursive practice itself.
>
> (Foucault, *What Is an Author?* 116)

Foucault's archive is not a fixed space, but an evolving discursive field. Critical to this chapter then is how, in adopting Foucault's theory of discursive formations and their dispersion, we can understand how the Trilogy opinions were influenced by statements that projected the Indians as hapless wards of the Federal Government, as opposed to acknowledging their fierce resistance to European-American expansionism over their lands. As I argued in my theoretical basis to this book, Foucault's *enunciative system* regulates statements. It is a system around those statements that can arguably regulate legal discourse. Critical in relation to Indian resistance is how Foucault's *archive* situated the Trilogy cases with discursive statements that excluded Cherokee resistance to European-American encroachment upon their land and specifically, by 1828, Georgia's attempts to illegally impose their state laws upon the Cherokee people.

Cherokee resistance

This research has demonstrated how the Trilogy cases established the American legal doctrines which rationalized the *legal* dispossession of Indians and how such legal doctrines were part of a long literary discursive tradition dating back to the early seventeenth century. What is also apparent is that many of the Native tribes fiercely resisted their depiction by Marshall in the Trilogy opinions as a race doomed to an inevitable demise in the face of superior and technologically more advanced European settlers.

Edward Said's theory of Orientalism accounts for the Cherokee resistance to the post-colonial American Government in the early nineteenth century. As part of this examination I engage Homi K. Bhabha's work in *The Location of Culture* to situate his criticism of Said's *Orientalism*. I then test Bhabha's theories of "anxiety," "ambivalence" and "mimicry" as they relate to the Cherokee resistance.[3] This chapter will focus on two particular areas of Cherokee resistance: the resistance against land pressures and resistance to the dominant American literary discourse. On a broader scale, this chapter examines the Cherokee resistance to cultural assimilation into the dominant European-American culture.

It is important to situate Said's Orientalist thesis in light of Bhabha's critique of colonialist strategies to explain how literature is used to not only define the Other, but to measure the parameters of this literary discourse. Only by assessing Said's Orientalist theory can we begin to understand the point of departure where Cherokee resistance extends into a dimension not captured by Said's approach. While I argue that Said provides a significant basis for assessing the role of literature and its connected discourses in relation to the colonized Other, my examination of Bhabha's work introduces a more nuanced appreciation of the dynamic interdependence within colonial discourse between the colonizer and the colonized. While I may use *colonizer* and *colonized* as terms to explain Bhabha's theory, use of Bhabha's theory does not necessarily mean that the relationship between the American Government and the Cherokee in the early nineteenth-century mirrored a colonial dynamic. This chapter attempts to demonstrate that neither Said nor Bhabha's theories of colonial discourse and *mimicry*, though helpful in positioning an important focus on discourse and resistance, account for the unique Cherokee resistance. The Cherokee resistance, which still persists today, always sought to camouflage its underlying strategic objective; namely, to preserve their culture and nation. Neither Said's Orientalism nor Bhabha's *mimicry* provide a theoretical explanation for the Cherokee resistance. Cherokee resistance exemplified a counter-discourse and political survival policies not to assimilate inevitably into the dominant American culture, but to preserve their status as a separate nation.

Said and Bhabha: Orientalism to mimicry

This research has shown that literary discourses, whether focused on the image of the Indian or on themes of wilderness, provided many literary archives about the Native Indian and the land before and during the Trilogy cases. While the literary discourses situated a discursive field upon which John Marshall could legally extinguish the *fee simple* land ownership of the American Indian in *Johnson*, these discourses failed to explain the persistent and lingering resistance by various Native tribes against European Americans. Our aim is not so much to document Indian resistance into the twentieth century, but rather to recognize that the resistance was nuanced at its most intense moment in the early nineteenth century; a century that nearly saw the complete eradication of the American Indians and their varied cultures.

These literary genres collectively sought to define the Other. As Edward Said attempted to show, literature produced by the colonial power sought to rationalize within the dominant mind (i.e., the West) both the imposed colonial system and the image of the conquered people. Said seeks to identify a literary perspective that projects an Orientalist worldview. It is this reality of the Other within the mind of the "cosmopolitan center" that Bhabha describes as the dominating power's attempt to define the Other in a way that solidifies their image. Said seeks to explain Orientalism as a system of identification by the West about the Orient. It is this identification, a process that projects the image and reality through literature of the Orient, which exemplifies Said's Orientalism:

> But at the outset one can say that so far as the West was concerned during the nineteenth and twentieth centuries, an assumption had been made that the Orient and everything in it was, if not patently inferior to, then in need of corrective study by the West. The Orient was viewed as if framed by the classroom, the criminal court, the prison, the illustrated manual. Orientalism, then, is knowledge of the Orient that places things Oriental in class, court, prison, or manual for scrutiny, study, judgment, discipline or governing.
>
> (Said, *Orientalism* 40–41)

What are the effects of the Orientalist discourse? What does the "study by the West" of the "Orient" illuminate? As I argue here, *a reality*. Said incorporates Nietzsche's expression about truth and language to capture the essential effect of Orientalism, that "truths are illusion" (203). It is the Orientalist initiative to marshal a collection of signifiers, codes, definitions and other translations as well as to explain, or define, a place. It is ultimately how that place is described through language and metaphors which produces the illusion. Said develops his important theoretical framework by stating that

> its objective discoveries—the work of innumerable devoted scholars who edited texts and translated them, codified grammars, wrote dictionaries, reconstructed dead epochs, produced positivistically verifiable learning—are and always have been conditioned by the fact that its truths, like any truths delivered by language, are embodied in language.
> (203)

Said explores how truths are embellished, transposed and rarefied over time by many rhetorical influences, some real and others illusionary, but ultimately, a canon is created in referencing Nietzsche. "Nietzsche once said, 'a mobile army of metaphors, metonyms, and anthropomorphisms—in short, a sum of human relations, which have been enhanced, transposed . . . which after long use seem firm, canonical, and obligatory to a people'" (203). Piyel Halder captures the essential element that explains Said's Orientalism.

> The Orient was made easier to rule once it had been reconnoitred and subjected to scholarly description. The cultural documents of Orientalism of which exist numerous novels, narratives, poems, plays, maps, paintings, photographs and works of translation, are what made Imperialism possible.
> (Halder 46)

Both Said and Halder's description of Said's Orientalism present tangible, albeit textually discursive, examples that help to detail how imperialism was able to essentialise knowledge about the Orient.[4]

Said's Orientalism establishes a one-dimensional relationship between the Occident and the Orient.[5] Daniel Martin Varisco questions Said's Orientalism for its inability to account for the counter-discourse of the Orient. "A pervasive assumption underlying Said's depiction of Orientalism-as-discourse is an unchanging, unifying hegemonic and pervasive influence that individual agency and self-critique by individual Orientalists were powerless to stop" (Varisco 252–3). As Valerie Kennedy explains, "Said's failure to acknowledge the heterogeneity of Orientalism may be one reason why his analysis of it becomes embroiled in contradictory definitions and redefinitions" (253). Said's narrowly framed Orientalism appears to omit a more nuanced explanation for the "heterogeneity" inherent in colonial discourses, Aijaz Ahmad examines Said's *Orientalism* in his book *In Theory* by noting among many critical observations that Said's *Orientalism* posits the West as a cultural source with a seamless and fixed identity. Ahmad notes that Said sees the metropolitan center as a homogeneous place that, over time, has projected a need to establish its own identity by constituting the Orient as the Other. The Orient thus becomes the object of textuality:

> It is rather remarkable how constantly and comfortably Said speaks—not only in this particular sentence but throughout the book—of a Europe, or the West, as a self-identical, fixed being which has always had an essence and a project, an imagination and a will; and of the 'Orient' as its object—textually, militarily, and so on. He speaks of the West, or Europe, as the one which produces the knowledge, the East of the object of that knowledge.
>
> (Ahmad 183)

Said's theory is therefore limited for its one dimensional view of the colonial relationship between the colonizer and the Other. Said is being criticized by Varisco, Kennedy and Ahmad for his omission of a dynamic reflecting discourses that include the voices of the Other. Bhabha writes, "[a]n important feature of colonial discourse is its dependence on the concept of 'fixity' in the ideological construction of otherness" (Bhabha 94). Bhabha's theory of colonial discourse does not stop with a fixed view of the Other since he develops a theory of *ambivalence*; namely, that discourses about the colonized seek to fix the ideological image of the Other while at the same time the discourse seeks to confirm "the disorder, degeneracy and daemonic repetition" of the "other" (94).

While Said's Orientalism presents a way to see how literary discourses situated the Trilogy cases, the Cherokee resistance is not explained either by Said's Orientalism or by the dominant literary discourses characteristic of the early nineteenth century. In this sense, Bhabha in his *The Location of Culture* accepts Said's Orientalism as far as it might seek to depict the Other. Yet Bhabha also seeks to reveal a reality that Said does not capture in his *Orientalism*; namely, that oscillating struggle at the margins of conquest does not necessarily fix the ideological image of the conquered. There is a space within colonial discourses where the dominated Other refuses to be defined. While counter-discourses of the Other, or as Bhabha terms it *mimicry* and resistance, manifest themselves, they are not shared by the dominant literary discourse. Bhabha examines colonial discourse as:

> an apparatus that turns on the recognition and disavowal of racial/cultural/historical differences. Its predominant strategic function is the creation of a space for a 'subject peoples' through the production of knowledges . . . [T]he objective of colonial discourse is to construe the colonized as a population of degenerate types on the basis of racial origin, in order to justify conquest and to establish systems of administration and instruction.
>
> (100–101)

Said and Bhabha would agree that Orientalist discourses seek, at least from the dominant power's point of view, to construct images of the Other through the "production of knowledge." In making this point, Bhabha quotes Said in order to situate *his* own criticism of Said. Bhabha *In Location of Culture* quotes Said:

> Philosophically, then, the kind of language, thought, and vision that I have been calling orientalism very generally is a form of *radical realism*; anyone employing orientalism, which is the habit for dealing with the questions, objects, qualities and regions deemed Oriental, will designate, name, point to, fix, what he is talking or thinking about with a word or phrase, which then is considered either to have acquired, or more simply to be, reality . . . The tense they employ is the timeless eternal; they convey an impression of repetition and strength . . . For all these functions it is frequently enough to use the simple copula *is*.
> (101–2)

Here, Bhabha's use of *mimicry* presents a dynamic that relates to his idea of *ambivalence*. The sense of ambivalence experienced by the colonizer is a reflection of both the static "is" of the colonized and, simultaneously, the elusiveness of the colonized in their continued ability to mimic the institutional persona of the dominant power.[6] The coexistence of both the "is" and the evolving nature of the colonized present an unsettling *internal* ambivalence for the dominant power:

> Which is to say, that the discourse of mimicry is constructed around ambivalence; in order to be effective, mimicry must continually produce its slippage, its excess, its difference. The authority of that mode of colonial discourse that I have called mimicry is therefore stricken by indeterminacy: mimicry emerges as the representation of a difference that is itself a process of disavowal. Mimicry is thus the sign of a double articulation; a complex strategy of reform, regulation and discipline which 'appropriates' the other as it visualizes power. Mimicry is also the sign of the appropriate; however, a difference or recalcitrance which coheres the dominant strategic function of colonial power, intensifies surveillance, and poses as imminent threat to both 'normalized' knowledges and disciplinary powers.
> (122–3)

The underlying tenet in Bhabha's mimicry relies on the dominant power's ability to demand the replication of its traits by the colonized, *although* only *to a point*. There must remain a gap. There must remain an intrinsic and discernible difference between the colonizer and the colonized. A difference ensures that while there is mimicry of the dominant power's civilizing attributes, no affirmation of equality or parity between the colonizer and the colonized can be acknowledged by the dominant power. As Bhabha states "mimicry is at once resemblance and menace" (123). Bhabha's account attempts to explain how the dominant power actively encourages a civilizing endeavor; recruiting agents from the colonized realm to promote a civilizing mimicry, but simultaneously maintaining a difference between the dominant power and the conquered.

It is at the juncture between *resemblance* and *menace* that our subject extends beyond the Said and Bhabha theories through the Cherokee mimicry of American culture and politics in the early nineteenth century. As I argue here, the Cherokee resistance to land pressures, Jeffersonian acculturation policies, and Jacksonian removal policies, while certainly incorporating mimicry of the European-American religions, politics, law and governmental institutions as a strategy to thwart land encroachments and cultural dilution, used mimicry as *deception*. After 1816, they used a conscious strategy to preserve their cultural identity and independence by adopting many of the civilizing attributes of the dominant American culture. Bhabha's *mimicry* draws attention to the "sign of a double articulation," where the Cherokees chose to mimic American culture, literary discourses, religion or political institutions to obscure their disavowal of American culture. The Cherokee adopted parts of American culture by disguised acculturation.[7] The Cherokee objective was to present the appearance of a sovereign people who owned their land. Such ownership would be preserved by virtue of the mimicry of perfecting the civilizing tenets of American culture and politics. This analysis will show that while the Cherokee adopted mimicry to disguise their strategy to preserve their land, their adoption of the American-type political institutions and their Constitution of 1828 was not an embrace of that culture but a means to preserve their own identity and clan society.

Bhabha does not clarify whether or not the mimicry of the colonized is a strategy for self-preservation, but merely that it exists. Bhabha's recognition of mimicry by the Other denotes its existence within colonial discourse without explaining the inherent reason for the mimicry. The closest utility of Bhabha's theory in terms of helping to account for the nature of Cherokee resistance lies with Bhabha's use of Jacques Lacan's in 'The line and light,' *Of the Gaze*:

> Mimicry reveals something in so far as it is distinct from what might be called an itself that is behind. The effect of mimicry is camouflage . . . It is not a question of harmonizing with the background, but against a mottled background, of becoming mottled—exactly like the technique of camouflage practised in human warfare.
>
> (121)

Unlike Said's Orientalism which seeks to explain how literature, through the colonizer's institutional apparatus, can essentialise the colonized, Bhabha's mimicry highlights the unsettled interdependence between the dominant power and the conquered. Bhabha's mimicry describes a type of resistance by the colonized that pretends to mimic the dominant power. While Bhabha does not assign a reason for this mimicry, he does expose this type of resistance in various guises, ranging from jokes to *camouflage*. Bhabha feels a level of resistance is attained by virtue of mimicry. This is a crucial juncture because, while Bhabha does identify mimicry relating to ambivalence within the context of colonialism, his theory does not explain how mimicry can be used within the context of resistance other than to show how the colonized can use mimic practices, perhaps in the form of jokes or other replications of the dominant culture, to increase the sense of insecurity or ambivalence within the *colonizer's* mind. "The menace of mimicry is its double vision which in disclosing the ambivalence of colonial discourse also disrupts its authority" (126). In this sense, Bhabha's mimicry transcends Said's one-directional subject-object dominant discourse by incorporating a dynamic between the colonizer and colonized. Bhabha's theory, unlike Said's, seeks to account for and explain the internal tension and inherent contradictions in the mimicry–ambivalent relationship he identifies. It is this ambivalence which upsets Said's colonial discourse theory by dismantling the premise that colonial literature can define the reality of dominance of the colonized by virtue of textual discourses. Bhabha's theory of mimicry and ambivalence introduces a far more nuanced interdependence between the colonizers and colonized with each seeking to project their own identity both within and beyond their respective cultures. Bhabha elaborates upon this dynamic when he writes:

> It is from this area between mimicry and mockery, where the reforming, civilizing mission is threatened by the displacing gaze of its disciplinary double, that my instances of colonial imitation come. What they all share is a discursive process by which the excess or slippage produced by the ambivalence of mimicry (almost the same, but not quite) does not merely 'rupture' the discourse, but becomes transformed into an uncertainty which fixes the colonial subject as a 'partial' presence.
>
> (123)

Bhabha moves beyond Said's analysis of colonial discourse by identifying both a fixed and an ambivalent dynamic between the colonizer and the colonized; however, Bhabha's theory of mimicry does not help explain why mimicry, within the context of the Cherokee resistance, was used to both mimic European-American culture and preserve Cherokee culture through political machinations. While Bhabha's theory may shed light on the internal *psychological* dynamic between the colonizer and the colonized, this does not provide an explanation of the broader Cherokee resistance. Cherokee resistance was not built on individual mimicry, but on the illusion that the Cherokee were becoming civilized through a vigorous acceptance of the European-American culture. To the extent that the European-American culture felt any ambivalence, it was not because its relationship to the Cherokee as a superior power was threatened, but rather because of the unsettling realization that Bhabha's cultural gap between dominant culture and the Other was closing, that differences between the European-American and Cherokee culture were becoming less distinct. Bhabha identified mimicry from the perspective of the dominant power as encouraging the replication of the dominant culture by the Other. Even though the colonizer encouraged acculturation by the colonized, racially the colonizer could never accept cultural parity. Bhabha described this internal contradiction by the dominant culture: "colonial mimicry is the desire for a reformed, recognizable other, as a subject of a difference that is almost the same, but not quite" (122).

One of the limitations of Bhabha's theory is his focus on the colonial text to evidence mimicry and ambivalence to explain colonial discourses. Like Said, Bhabha uses examples of literature to apply his theory; however, as with Said, so too with Bhabha, using literature to apply a colonial theory leaves too much ambiguity between the imaginative and psychoanalytical and the nature of resistance that is integrated into action based not on notions of internal mimicry and mockery, but on strategic struggles to preserve a culture. Instead Bhabha relies on literature and individual psychology to advance his theory of colonial resistance.

Bhabha maps a genealogy of "mimic man" through other writers. He states "the line of descent of the mimic man can be traced through the works of Kipling, Forster, Orwell, Naipaul, and to his emergence, most recently, in Benedict Anderson's excellent work on nationalism, as the anomalous Bipin Chandera Pal" (125). What appears to be ironic is that Bhabha, in citing these writers as examples of "mimic man," also mocks them as "the parodist of history." On the one hand Bhabha criticizes literature written by "parodists," yet he uses such works as examples of mimicry (126). An example of Bhabha's use of literature to apply this mimicry, notwithstanding the preceding criticism of such texts, is Naipaul's novel *The Mimic Men:*

> I paid Mr. Shylock three guineas a week for a tall, multi-mirrored, book-shaped room with a coffin-like wardrobe. And for Mr. Shylock, the recipient each week of fifteen times three guineas, the possessor of a mistress and of suits made of cloth so fine I felt I could eat it, I had nothing but admiration. . . . I thought Mr. Shylock looked distinguished, like a lawyer or businessman or politician. He had the habit of stroking the fore of his ear inclining his head to listen. I thought the gesture was attractive; I copied it. I knew of recent events in Europe; they tormented me; and although I was trying to live on seven pounds a week I offered Mr. Shylock my fullest, silent compassion.
>
> (Naipaul 1–2)

Naipaul describes a lodger who is both a tenant and an admirer of the fine clothes worn by his landlord, Mr. Shylock. While the tenant acknowledges the financial dominance of Mr. Shylock in comparison to himself, he also judges his landlord's lifestyle "the possessor of a mistress." Immoral perhaps, but the renter still seeks to copy Mr. Shylock's many attributes. While the lodger may not have any personal admiration for his landlord's personal lifestyles beyond fine suits, the reference to "recent events in Europe" alluding perhaps to the European holocaust, prompts the renter to offer "Mr. Shylock my fullest, silent compassion" (2). On the surface, the illusion of replication may be there, but the inner resistance, in part, is tempered by the renter's sympathy for the tragic events in Europe that plagued Mr. Shylock's people. The critical point is that Bhabha's theories of *mimicry* and *menace* are formulated on a fictional and textual basis. While transcending Said's Orientalism beyond the domination of the colonial Other through literature, Bhabha develops a theoretical space to humanize the one-dimensional colonial discourse by representing the counter-discourses of the colonized.

In using narratives written by authors such as Naipaul to reveal how mimicry operates, Bhabha seeks to create a theoretical space for his discursive and psychoanalytical analysis on the basis of text—text that is fictional in explaining how mimicry operates within the mind of the colonial subject. In comparison, the ambivalence of the dominant colonizer results from what Bhabha terms as *hybridist.* Hybridity extends beyond the cross-cultural mixing of the colonized with the dominant culture; it is more than mixing dominant and colonized cultures; I argue that hybridity produces *menace* rather than resemblance:

> What is left, according to Bhabha, is the trace, the impure, the artificial, the second-hand. Bhabha analyzes the slippages in colonial political discourse, and reveals that the Janus-faced attitudes towards the colonized lead to the production of a mimicry that presents itself more in the form of a "menace" than "resemblance"; more in the form of a rupture than consolidation.
>
> (Beya)

Bhabha's focus on mimicry as a reflection of hybridity produces a menace, an ambivalence within the dominant colonial culture:

> In mimicry, the representation of identity and meaning is rearticulated along the axis of metonymy. As Lacan reminds us, mimicry is like camouflage, not a harmonization of repression of difference, but *a form of resemblance* [my emphasis], that differs from or defends presence by displaying it in part, metonymically. Its threat, I would add, comes from the prodigious and strategic production of conflictual, fantastic, discriminatory 'identity effects' in the play of a power that is elusive because it hides no essence, no 'itself.'
>
> (Bhabha 128–9)

Bhabha implies that mimicry by its very presence, by its very "play of power" itself is sufficient to establish a "menace" to make the colonizer ambivalent. The limitations of Bhabha's theory emerge within our study of Cherokee resistance. This research is concerned with the "menace" felt by the American Government in relation to the Cherokee resistance.

In seeking to explain the interdependence between the colonizer and colonized, it is not enough to psychoanalyze the structure and source of the "menace" felt by the dominant power. Unlike a psychoanalytical examination, the Cherokee resistance was a *collective* reaction, a meta-cultural resistance of varied clans within the Cherokee Nation to the pressures of European-American conquest. American conquest was exemplified by the land pressures from the agents of the American Government and by the collective breach of Cherokee land boundaries by American frontiersmen, prospectors and the State of Georgia. Stated otherwise, the internal psychological and cultural dynamic between the dominant power and the colonized does not provide a theoretical framework to explain the collective Cherokee resistance to the conquest forged by the American Government. The political and economic pressures that shaped the Cherokee resistance extend beyond the literary and psychoanalytical Orientalism of both Said and Bhabha.

The nature of Cherokee resistance

Bhabha's *ambivalence* and *mimicry* only partially help to explain the Cherokee resistance to the land pressures imposed by the white frontiersman and the American Government in the late eighteenth and early nineteenth centuries. The Cherokee resistance exemplified the hybridity Bhabha identified in the greater colonial resistance. For example the Cherokee replicated elements of Euro-American culture and political institutions by permitting Christian missionaries onto their land to establish schools; by establishing political general councils to represent the seven Cherokee clans in their negotiations with Federal agents; by establishing a Cherokee alphabet and Cherokee newspaper, *The Cherokee Phoenix*; by establishing the Cherokee Constitution in 1828 and by developing a Cherokee Supreme Court that established criminal jurisdiction over non-Cherokee on Cherokee lands. While such acculturation by the Cherokee seemed to evidence the "civilizing" attributes of the Cherokee people, European Americans could not acknowledge cultural, political, or national parity. By contrast, some Americans did openly acknowledge the cultural parity of the Cherokee in relation to European-American culture. Sam Houston, for example, said of Major Ridge and his son: "these Indians are not inferior to white men. John Ridge was not inferior in point of genius to John Randolph" (Wright 214). Yet while men like Sam Houston acknowledged the cultural and intellectual parity between Cherokee and European-American cultures, those in power projected a fiercely ambivalent and overtly hostile attitude toward any notion of parity between the European-American and Cherokee cultures. American war hero and President Andrew Jackson remarked that the Cherokee "have neither the intelligence, the industry, the moral habits, nor the desire of improvement . . . Established in the midst of another and superior race . . . they must necessarily yield . . . and ere long disappear" (214). One can well appreciate how power relations, typified by Jackson's quote and in the Foucauldian sense, ensured that discourses were permitted into the American Indian *archive* would also be steadfast in their exclusion of any civilized discourses of the American Indian as expressed by Sam Houston.

The denial of civilizing equivalence of the Native Indian by the European-American culture was derived from several sources. For Jefferson, cultural equivalence would undermine his objective of pressuring the Indians into moving west of the Mississippi. For Chief Justice John Marshall, cultural equivalence would contradict the premise that Indians could never attain the *legal capacity* to own their land. Jackson felt that the Indians could not attain the civilized attributes of the dominant European-American culture to a degree that would enable them to retain their land. Speaking to the Cherokee in 1835 Andrew Jackson wrote:

> Circumstances that cannot be controlled, and which are beyond the reach of human laws, render it impossible that you can flourish in the midst of a civilized community . . . You have but one remedy within your reach. And that is, to remove to the west.
>
> (Jackson, *Andrew Jackson to the Cherokee Tribe* 1835)

For several reasons, the Cherokee could not attain full civilized replication since the *menace* of *resemblance* haunted the dominant American powers, in particular, the State of Georgia.

Whether depicted by Thomas Jefferson in his Indian acculturation policy, by John Marshall in his profuse denial of cultural and constitutional equality in relation to the civilized European-American race, or by Andrew Jackson in his Indian removal policy of the 1830s, collectively these *ambivalent* reactions toward the Cherokee resistance suggested that American power would not acknowledge Indians as being sufficiently civilized to retain their own lands. While Bhabha may interpret Cherokee mimicry as a location of resistance, for the Cherokee it was also a practical necessity to replicate European-American notions of land ownership by attaining attributes and practices of the dominant culture. Cherokee resistance camouflaged the acceptance of acculturation, that is, replicating the attributes of American civilization where such acculturation was an essential component for promoting their own sovereignty, and by extension their land boundaries, with the American Government or with states such as Georgia. Bhabha identifies an inherent contradiction within the civilizing process—seeking to replicate the dominant power's culture. Loomba writes "thus there is a fundamental contradiction at the heart of the attempt to educate, 'civilize' or co-opt the colonial 'other'" (Loomba 79). This contradiction can be exemplified within the Cherokee context through our analysis of how Jackson and the State of Georgia repudiated the acculturation efforts of the Cherokee. "The ideals the Cherokee had adopted with such fervor were no longer held by those in charge. Emboldened by this, Georgia declared the Cherokee Nation's existence null and void" (Wright 218). The nature of Cherokee resistance cannot be fully explained within the boundaries of Bhabha's *mimicry*.

Loci of Cherokee resistance

While the nature of Cherokee resistance was driven by conflicts and pressures over their land, it was their *mimicry* of the dominant European-American culture that exemplified their different resistance locations. Said's Orientalism may be perceived as too limited to explain the nature of the Cherokee resistance since his theory seeks to identify literature as the mode of discourse to represent the knowledge and power relations between the colonizer and the colonized (Loomba 83). Ania Loomba elaborates by interpreting Said's *Orientalism* as both a text and a discourse where both can be employed by colonial institutions, such as education, to represent the colonized in ways that created their reality from within the colonized realm. Literature and history foreground the need to connect "the local to the global." Said refers to this as a "contraption" whereby the very text, not the author, take on a meaning beyond the author. Loomba's point is that we can utilize Said's Orientalism to contextualize discourse and thus gain a better understanding of the nature of both colonizer and colonized. Loomba writes, "in any colonial context, economic plunder, the production of knowledge and strategies of representation depended heavily upon one another" (85). When examining Cherokee resistance, it is not enough to base our analysis on the literary discourses we have surveyed throughout this research. We must also understand Cherokee resistance within the context of the political pressures of the early nineteenth century. By understanding the political context which led to Cherokee resistance, we can begin to appreciate the nature of their resistance. Understanding the nature of resistance can help to explain why the Trilogy cases excluded discourses that evidenced a resistance by *mimicry* rather than by physical violence.

The Trilogy cases present a dominant discourse of the American Indian. In order to repudiate the Trilogy depiction of the Indian one has to evaluate Cherokee resistance not as a reaction to discourse, but as a reaction to the practical issues related to their land. While the dominant European-American protagonists, from the State of Georgia to President Jackson, sought to shield their ambivalence towards the Native Americans, the *mimicry* by the Cherokee was a conscientious strategy to resist land pressures and preserve their cultural identity and national sovereignty under pressure from European-American land acquisition. The placement of the literary discourses was centered by the dominant European-American culture both before and after the American Revolution. To the extent that one seeks to situate a discursive context for the Trilogy cases, our research has identified both textual and visual sources of this discourse. To measure the impact of these dominant American discourses as they relate to the Native Americans we can utilize Bhabha's theories of *ambivalence* and *mimicry* not as a psychological dynamic, but as a reflection of the broader political and cultural Cherokee resistance. Cherokee resistance presented a counter-discourse to the narratives of the American Indian culture and sovereignty articulated by the Trilogy cases.

Political replication as resistance

Bhabha's *mimicry* appears to explain why the Cherokees adopted political institutions and a constitution to replicate the political machinery of the American Government; however, this is only one dimension of what the Cherokee were seeking to accomplish. The Cherokee were also interested in the preservation of their land and culture. It has been explained throughout this book that part of the civilizing process was the Cherokee desire to mimic American institutions because such an imitation would help to produce the appearance of the advanced and civilized state of the Cherokee Nation to European Americans. If the Cherokee were deemed civilized, either because they formed a National General Council or a written constitution, such civilizing features would advance their credibility insofar as they could claim ownership of their own land. From the dominant American viewpoint, being *civilized* was a necessary condition to establish the legal capacity to own property. Cherokee *mimicry* sought to counter the dominant discourse that portrayed Indians as savages and heathens. Such depictions by the dominant European-American discourses are what untethered Indians from ownership rights to their land. To counter the dominant discourse, the Cherokee formed a National General Council and developed a written constitution; this was institution building designed to evidence the positive civilizing effects of American culture.

While the Cherokee were seeking to convince the Americans that they were civilized, there also remained a concurrent and competing cultural universe inside Cherokee jurisprudence—the *retention* of the clan-based system of Cherokee law and justice.[8] Led by John Ross, the Cherokee adopted a duel strategy of resistance; they built an Americanized version of their political structures while retaining the decentralized clan-based system.

Theda Perdue, for example, writes about a woman named Chickaw, a black slave given to the family of a murdered woman by her murderer and white husband shortly after the beginnings of the American Revolution as a way to compensate the family. He offered Chickaw to avoid clan vengeance against himself. Cherokees maintained a system of clan justice, especially where based on the decisions of a matriarchal system. Cherokee society would consider vengeance as justice against a murderer, unless he offered an equivalent form of compensation. In this instance, Chickaw was offered by the husband to the slain wife's Cherokee family not only to replace the murdered woman, but to avoid what he knew would be an act of retaliation against himself. In short, clan justice operated within the Cherokee Nation in the late eighteenth century. By 1833 Chickaw, was accepted into the Cherokee clan in exchange for the slain wife's husband. While Chickaw bore children over the subsequent decades and was integrated as a free person within the Cherokee clan, she found herself a target of disputed slave title by a white Cherokee. To settle the claim and to protect her freedom the Cherokee clan that had adopted her appealed to the new Cherokee Court to deny any ownership claim against Chickaw. The Court sided with the clan and thus revealed the retention of traditional clan law while simultaneously moving to produce a new legal institution. In this context Bhabha's theory of *mimicry* to explain Cherokee resistance indicates that Cherokee resistance was not only designed to replicate American institutions, but to also retained traditional Cherokee clan institutions:

> The experience of Chickaw and Isaac demonstrates that Cherokees not only recognized the importance of clans and matrilineal kin ties but they also used political innovations to confirm traditional social relations and values. The decision, along with other evidence, suggests that two legal systems operated simultaneously in the early Cherokee republic. The ready availability of sources for the newer system of written constitutions and laws, redefined citizenship, and differentiated authority may lead us to ignore that other system that extends back into an ancient Cherokee past. Scholars must remember that the surviving record does not always correlate precisely to the human past, and they must be ever alert to opportunities to redress imbalances. Unless we are vigilant, stories like that of the slave girl Molly who became the Cherokee woman Chickaw will be lost because they run counter to the preponderance of evidence. Even more seriously, we will miss the opportunity to challenge the master narrative that Cherokee society abandoned its own values and institutions for those of Anglo-Americans. By constructing alternative narratives, we begin to make amends for the removal of Cherokees from their own history.
>
> (Perdue, *The Cherokee Nation and the Trail of Tears* 568)

Perdue's discovery is critical to assessing whether the premise of Bhabha's *mimicry* is consistent with the nature of Cherokee resistance; namely, that resistance is reflected in many ways by *mimicry*. Although the Cherokee sought to replicate elements of the American institutions to appear more civilized in order to strengthen their legal and political sovereignty with respect to their land, they maintained two systems of law: one based on Cherokee clan justice and the other on the new Cherokee constitution based on institutions similar to the prevalent European-American culture. One must avoid the mistake of perceiving Cherokee replication of American political and legal institutions as encompassing the full spectrum of Cherokee resistance. On the contrary, the amalgamation of the clans into a General Council was a strategy to unify the Cherokee Nation—a strategy outside the purview of the *mimicry* Bhabha would assign to their resistance:

> To the extent that Cherokee nationalism required new legal and political procedures, it constituted an acceleration of acculturation (or biculturalism) traceable in the Cherokees' developing adoption and adaptation of American political and economic practices; but to the extent that it protected geographical integrity, participatory self-government, and the ethic of consensus, it also preserved basic aspects of Cherokee values, beliefs, and practice.
>
> (McLoughlin 550)

Rather than viewing Cherokee resistance through the lens of Bhabha's *mimicry*, whereby the colonialized seek to project the replication of the dominant culture, albeit with a Janus-faced mockery, it is relevant to consider the political cultural context. Cherokee resistance was also a strategy to unify and strengthen their *collective* political and cultural system, that is the Cherokee General National Council and the clan system. Cherokee resistance was not only a fight against acculturation; resistance further altered their sense of political organization as a reaction to the threats upon their land by the State of Georgia. Institution building in this sense was not merely a plan to replicate American culture. Editor Elias Boudinot of *The Cherokee Phoenix*, rather than embracing Cherokee strategy as evidence of resistance, sought to project tribal unification as a form of flattery of the Euro-American culture. Here the similarity to Bhabha's mimicry ends as Boudinot's projected Cherokee resistance is evidence of acculturation by the Cherokee *absent* the Janus-faced mimicry. Boudinot distorts the Cherokee history of resistance. Jefferson's land pressures of the early nineteenth century (1806–1809) and legislative attempts to usurp Cherokee sovereignty by the State of Georgia after 1828 helped to solidify Cherokee nationalism. Cherokee *nationalism* outside the context of colonialism, rather than *mimicry*, explains the nature of Cherokee resistance beyond Bhabha's colonial-centered theory.

Judicial resistance

The Cherokees, once all hope of protecting their land against advances by the State of Georgia was lost in Congress with the passage of the 1830 Indian Removal Act, felt compelled to file an appeal with the U.S. Supreme Court against the State of Georgia in the case of *Cherokee Nation v. Georgia.* Simply filing a Supreme Court appeal was a remarkable achievement for an *uncivilized* tribe. How could such "hapless" wards of the state, "savages" who could not farm according to the European-American way, have any inkling of American jurisprudence? This remarkable litany of achievement is the Cherokee judicial resistance.

By 1828, the Cherokee Nation had adopted a written constitution, set up schools and sought to embrace the type of political institutions promoted by the Federal Government of the United States. In particular, the Cherokee permitted the building of several American religious missionary schools on their land.[9] While the emergence of missionary schools on Cherokee land appeared to confirm that the American Government's attempts to civilize the Cherokee were working, beneath this *mimicry* lay a political strategy that feigned the acceptance of American institutions and Christianity based on the practicalities of the Cherokees' strategy to retain their lands. This strategy was paramount in protecting the Cherokees' existence and the survival of their culture. Given the military superiority of the Americans after the War of 1812, the Cherokee leaders embraced the incorporation of American institutions as their most realistic opportunity of retaining ownership of their land. The elements of this realization necessitated that the Cherokee superficially undermined matriarchy, and changed the way their agricultural practices differed from those of European Americans (women were to avoid farm work and instead men were to devote more time to the field and less to hunting). Women and children were expected to embrace Christianity and, to this end, various relationships were developed with several of the U.S. Government's supported missionaries who lived and proselytized among the Cherokee.[10] Additionally, the adoption of *laws* rather than clan revenge was to become the hallmark of the kind of justice Cherokees would need in order to promote the appearance of acculturation in the eyes of the American missionaries and commissioners. Some of the "good advice" received by the Cherokees is worth quoting at length in order to demonstrate the scope of cultural change pressured by the United States:

> To achieve this model of civilization, presidents, federal agents, and federally subsidized missionaries ceaselessly recommended that the Cherokee abandon clan revenge for written law enforced by elected public authorities, paying particular attention to laws governing the descent of property. They recommended that the Cherokee allot their

> lands-held-in-common to individual, male family heads; that men rather than women take major responsibility for farming; that these potential patriarchs use the plow and fence their fields. Women should abandon agriculture in favor of the wheel and the loom, so that their husbands need not hunt an ever-diminishing supply of game to trade for civilized clothing. Children, meanwhile, should be at school, learning to spin and weave, if female; or plow and reap, if male. Both sexes should discover how to count their money and read understandingly in the New Testament. Thus might sloth give way to industry; and magic, superstition, heathen dance, and conjuring, to reason, reflection, and revealed religion. Thus might American natives become model Americans.
>
> (Young 504)

The Cherokee Nation had to balance appeasing the American Government while looking for ways to protect their lands and culture. The Cherokee decision to appeal to the U.S. Supreme Court was in part a strategy to use the American law and its legal system to protect Cherokee land. *Cherokee Nation v. Georgia* is an example of how Bhabha's *mimicry* appears to provide an explanation of how the Cherokees were seeking to replicate the dominant culture while using its institutions, perhaps mockingly, to undermine the land pressures by the State of Georgia. Bhabha's theory of resistance within colonial discourse in *The Location of Culture* does not explain the nature of Cherokee resistance. Bhabha's theory of *mimicry* seeks to accent the mockery side of resistance, in particular, the use of jokes to humiliate the colonizer. Bhabha's *mimicry* does not account for another kind of resistance that is organized as a national strategy for survival. Unlike Bhabha's *mimicry*, the Cherokee resistance was not based on psychoanalytical reasons, but stems from a wider political and cultural decision to preserve Cherokee clan culture. The latter helps to account for the nature of Cherokee resistance. Bhabha's theory of *mimicry*, while useful in pinpointing resistance within colonial relations, stops short of being able to account for the precise nature of Cherokee resistance. In the Cherokee experience, their *mimicry* was a strategic calculus to protect the Cherokee Nation in the face of aggression by the State of Georgia over Cherokee lands.

The Cherokee Supreme Court

While the Cherokee litigation at the U.S. Supreme Court exemplified a more public display of their resistance, what was not appreciated until very recently was the jurisprudence of criminal law developed by the Cherokee Supreme Court (between 1823 and 1835). J. Matthew Martin, in his article *The Nature and Extent of the Exercise of Criminal Jurisdiction by the Cherokee Supreme Court 1823–1835*, reveals the little-known application of criminal jurisprudence over non-Indian U.S. citizens on Cherokee lands. Citing the

U.S. Supreme Court ruling in *Oliphant v. Suquamish Indian Tribe* (1978), Martin shows how the court held that the Cherokee Nation did not have jurisdiction over non-Indian U.S. citizens based on treaties with the Indian nations and the United States. As Martin notes "the Supreme Court has also determined that Tribal Courts may not attach criminal jurisdiction over non-Indian citizens of the United States" (Martin 31). Notwithstanding the court's ruling in *Oliphant,* Martin highlights Cherokee Criminal court reports and proceedings that clearly evidenced personal jurisdiction over non-Indian U.S. citizens during the period 1823 through 1835. Incorporating *Cherokee Nation*'s ruling where it described the Cherokee as a "dependent nation," Marshall predicated Cherokee status on the "actual state of things" in his earlier ruling in *Johnson.* Martin posits that the Cherokee Supreme court did attach personal jurisdiction over non-Indians in criminal cases.

> Perhaps the exercise of criminal jurisdiction by some Tribes might be inconsistent with their dependent status at this time. Nevertheless, the historical record suggests that the time has come for another look at *Oliphant,* at least in the light of Cherokee Tribal Court jurisdiction. (63)

Martin's point reveals how the counter-discourses citing Cherokee criminal jurisdiction over non-Indians were excluded by John Marshall in both *Johnson* and *Cherokee Nation* as they did not fit with his acceptance of discourses which depicted the Cherokee as "savages" and a "dependent nation."

Given the record of criminal jurisprudence by the Cherokee, the formation and application of criminal law demonstrates yet another mode of Cherokee resistance—the application of jurisprudence to demarcate Cherokee law and sovereignty whilst the Cherokee Nation was pressured politically, culturally and violently by states such as Georgia. Evidence of Cherokee criminal personal jurisdiction on one side might be viewed by Bhabha as *mimicry;* however, the aim to delineate Cherokee law and sovereignty was not a psychologically based resistance but a practical form of national resistance to unite Cherokee clans by the application of *Cherokee law* over non-Indians. The unity of nineteenth-century Cherokee law was itself a collective resistance because, prior to Georgia's encroachment on Cherokee land, individual clans retained their own decentralized form of justice. Collective resistance is a type of resistance that Bhabha's theory does not account for.

American ambivalence to Cherokee resistance

I argue that Cherokee resistance obscured a strategy to retain their land and culture, all the while replicating many European-American political institutions. The *ambivalence* and *anxiety* felt by some of the major American actors in shaping Indian policy help to assess how the Cherokee resistance was viewed by the dominant leaders, from President Jefferson to President Jackson. Bhabha's theory of *ambivalence* helps us to appreciate the various reactions by American officials to Cherokee resistance.

Jefferson's quest for Indian land

President Jefferson's anxiety about American Indians surfaced because they embraced a form of non-violent resistance, which was of the kind Jefferson himself asked of the Indians. Jefferson's personal relations with the Indian delegations were structured around negotiation rather than conflict. While Jefferson sought to encourage Indians to farm, learn the ways of the white man, educate their people and embrace the inevitable European-American encroachment, the Jeffersonian reality was quite the opposite of his private consultations with Indian delegations:

> To this end he placed his famous plan before one delegation after another: They should give up the chase, dispose of lands needed only for hunting, become tawny yeomen farmers, and intermix with the white population. Since they were "now reduced within limit too narrow for the hunter's state," as he said in this second inaugural address, 'humanity enjoins us to teach them agriculture and the domestic art (March 4, 1805).'
>
> (Drinnon 83)

Jefferson's humane concern for the Indian amalgamation into European-American culture was a pronouncement intended for public consumption. His real effort to incorporate the American Indians was not built on humanity, but on the economic practicalities of overcoming any resistance they might offer. In a letter to Benjamin Hawks (1803) Jefferson wrote "incorporating themselves [the Indians] with us as citizens of the U.S., this is what the natural progress of things will bring on, and it will be better to promote than to retard it" (Conser 202). Jefferson did not expound upon his meaning of "natural progress," but it appears to have been based on the critical assumption underlying his policy of promoting Indian assimilation.[11] If the Indians resisted the "natural progress" destined for them by Jefferson, they would be seen as a threat and would be removed by American officials from their land. The relevance of this analysis is not to highlight Jefferson's true intentions with respect to Indian removal or assimilation, but to highlight his *anxiety* towards Indian resistance. Jefferson's anxiety was exemplified by his need to project a humane approach in order to reveal the ambivalence of American officials in their dealings with the Indians. Past violent resistance by the Indians, coupled with post-Revolutionary war treaties with the American Government, reminded Jefferson that the Indians were not going to abandon their lands without opposition. What better way to prepare the American mind for the ultimate appropriation of Indian land, whether by blood or treaty, than to cast the relationship between the American Government and Indians as preordained by *natural progress*. Incorporating a public theme of benevolence toward the Indians under the guise of natural progress helped to camouflage the American Government's dealings with the Native Indians. This sanctification was created by the *ambivalence* cited by Bhabha, when the dominant power tries simultaneously both to fix the image of the Other and to engage the "disorder" of the Other. This *ambivalence* is where Bhabha's theory of *anxiety* is formed. The *anxiety* felt by the dominant power not only relates to the disorder of the Other but also highlights the colonizer's insecurity by virtue of rationalizing racial superiority relative to the colonized Other.

Some Indians followed Jefferson's advice, making it necessary for him to adopt a covert discourse with Congress and U.S. Indian Commissioners to pursue policies that would dilute Indian populations, undermine their culture and encourage easy trading credit. For example, Jefferson promoted easy credit terms to Indians. By offering easy credit Jefferson knew Indians would accumulate debt that could not be paid back in the normal course of trading, unless Indians exchanged their land to pay off their debts:

> In early 1805, while he (Jefferson) proposed incorporation in his inaugural on March 4, he suggested removal to a Chickasaw delegation on March 7: "We have lately obtained from the French and Spaniards all the country beyond the Mississippi called Louisiana, in which there is a great deal of land unoccupied by any red men. But it is very very far off, and we would prefer giving you lands there, or money and goods, as you like best, for such parts of your land on this side of the Mississippi as you are disposed to part with."
>
> (Drinnon 83–4)

Jefferson attempts to exhibit an equitable approach with the Chickasaw delegation for their land. His offer seeks to buy land from Indians so they would relocate west to Louisiana.[12] Jefferson's offer was disingenuous and the official government policy of establishing additional trading posts near Indian lands to encourage further trade, dependence and debt upon Indians fulfilled his wishes. The true aim of Jefferson's official Federal Indian policy was the acquisition of Indian land using liberal credit through trading posts and debt as a tactical tool to disguise the Government's real intent with respect to *dispossessing* Indians from their land:

> In his message of January 18, 1802, he (*Jefferson*) expressed his opinion that trading posts should be multiplied and used as a means of keeping the Indians quiet. The growth of the trade would lead them

> to agriculture so that they would not need so much land. In private, Jefferson urged the plan of encouraging the Indians to incur debts which they would be forced to get rid of by land cessions. To this end he was prompt in establishing more trading posts.
>
> (Cotterill 342)

Jefferson's duplicitous policy toward the Indians can also be understood by reference to Bhabha's theory of *anxiety;* Jefferson sought to fix the image of the dispossessed Indians as the inevitable result of American westward expansion across America. Jefferson was also anxious that tribes, such as the Cherokee, were establishing institutions and forms of government in a manner that directly challenged the image of the helpless Indian.

American Indian resistance was complex and was epitomized by violent opposition, with the exception of such tribes as the Cherokee and Chickasaw. The mimicry described here is the one observed from a distinctly American point of view. It is strange then that the act of cooperating with Jefferson's initiative and following the ways of the European American would in itself become a form a resistance for the Cherokee. Walter H. Conser, Jr. writes

> few have noticed that, unlike the opposition of the Creeks and Seminoles, the resistance to removal by the Cherokees was nonviolent. Similar to traditional religious nonviolence, yet amenable to questions of efficacy as well, the Cherokee resistance campaign belongs to that unique type of struggle called nonviolent action.
>
> (Conser 191)

Conser notes the non-violent opposition of the Cherokee. I would extend Conser's observation to that of a nuanced resistance, thereby projecting not only a unique type of resistance not only for the early nineteenth century but one that has an interesting parallel with the Natick Indians and the Massachusetts Bay Colony in the early seventeenth century. Like the Cherokee, the Natick were under intense land pressure by English settlers. As more and more English settlers arrived and settled Natick, as well as neighboring towns such as Nedham, the local Indian populations quickly adopted to the English method of land ownership to protect what little land they could defend from encroachment. In addition to assuming the use of English land ownership titles, the Natick also positioned themselves to serve as the praying Indians to portray themselves as capable of finding religious salvation in accord with English Calvinism. Jean O'Brien's book *Dispossession by Degrees* suggests some interesting parallels with the Natick Indians:

> Over the course of 140 years, Natick Indians had continually redefined their vision of the future in creatively resisting erasure by the English colonial order. Recognizing their precarious position

> after the permanent arrival of the English, they considered English Calvinism in order to secure some of their lands within the imposed English system that dictated procedures with regard to the legal tenure of land. They used their connection to the English religion as well as their military alliance with the English during King Philip's War to make claims for special treatment within the colonial relationship. When rapid proliferation of English colonists undermined Indian economies, they selectively adopted and shaped English ways, and when they struggled demographically, they intermarried with African Americans, which sustained their numbers.
>
> (O'Brien 213)

Strategic non-violent resistance by American Indians did not start with the Cherokee; O'Brien's research reveals as much regarding the Natick response to the English settlers in New England.

The Cherokee adoption of European-American religion, for example, was recognized as a form of resistance by European Americans because the American frontiersman and the American Government never intended to cooperate. The American Government never intended to share the land with the Indians and, as such, the Americans viewed actual replication of their society by the Cherokee as an obstruction. John Ross and the other delegates representing the Cherokee people traveled in the winter of 1816 to Washington, D.C. to protest against their harsh treatment by General Andrew Jackson over the Treaty of Fort Jackson at the close of the Creek War. Upon meeting with U.S. Secretary of War Crawford, the delegation was able to attract just compensation from the U.S. Government with the Treaty of Washington, where new boundary lines were established together with a payment of $2,500 for damages incurred during the Creek War upon the Cherokees. General Jackson, one of the U.S. agents negotiating the end of the Creek War, was not amused by the Cherokees' actions and he was by no means alone. The notion of Indians becoming civilized caused great concern among land speculators and American politicians:

> The fact that the Indians were becoming civilized and showed evidence of the ability to develop into good American citizens, thereby adding strength to the whole American nation, did not appeal to politicians who coveted Indian lands. In truth this class of men opposed any policy for civilizing the Indians, since it would tend to attach them more firmly to the soil. And to many a white man just over the border the Indian country was the promised land of wealth and plenty which he hoped some day to possess. If the delegates returned home with the belief that their territorial boundaries were permanently fixed they were soon undeceived.
>
> (Eaton 28)

In order to rationalize the dispossession of Indians as if it were in the best interests of those tribes, the Americans had to project a benevolent and humane attitude toward the Indian tribes. Treaties between the American Government and Cherokees, for example, were nothing more than public relations manoeuvres to avoid direct confrontation and bloodshed. The Federal Government knew full well that frontiersmen had settled on Cherokee land while the treaties were being signed. Any peace pipe shared between American negotiators and Indian chiefs were in reality a strategy to turn agreements and accommodations into opportunities for the American Government to dispossess Indians from their land one treaty at a time: the policy to remove the Indians from their land had a long presence in American history:

> Between 1721 and 1819, over 90 percent of our traditional territories had been ceded over to the settlers. Thomas Jefferson knew he wanted to create a new Indian Territory within the new Louisiana Purchase, and planned to move them there. Jefferson warned John Adams in a letter that despite the progress of some Indian nations, such as the Cherokee, to adopt representative government, many Native Americans "will relapse into barbarism and misery, lose numbers by war and want, and we shall be obliged to drive them with the beasts of the forest into the Stoney mountains."
>
> (Kingfisher 208)

While Jefferson encouraged Indians to adopt forms of representative government, to his surprise and that of government officials, tribes like the Cherokee moved to adopt such institutions. Viewed from an American perspective, the Indian adoption of representative government created the *anxiety* that Bhabha describes. Such *anxiety*, whereby Indian tribes sought to adopt the institutions that Jefferson encouraged, fostered the need for sham treaties to manipulate tribes like the Cherokee to cede land before they adopted the political institutions Jefferson promoted. Treaties with the Cherokee and other tribes were a sham because the American Government knew that it could not prevent frontiersman from encroaching upon Indian land. Treaties would only serve to provide the appearance of protection of Indians lands by the American Government. According to Ronald N. Satz:

> As the demand for Indian lands grew, American officials increasingly resorted to bribery, deception, economic coercion, threats, and sometimes brute force to secure Indian signatures on land cession treaties. The treaty-making process served as a convenient means of sanctioning federal land grabs under the guise of diplomacy.
>
> (Prucha, *American Indian Treaties: The History of a Political Anomaly* 10)[13]

It was to be just a matter of time before new treaties would be signed by Indians ceding yet more land in the false hope that further incursions by frontiersman would be contained by the American Government.

John Marshall's anxiety in legal discourse

Fifteen years after President Jefferson's 1805 inaugural address, John Marshall would echo his discursive refrain of "humanity" in the *Johnson* opinion. While *Johnson* sought to establish a humane legal doctrine with respect to "conquest," what was missing from it is not a legal doctrine to justify the conquest and amalgamation of American Indians, but any express hint of the *anxiety* that Bhabha speaks of in the struggle between the colonizer and the colonized. This did not mean that Marshall felt no anxiety toward Indian resistance, for surely Jefferson's duplicitous dealings with Indian tribes were a testament to the internal struggle felt by American officials in retaining their sense of domination in the process of eradicating the Indians from their land. Was John Marshall naive enough to think that history and his legal Doctrine of Conquest could only justify conquest through discovery? *Johnson* was a case that dealt with issues of land purchases between Indians and pre-Revolutionary purchases of land. In establishing a legal theory of property ownership, Marshall also attempted to develop an American jurisprudential theory of land title based upon a legal fiction whose roots extended to the European Doctrine of Discovery. The European Doctrine of Discovery was founded on religious bias and Christianity—hardly a doctrine that would accede to incorporating Indians.[14] In the *Johnson* opinion, cited below, Marshall's rhetoric speaks about a humane theme not to embrace the American Indian but to help justify a legal doctrine of how conquest *should* operate in relation to the Indian. Marshall's opinion in *Johnson* attempted to justify a legal doctrine of conquest by associating such a doctrine with a theme of benevolent charity toward a conquered race. The role of benevolent charity implicitly denies any resistance by the Indians; hence, it provides a rationale for conquest within the American mind. Marshall's view of history was grounded on the notions of historical inevitability and religious bias:

> Humanity, however, acting on public opinion, has established, as a general rule, that the conquered shall not be wantonly oppressed, and that their condition shall remain as eligible as is compatible with the objects of the conquest. Most usually, they are incorporated with the victorious nation, and become subjects or citizens of the government with which they are connected. The new and old members of the society mingle with each other; the distinction between them is gradually lost, and they make one people. Where this incorporation is practicable, humanity demands, and a wise policy requires, that the rights of the conquered

> to property should remain unimpaired; that the new subjects should be governed as equitably as the old, and that confidence in their security should gradually banish the painful sense of being separated from their ancient connexions, and united by force to strangers.
>
> (*Johnson v. M'Intosh* 589)

It is inconceivable that Marshall was ignorant of the land seizures and illegal appropriations of Indian territory prior to *Johnson.* Treaties between the Cherokees and American Government for example had to be renegotiated anew numerous times in order to account for the constant border infringements by white frontier settlers whom the American Government was either unable or unwilling to remove from Cherokee land. [15] Marshall would also have been well aware of the countless broken treaties between the American Government and various Indian Nations from the 1790s until *Johnson.* Marshall completely omits to cite these inhumane and illegal practices by the American governmental negotiators and frontier settlers. This research argues that Marshall glossed over the sordid history of Indian treaties on Indian land because *Johnson* was also an attempt to establish a legal facade for the conquest of Indian lands. In *Johnson, anxiety* could not be acknowledged by Marshall. The humane theme in the court's ruling exemplifies a *silent* anxiety that Marshall felt jurisprudentially, given the court's omission to cite the human cost incurred by the Indians in their treaty dealings with the British and the United States.

Jackson's humane theme

To appreciate the importance of the humane theme as to the dispossession of Indian land, one needs to understand the literary genealogy from Jefferson to Marshall to Andrew Jackson. Jackson, in particular, used the humane theme to justify his Indian removal policy. Before quoting Jackson it is important to recall that the themes of charity and melancholy used to situate the Indians were examples of Jefferson's and Marshall's *anxiety*; that is, while attempting to "fix" the image of the Other, the dominant power experiences a sense of insecurity concerning its own identity. Situated within this theoretical construct, the humane theme adopted by Jackson had two objectives: to lay down a rationale within the American mind justifying forced removal of the Native Americans and to reinforce the benevolent image of the American Government. That latter objective in particular is relevant because Bhabha's *anxiety* demonstrates Jackson's attempt to reshape and further ground European-American identity in relation to the American Indian. Jackson's humane theme could not be sustained without the existence of the Indian—the two are intrinsically and symbolically connected. Walter H. Conser, Jr. notes from Jackson's second annual message. "'Toward the aborigines of the country . . . no one can indulge a more friendly feeling than myself.' Yet in the end '[t]he waves of population and civilization are rolling to the westward' and from this conjunction of inevitability and expectation, paternalism and resolve, Jackson fashioned his policy of Indian removal" (Conser 194).

Our examination of the Cherokee tribe analyzed the nature and extent of their resistance to the pressures inflicted upon them by the U.S. Federal Government and the State of Georgia. What has been overlooked in the post-*Worcester* literature is the fact that the Cherokee, by virtue of taking their case to the Supreme Court in *Cherokee Nation*, exemplified resistance in jurisprudential terms. Cherokee resistance undermined the basis of the literary discourses that preceded *Johnson* regarding Native Americans. I have argued that, despite the literary discourses that framed much of the Marshall opinions about Indians and despite Marshall's legal history, conventional interpretations of the Trilogy cases have failed to acknowledge that *Johnson* was distinguished by *Worcester*. While the *Johnson ruling* depicted American Indians as "hapless wards" and the *Cherokee Nation* ruling classified American Indians as a "domestic dependent nation," both court decisions about Native Americans were repudiated, at least with respect to U.S. states. In 1832 the Cherokee saw their sovereignty reaffirmed in *Worcester* where the U.S. Supreme Court held that Cherokee sovereignty could not be abrogated by the state laws of Georgia.

Notes

1 "Antonio Gramsci uses the term 'subaltern' interchangeably with 'subordinate' and 'instrumental' in his class analysis. Its sense of 'inferior rank' means that it is particularly well suited to describe the diversity of dominated and exploited groups who do not possess a general 'class consciousness.' . . . Spivak found it necessary to insist on the extension of subalternity to women's and gender issues; in post colonial studies generally, the subaltern has become a synonym for any marginalised or disempowered minority group, particularly on the grounds of gender and ethnicity" (Young, 353–4).

2 Homi K. Bhabha quoting Edward W. Said 'The Text, the world, the critic' in J.V. Harari (ed.) *Textual Strategies* (Ithaca: Cornell University Press, 1979), p. 184.

3 Use of the term "resistance" in this research focuses on the push back against Orientalizing and colonizing narratives depicted by the post-Revolutionary American literary discourses with respect to the Native Americans, in particular, the Cherokee Nation. Resistance in this research should not be conflated with present day Arab Spring resistance movements.

4 "Essentialise" means a certain or fixed knowledge about a subject, to know it inside and out. It also implies that complete knowledge of a subject translates into control or power over an object or subject.

5 By "Occident" Said refers to the metropolitan centers, or the colonial capitals. In contrast, the Orient is that Other place that is essentialised by colonial discourse. The Orient is that Other place that is defined from within the "metropolitan center."

6 Bhabha incorporates Franz Fanon's "stare" from Fanon's book *Black Skin, White Masks* to express the ambivalence felt by the colonizer when the daughter of the

French family stares at a black man only to have the black man return her stare. It is the reciprocal stare that Fanon, and later Bhabha, cite as a point of anxiety and ambivalence. Bhabha writes in relation to Fanon, "the demand of authority cannot unify its message nor simply identify its subjects . . . It is from such tensions—both psychic and political—that a strategy of subversion emerges. It is a mode of negation that seeks not to unveil the fullness of Man but to manipulate his representation. It is a form of power that is exercised at the very limits of identity and authority, in the mocking spirit of mask and image" (Bhabha 89).

7 Disguised is used as a proxy for Bhabha's mocking.

8 Just prior to the 1830 Indian Removal Act, efforts by the Cherokee to ward off attempts by the State of Georgia to impose Georgia law over Cherokee land were seen by many in the Northeast as a naked land grab against a civilized and educated Cherokee Nation. The Cherokee "appealed to the general public through an address drawn up by the Committee and Council of the entire Cherokee Nation. They begged the American people to listen to their cries for justice" (Remini 254). Senator Theodor Frelignhuysen of New Jersey opposed President Jackson's Indian Removal Bill—Frelignhuysen "castigated the Democrats for their hypocritical attempt to disguise the fact that they were intent on removing not just the southern tribes, but all Indians: and if those Native Americans refused, to subject them totally to state control" (233).

9 The Cherokee National Council agreed to permit the Moravians "to make an experiment" with a school "to instruct us and our children and improve our and their minds in the Nation" (McLoughlin 46).

10 "The variety of missionary denominations (Moravian, Presbyterian, Congregationalist, Baptist, Methodist) offered different ways of transition to new world views to the Cherokee between the late eighteenth and early nineteenth century" (Mcloughlin 10).

11 Assimilation was a policy first adopted by Henry Knox, Secretary of War under George Washington. Knox promoted this policy to dilute and insidiously break down Native American culture. To promote this strategy Knox, and later Jefferson, underwrote funding for religious missionaries, not as agents necessarily to Christianize the Indians, but as a method of diluting the Native American culture. "The linchpin of this civilization plan was that missionaries 'of excellent moral character, should be appointed to reside in the [Indian] nation.' Knox saw these missionaries as more than spiritual guides; they were government agents who would act as 'instruments to work on the Indians' and encourage assimilation" (quoted in Magliocca 881) quoting William G. McLoughlin, *Cherokees and Missionaries 1789–1839*, 33–4 (1984).

12 The United States purchased the claim to the Louisiana Territory from France in 1803 at a price of fifteen million dollars.

13 Francis Paul Prucha in *American Indian Treaties*, citing Ronald N. Satz's statement in *Chippewa Treaty Rights: The Reserved Rights of Wisconsin's Chippewa Indians in Historical Perspective*, Transactions of the Wisconsin Academy of Sciences, Arts and Letters, vol. 79, no. 1 (Madison: Wisconsin Academy of Sciences, Arts and Letters, 1991), p. 6.

14 "The doctrine of discovery is a doctrine of religious bias, which proclaimed that Indians were not capable of ownership of their land because they were not Christians. In *Johnson v. M'Intosh* the U.S. Supreme Court declared that the foundation of the U.S. claim to sovereignty over Indian land is the doctrine of discovery, thereby grounding that claim upon the quicksand of religious prejudice" (Kingfisher 124). Newcomb cites "Marshall's repetition of the phrases *Christian people* and *Christian prince or people* and the distinction he made between the two categories Christian people and natives, who were heathens enables us to grasp

the religious basis and context of discovery. This is also why it is accurate to refer to the main conception that runs through the *Johnson* ruling as a Christian discovery rather than simply discovery or European discovery" (Newcomb, *Pagans in the Promised Land* 86).

15 For example, the first treaty between the Cherokee Government and the British colonial Government in South Carolina was in 1721, when the Cherokees ceded 2,000 acres of land. The Treaty of Hopewell in 1781 established for the first time that the Cherokees would agree to Federal Government protection in exchange for the United States becoming the successor in interest on all treaty rights inherited by virtue of their victory over Great Britain. By the terms of this treaty, only Congress, not the United States, could regulate commerce with the Cherokees. In 1791, in the *Treaty of Holston,* the Cherokee Nation re-emphasized its national sovereignty within the body of the treaty, thus solidifying its status as a sovereign government entity. The treaty also ceded further land to the United States to deal with the pre-existing encroachments on Cherokee land by white frontiersmen. A further treaty was signed in 1794 to amend the *Treaty of Holston,* given the continued encroachments by white settlers on Cherokee land. In 1798 yet another treaty was signed between the Cherokee Nation and the U.S. Government to clarify boundary disputes from the *Treaty of Holston.* In 1806 the Treaty with the Cherokee, signed by Henry Dearborn, U.S. Secretary of War and the Cherokee, ceded yet more land north and west of the Tennessee River. Like previous treaties, the *Treaty of the Cherokee* was in reaction to the pre-existing encroachment of yet more white settlers on previously negotiated Cherokee land.

Conclusion

Reflections on *Johnson*

The primary purpose of this research was to provide an alternative reading of the Marshall Trilogy cases. To read the judgments is to also read a literary tradition in which authors such as Fenimore Cooper and Hawthorne helped to shape a narrative of American progress. To read the judgments is to see landscape paintings depicting wild and unruly lands. What I hope to reveal is the several layers under the dry legal texts—layers composed of several different artistic forms as well as of the traditional matter that informs the more conventional contexts of the Trilogy cases.

I was aided in this endeavor by several theorists of modernity, especially Michal Foucault, Edward W. Said and Homi H. Bhabha. Foucault situated the discursive statements and literary archive that preceded the Trilogy judgments with respect to the American Indian. In particular, this work demonstrates how Foucault's literary archive of Native Americans and the Doctrine of Discovery was accepted by John Marshall as "findings of fact" to support his legal doctrines. Said's Orientalism explains how literature was utilized to support British imperialism in the nineteenth century by defining the colonized Other. In this research Said's Orientialism helps to situate colonial and post-colonial literary representations of the Native American. Said provides a critical understanding of how literary discourses imagined a reality of the Other within the mind of the colonizer. Bhabha's theories of *mimicry*, *anxiety* and *ambivalence* incorporated Said's Orientialism to explain the dynamic of resistance within colonial discourses. Bhabha's theory provides an important framework to examine the Cherokee resistance during the late eighteenth and early nineteenth centuries. Having analyzed the varied literary genres preceding and concurrent with the Trilogy cases, we identified the literary findings of fact that formed the image of the Indian in the Trilogy.

These have contributed to what I also hope is an important political project. Understanding the literary and historical discourses that influenced John Marshall's rulings in the Trilogy helps to reflect on the past in order to facilitate a more humane and culturally accurate appreciation of the Indian cultures that still remain in North America.[1] We must also acknowledge that legal discourses regarding Federal Indian law were built on legal fictions. The Trilogy cases must be repudiated for the destructive doctrines they propagated, doctrines such as the Christian Doctrine of Discovery that form the bedrock of U.S. Federal Indian law.

It is the author's hope that this research has identified the false legal doctrines that were supported by findings based on varied literary discourses and propagated by the Trilogy. The Trilogy, in particular, *Johnson* and *Cherokee Nation,* dispossessed the Native Americans by branding them as mere occupants of their native lands; occupants whose very place on their soil was "dependent" on 'protection' by reputedly civilized European-American culture. From the American Founding Fathers to the massacre at Wounded Knee in 1890, a steady discursive onslaught of false images about the Indians was created to extinguish Indian culture under the guise of inevitability, humanity and Manifest Destiny. Derived from art, poetry, captive narratives, novels, historical studies and public speeches, the European-American settlers in North America spread the fabricated images of the Indian and the American wilderness for self-serving objectives, objectives, for example, devoted to taking and holding dominion over native land while using the pretext of Christianity and Doctrines of Discovery as legal justification to sanction Indian dispossession. The literary discourses that helped to situate the Trilogy must be addressed in ways that reveal the false histories and legal doctrines that were propounded by the U.S. Supreme Court. As Lindsay Robertson notes:

> The discovery of the Americas forced Europeans to adapt their traditional worldview to accommodate the Columbian landfall. For political and cultural reasons, the intellectual structure they ultimately applied to define the terms of their relationship to this "new world" was legal. Over a succession of generations, Europeans devised rules intended to justify the dispossession and subjugation of the native peoples of the Western Hemisphere.
>
> (Roberston ix)

Indian dispossession had its genealogy in literary discourses authored by the dominant cultures of England and the United States. As I will argue below, there needs to be a focused understanding of U.S. history with respect to how and why this dispossession was formulated in North America, in order to reclaim the rich culture of the American Indian. A re-examination and repudiation of the sordid Trilogy cases can first begin with education, media and the U.S. Supreme Court. If the U.S. Supreme Court still feels bound to *Johnson,* for example, then there are alternative political, religious and legislative arenas through which we can repudiate *Johnson's* legal precedent of "impaired" Indian claims to their land. Until *Johnson* and the Papal Bulls are renounced, it will be difficult to reclaim the truth and initiate cultural renewal, not only for the Native Americans, but for all post-colonial aboriginal peoples whose dispossession was grounded on *Johnson's* legal precedent. Coming to terms with a native dispossession based on Christian and legal doctrines will help to end today's disingenuous rhetoric of human rights and modernism in the United States. To proclaim a postmodern era means not only to question the efficacy of a teleologically reasoned Western conceptualization of the world, but the postmodern era must also acknowledge the false interpretation of progress that was built on the brute force of American colonialism.

Moving forward

In providing one final look at the Marshall Trilogy cases, it is important to trace the images of the Native Americans that were present in the previous two centuries. John Marshall employed language that described the Indian as a savage: "But the tribes of Indians inhabiting this country were fierce savages, whose occupation was war, and whose subsistence was drawn chiefly from the forest" (*Johnson* 590). Marshall's findings pivot on terms like "savage," "war" and "forest"—all metaphors that were incorporated into his rulings as sworn statements. Marshall was not the author of such native discourses, but his findings were derived from and accepted by the dominant American culture. These findings were based on a long literary tradition about Indians that dwelt in Foucault's *archive.* While such images of the Native American harken back to Christopher Columbus' arrival in the New World in 1492, this study has drawn on more recent racial depictions of the Indian, beginning first with the English colonies in New England and then through the cultural and political ascent of the American Republic. Unlike other post-colonial revolts against former imperial powers by indigenous peoples, the American Republic sought to depict its new history as a distinctly "post-colonial" era; however, the evidence reveals that the new American Republic was an imperial power encroaching westward as it pursued the internal dispossession of the Indians (Loomba 22). Reflecting, in part, on America's unique place in post-colonial literature, America's westward movement was shrouded in the subterfuge of divine providence, divine will and ultimately a 'Manifest Destiny.' In their westward expansion, European-American settlers utilized an effective religious justification for the virtual extinction of the Native Americans or, as Ward Churchill has argued, the genocide of Native Americans:

> Against the Indians, there's not a law the United States hasn't broken, not a Crime Against Humanity it hasn't committed and it's still going on . . . On October 12th, 1492, the day Christopher Columbus

> first landed in what came to be called the 'New World,' the Western Hemisphere was inhabited by a population of well over 100 million people. Two centuries later, it is estimated that the indigenous population of the Americas had been diminished by some 90 percent.
>
> (Churchill 97)[2]

Churchill's lament of Indian "genocide" rests on an intrinsic European-American disregard for the law. Implicit in Churchill's view is that laws were established only to be "broken" by the United States. Churchill seems to describe what is implicit, namely the facade of law was used as a justification to dispossess and eradicate American Indians.

The legal history described by John Marshall in *Johnson* expanded the false image of the Native Americans and resulted in the growth of the discursive archive of Indians. But unlike the false representations about Indians, the rulings in the Trilogy cases provided a *legal* basis by which the Federal Government could displace the Indians one tribe at a time. Andrew Jackson's rhetoric added to the discursive hypocrisy of the helpless Indians falling victim to the inevitable march of history. In reality, however, Jackson had a sordid record of Native American torture and extermination:

> [n]otably Jackson led some two thousand Tennessee and Kentucky militia and Cherokee, Choctaw, and Chickasaw forces on a scorched-earth campaign down the Coosa River. In a March 1814 assault on a fortified town at Horseshoe Bend, his combined forces slaughtered nearly eight hundred Red Stick men, women and children.
>
> (Richter 232)

Jackson's notable disdain for Indians is relevant since his rhetoric was aimed at a Congress and a literate American public which included the Justices of the U.S. Supreme Court. Jackson's passive rhetoric of defining the place of the Indians in the new American landscape sought to emphasize the Government's humane policy to save the Indians from themselves. "Towards the aborigines of the country no one can indulge a more friendly feeling than myself, or would go further in attempting to reclaim them from their wandering habits and make them a happy, prosperous people" (225). Buried within Jackson's statement is the notion of the nomadic nature of Indians. Jackson describes their "wandering habits," as if equating a nomadic existence with abject poverty. Jackson's apparent lament for the Indians is situated in the illusion that their wandering habits made the Indian poor in relation to the European American. Jacksonian policy towards the Indian tribes was one of structured dehumanization, displacement and genocide that discarded the veneer of prior treaties and discussions of co-existence. While the *de facto* disregard of prior treaty relations between the United States and Indian nations was promoted by Jackson's administration, it was the U.S. Supreme Court which provided the legal doctrines in *Johnson*, enabling Jackson to lead his southern supporters in Congress to pass the Indian Removal Act of 1830. The Indian Removal Act established the legal basis for the U.S. Army to forcibly dispossess 15,000 Cherokee from the mountains of western North Carolina in a blatant campaign to seize their land.[3]

The American Republic was not a post-colonial nation built upon indigenous independence, but rather on the pursuit of liberty and happiness for the Protestant male. Obstructing the path of that pursuit were several significant obstacles. Native American tribes indigenous to New England presented an obstacle to the pursuit of Protestant male possession. In the early colonial period, for example, New England settlers like John Winthrop moved to create a religious justification for English settlement and expansion through warfare with such tribes as the Pequot Indians in Massachusetts and Rhode Island:

> England's imperial competition with Spain had early consequences for New England. As Karen Kupperman points out, in 1640 and 1641, Lord Saye debated John Winthrop as to where God had intended the English to plant, arguing that at most New England would be a temporary 'way station' where colonists would await a fit time for settling Spanish holdings . . . Winthrop of course, disagreed, contending that New England was also intended by God as a permanent /Christian settlement.
>
> (Bross 15)

Here Winthrop alludes to divine purpose to explain why "settlement," rather than seeking "Spanish holdings," justified the English settlement of New England. Winthrop's quote implicitly makes the English appear more altruistic in their endeavors in the New World, when compared to the Spanish conquistadors whose purpose in the New World was to acquire "holdings" of gold. Rationalization for the New England settlements was later grounded in a messianic form by proselytizing the indigenous Indians into noble savages.[4]

The "divine purpose" theme endures in America to the present day; namely, that a divine mission was bestowed upon the New England settlers to promote the work of God. John Winthrop's *A Shining City on a Hill* established an English interpretation of the settlers' destiny as God inspired (*Native Blood*). "The Lord makes it like that of New England: for wee must Consider that wee shall be as a Citty upon a Hill, the eies of all people are upon us" (Winthrop). Here Winthrop's observation "the eies of all people are upon us" alludes to the experiment that is exemplified by New England's settlement and how that experiment was being watched by the European. Being a "citty upon a Hill" seems to also imply that English settlers are being held up on a "hill" as an example and where everyone can see them. Winthrop's zealous interpretation of his mission led him to interpret the widespread impact of smallpox on American Indians as divine justice. In retrospect, it mattered little that it was the English colonizers who imported and infected the American Indians with smallpox.[5] This research has shown, in part, that *religious* literature helped project false images and discourses that were later incorporated as findings of fact in the Trilogy cases. "For two hundred years to come Washington, Jefferson, Jackson, and other leaders, representing the wishes of virtually the entire white nation, followed these minister's genocidal instructions with great care. It was their Christian duty as well as their destiny" (Stannard 241). As Stannard notes, the religious discourses about the Indian helped to establish a divine pretext to Native American dispossession.

This book seeks to bring to light a major myth in American Jurisprudence; namely, the myth that American jurisprudence was neutral and just in the early nineteenth century with respect to Indians and their lands: a legal myth that camouflaged the literary genesis to the false representations and discourses of the Native Americans. In examining American jurisprudence we are also analyzing the historical context and literary representations that helped to forge the fiction of the infant nation as one obtaining independence from a colonial power, rather than as an American imperial power moving westward. The U.S. Supreme Court played a critical role in legally establishing the moral veneer through legal judgment that led to the dispossession and virtual extermination of the Indian population between the 1820s and 1890. During the era preceding the Trilogy cases, writers like Fenimore Cooper and Cullen Bryant described the Indian through Romantic constructions. Bryant's *The Disinterred Warrior* evokes a poignant description of the vanishing Indian:

> A noble race! But they are gone
> With their old forests wide and deep,
> And we have built our homes upon
> Fields where their generations sleep.
> Their fountains slake our thirst at noon,
> Upon their fields our harvest waves,
> Our lovers woo beneath their moon—
> Then let us spare, at least, their graves!
>
> (Quoted in Bross 187)[6]

When religion and literature are used to dehumanize and dispossess millions of Native Americans, it is vital to understand the conqueror's fiction. By understanding the discursive fiction we not only gain an appreciation of how colonialism works through literature and language, but this understanding also helps to decode the insidious logic of legal judgment with respect to indigenous dispossession. This research does not seek to pronounce universal truths, but rather to interpret how the law was fictionalized in the Trilogy cases, through literary representations of the Indian, to propagate arguably one of the greatest indigenous dispossessions in human history. Although European-American settlers and the American Government dispossessed Indians of their land, the theme of "historical inevitability" was utilized by the early nineteenth-century Romantic writers and later incorporated by jurists like John Marshall in the Trilogy to propagate the vanishing Indian myth. As Bross notes, "However much nineteenth-century authors may have lamented the disappearance of the Indians, they agreed with seventeenth-century writers that Indian deaths were necessary and inevitable—whether because of divine will, 'natural' inferiority to white, or manifest destiny" (187). Such American mythology distorts the stark reality of what happened to Native Americans between the arrival of Columbus in 1492 and the late nineteenth century: virtually 95 percent of the native population was killed during this time period and what remains today is an internally displaced *refugee* population that has been relegated to reservations throughout the United States. According to Stannard and Churchill, the pre-Columbus population was estimated to be between 120,000,000 and 125,000,000 people, but by 1892 the U.S. Census estimated the native population inside the United States to be approximately 250,000.[7]

Revoke the Papal Bulls

If *Johnson* is to be repudiated the Papal Bulls which provided the legal and religious foundation to the European Doctrine of Discovery must be revoked by the Vatican.

> The Papal document called for our Nations and Peoples to be subjugated so the Christian Empire and its doctrines would be propagated. The U.S. Supreme Court ruling in *Johnson* adopted the same principle of subjugation expressed in the Inter Caetera Bull.
>
> (J. Reynolds, *Revoking the Papal Bull of 1493*)

As Steven Newcomb notes in *Pagans in the Promised Land,* the bulls provided the *Christian* Doctrine of Discovery with religious and legal justification to conquer an entire hemisphere in the name of Christianity (Newcomb 86–7).

> Mr. Newcomb tracks *Johnson vs. McIntosh* back to the Doctrine of Discovery, but with a nuance. He calls it the 'Doctrine of Christian Discovery,' because it denies sovereignty to non-Christians. "That's the

> key point here," Mr. Newcomb said, "If it's not in the possession of any Christian lords, they have the right to go in and take the land. That was the principle that John Marshall adopted into a United States Supreme Court decision."
>
> (J. Reynolds)

Therefore, the Doctrine of Discovery denied both sovereignty and ownership of land to indigenous non-Christian peoples according to this European legal doctrine.

Dispossession may sound like a harsh indictment of a religious document, but when viewed as a literal declaration of war upon indigenous people in the late fifteenth century it may strike the reader from the twenty-first century as a remarkable commentary. Furnished with decrees from King Ferdinand and Queen Isabella, Spanish invaders were required to announce their intentions before the commencement of hostilities against aboriginal peoples in the New World in Spanish or Latin even though these were foreign languages and incomprehensible to native peoples. For example, part of the Spanish announcement stated:

> but if you do not do this, and maliciously make delay in it, I certify to you that, with the help of God, we shall powerfully enter into your country, and shall make war against you in all ways and manners that we can, and shall subject you to the yoke and obedience of the church.
>
> (Shatzman 80)[8]

Spain was not alone in using decrees based on the edicts of Papal Bulls. Shortly after the *Inter Caetera* of 1493, England's Henry VII issued his own charter of exploration to subjugate non-Christian peoples in North America.[9]

Johnson was directly linked to both the *Inter Caetera* and to the English issued letters patent to John Cabot in 1496.[10] In *Johnson* "the chief justice's opinion leaned on English charters of exploration, among them the one granted by Henry VII to John Cabot in 1496. Cabot's charter, and those of English explorers after him, contains a language of subjugation derived from papal decrees of the mid- to late 15th century" (J. Reynolds, *Revoking the Papal Bull of 1493*). These religious and monarchical commands served as *de jure* grounds to subjugate indigenous people. In *Johnson* these orders were incorporated as findings of fact to answer questions of law.

The Christian tenets of the Papal Bulls were integrated into the Trilogy as findings of fact in *Johnson*. In *Johnson*, Marshall cited the Royal Charters granted to John Cabot and Sir Walter Raleigh on the same religious principle established in the Bulls issued by the Vatican:

> The documents upon this subject are ample and complete. So early as the year 1496, her monarch granted a commission to the Cabots

> to discover countries then unknown to Christian people and to take possession of them in the name of the King of England. Two years afterwards, Cabot proceeded on this voyage and discovered the continent of North America, along which he sailed as far south as Virginia. To his discovery the English trace their title.
>
> (*Johnson v. M'Intosh* 576)

Marshall's ruling expressly ties the American chain of title to land ownership to the English "monarch" who granted John Cabot entitlement to "discover countries then unknown to Christian people." The Doctrine of *Christian* Discovery, then, must be identified for its role in dispossessing Native Americans from their land.

While we cannot change the past, we can reconstitute how the past is framed to underscore the myth of Christian civilizing and dispossession of the native people of North America. Catholics and Protestants can renounce the role played by Christian Discovery and English colonialism as a stratagem to achieve conquest over native peoples. Indian dispossession must be acknowledged not as an inevitable demise in the guise of Manifest Destiny or as John Marshall's march of history over a dependent nation of savages, but as a pretext to legally conquer indigenous lands.

Johnson alive and well

Johnson is still the jurisprudential source of U.S. Federal Indian Law. In 2005 the U.S. Supreme Court in *New York vs. Oneida Indian Nation of New York* upheld the Doctrine of Discovery. In *Oneida* the issue was whether New York State's original land title and taxing authority extended over lands re-purchased by the Oneida nation. While the land was originally owned by the Oneida in the early nineteenth century the issue was whether they were exempt from New York State property taxes after their re-purchase of the same land. Justice Ruth Ginsburg's majority opinion (8–1) held that the Oneida had relinquished their sovereignty when they sold their land to New York State in the early nineteenth century. Ginsburg based her ruling on the Doctrine of Discovery and the original treaties *negotiated* between New York State and the Oneida during the time just after American independence from England. In footnote number one to Justice Ginsburg's opinion the court held:

> Under the "doctrine of discovery," *County of Oneida v. Oneida Indian Nation of N.Y.*, 470 U.S. 226, 234 (1985) *(Oneida II)*, "fee title to the lands occupied by Indians when the colonists arrived became vested in the sovereign—first the discovering European nation and later the original States and the United States," *Oneida Indian Nation of N.Y. v. County of Oneida*, 414 U.S. 661, 667 (1974) *(Oneida I)*. In the original 13

> States, "fee title to Indian lands," or "the pre-emptive right to purchase from the Indians, was in the State." *Id.*, at 670; see *Oneida Indian Nation of N.Y. v. New York*, 860 F. 2d 1145, 1159–1167 (CA2 1988). Both before and after the adoption of the Constitution, New York State acquired vast tracts of land from Indian tribes through treaties it independently negotiated, without National Government participation.
>
> (City of Sherrill 3, Footnote 1)

Ginsburg's use of the phrases "fee title to the lands occupied by Indians" and "became vested" is quite revealing because it suggests a seamless and inevitable transition from English to American land ownership. Ginsburg's use of the term "occupied" mirrors the *Johnson* holding that Indians occupy their land as tenants rather than as fee simple owners. Ginsburg does not relate her use of the term "occupied" to *Johnson,* but instead adopts the term as if to imply that upon discovery by Europeans, Indians merely *occupied* the land in the New World—a strange reality where land was deemed occupied but not owned by Indians.

Following Ginsburg's legal reasoning, the ownership of such occupied fee title land is established only when the "colonists arrived." Ginsburg argues that it was upon "arrival," not upon purchase, that England obtained legal fee simple title to Indian lands. As explained in earlier chapters, payment of money or the barter of goods to Indians by English settlers and, later, by American land speculators on the pretext of making purchases were designed to avoid bloodshed. As far as European Americans were concerned the ultimate dispossession of Indian lands was a central long-term strategy. Ginsberg's historical interpretation of Indian occupation makes English claims to the fee simple ownership at the time of discovery (i.e., "colonial arrival") seem creditable. Ginsburg then attests that the fee simple title of Indian land upon discovery "became vested." What became historically vested was the English Doctrine of Discovery claim over Indian lands, which re-emerged under American control as pre-emption rights. Pre-emption rights granted exclusive rights, either to pre-Revolutionary European colonists or to the U.S. Federal Government after 1783, to purchase Indian lands, even though these lands were still inhabited by Indians. Seen from an Indian perspective such pre-emptive rights meant they could only sell their land to rightful holders or rather to the U.S. Federal Government exclusively. The latter undermines Ginsburg's next section in her opinion wherein she cites that New York State "acquired vast tracts of land from Indian Tribes through treaties it *independently negotiated*" [my emphasis]. Justice Ginsburg's reliance on the premise that New York obtained good title to Oneida land pivots on the phrase "independently negotiated." Justice Ginsburg's attempt to project New York's purchase of Oneida land as fair negotiation is a remarkable example of historical amnesia. Ginsburg's use of the term "negotiate" is especially misleading because it obfuscates the real pressures exerted by State land commissioners and U.S. Federal agents upon Indian tribes to sell their land. This research has revealed that such negotiations were not "independent" nor "negotiated" between two equal parties. The essential point is to foreground that *Johnson's* use of the Doctrine of Discovery as a basis for American land ownership of Indian land is still used by the U.S. Supreme Court to assert Federal and state sovereignty over Indian lands. Justice Ginsburg's incorporation of the Doctrine of Discovery, first articulated under *Johnson*, was re-established in *Oneida*.

Oneida presents a challenge to American jurisprudence to rid the last vestige of indigenous legal dispossession from the law. In *Brown v. Board of Education of Topeka*, 347 U.S. 483 (1954), the U.S. Supreme Court overturned *Plessy v. Ferguson*, 163 U.S. 537 (1896) to strike down the "separate but equal" clause that permitted segregated schools based on skin color. After the Second World War, the U.S. Congress atoned for the forced internment of Japanese Americans by providing reparations of $20,000 to each victim. The Native American, however, continues to be regulated by Supreme Court decisions that still sustain racist and prejudiced assumptions about their culture. While the ruling in *Worcester* restored some degree of sovereignty to Indian nations, later Supreme Court rulings disregarded *Worcester* and instead continue to rely on the precedent of *Johnson*. As Echo-Hawk notes:

> Even though colonialism was rejected as repugnant by the international community shortly after World War II, the legal underpinnings of colonialism remain implanted in the domestic law of the United States. In addition, the Supreme Court continues to rely upon legal doctrines infected with bare race-based notions as it decides contemporary Indian cases, long after the ideology of race has been discarded by virtually every other governmental institution in the country. Thus, the legal system ironically remains one of the last to perpetuate a form of racism.
>
> (Echo-Hawk 5)

Echo-Hawk notes that the American legal profession continues to base Federal Indian law on racist notions. From American slavery to the forced Japanese internment during the Second World War, American political and legal institutions have attempted to address the injustices inflicted upon oppressed peoples; however, the American legal profession still clings to "bare race-based notions" of Indians to *justify* American land ownership (5).

This book has demonstrated how literary discursive formations established false images of the Native American, discursive images that were accepted as findings of fact by state courts and the U.S. Supreme Court, in particular *Johnson*. In like fashion, counter-discourses of the American

Indian can contest the racist legal precedents in American law with respect to Indian land. The contribution this research seeks to make to understanding the Trilogy cases is to explain how literature and law can become blurred when courts accept findings of fact that are built on distorted and regulated discourses that exclude alternative discourses. The danger is that narrowly regulated discourses over time become, as Foucault demonstrates, *unity of statements* or "fact" which can lead to racist assumptions about peoples. Once these assumptions acquire the status of "findings of fact" it is but a short step to the "legal" dispossession or oppression of a group of people. The tragic consequences of this discursive genealogy are only too familiar to the Native Americans; however, the literary genealogy of legal dispossession can be countered with discourses that reveal the poverty of the law's claim to justice.

Notes

1 According to the U.S. Census Bureau, the indigenous Indian population in the United States was 2.9 million in 2010 (U.S. Census Bureau).

2 Churchill's estimates are by no means universally accepted within the academic community. As Brenden Rensink cites in his chapter contribution titled *Genocide of Native Americans: Historical Facts and Historiographic Debates*, "Although the consensus on such estimates has been tenuous, much of the related demographic debate over pre-contact and post-contact population statistics asserts per capita loss percentages unparalleled in human history (Dobyns, 1983, and Stannard, 1992). If taken at face value and as the only criteria for assessing genocide, one might conclude that Native American history should stand as *the* archetype. However, the accepted legal definition of genocide entails a second important factor: the *intent* to destroy a targeted group in whole or in part. This consideration greatly complicates the issue" (quoted in Totten and Hitchcock 17).

3 In addition to the 1830 Removal Act, President Andrew Jackson procured and accepted a sham Treaty signed by the minority pro-removal faction of the Cherokee. Despite protests from the recognized Cherokee leader John Ross, and thousands of signatures from Cherokee members, the Treaty of Echota in 1838 was used as a legal fig leaf to initiate the forced removal of 15,000 Cherokee by the U.S. Army from western North Carolina, Tennessee and Georgia to Oklahoma, an event otherwise known as the "Trail of Tears." Some 4,000 Cherokee died during their forced removal.

4 In commenting on the film *Avatar*, Catherine Cutcher and Siphokazi Magadla, in their article *Avatar: Noble Savages Meet the White Messiah in Colonial Struggle*, write "As post-colonial scholars, we must deconstruct these condescending myths of the 'Noble Savage' and the 'White Messiah.' *Avatar*'s colonialist fantasy replays common themes found throughout U.S. media, including films like *Dances with Wolves*, *The Last of the Mohicans*, *The Last Samurai*, *Pocahontas*, and *Fern Gully*. The story goes: a White man travels to a different culture, learns their customs, falls in love with a local woman, becomes disgruntled with his own culture, and goes AWOL. He then becomes the most awesome warrior in his new culture, and saves them from the greed and violence of his own people. Despite his betrayal, he is forgiven and accepted to join the clan as an honorary member or a new chief" (Cutcher and Madadia).

5 John Winthrop considered this wave of illness and death among the New England tribes to be a divine miracle. He wrote to a friend in England, "but for the natives in these parts, God hath so pursued them, as for 300 miles space the greatest part of them are swept away by smallpox which still continues among them. So as God hath thereby cleared our title to this place, those who remain in these parts, being in all not 50, have put themselves under our protection" (*Native Blood: The Myth of Thanksgiving, Revolutionary Worker*).

6 Quoting William Cullen Bryant, "The Disinterred Warrior," in *The Poetical works of William Cullen Bryant* (1903); rpt. (New York: AMS Press, 1969), p. 107.

7 By the late nineteenth century the American Indian population in the United States was about 1% percent or 250,000 of the total U.S. population (Stannard 146). By 1892 when the U.S. Census Bureau estimated that approximately 250,000 indigenous people lived within the borders of the U.S., according to Ward Churchill, "a hemispheric population estimated to have been as great as 125 million was reduced by something over 90 percent" (Churchill 1). Churchill cites the study by Henry R. Dobyns "Estimating Aboriginal American Population: An Appraisal of Techniques with a New Hemispheric Estimate," *Current Anthropology*, No. 7, 1966 where estimates set aboriginal population ranges in the 112 million to 125 million in 1492 (Churchill 13). Other scholars, such as Russell Thornton (2000) in "Population History of Native North Americans," estimate the pre-contact figures for the indigenous North American population to have been between 1,000,000 and 10,000,000. This had reduced to 600,000 by 1800 and 237,000 by the end of the nineteenth century (Hacker and Haines).

8 The Decree was known as El Requierimento.

9 One of the significant differences between a Papal Bull and Letters Patent or Charters was that the former established control of indigenous non-Christian heathens while the latter established control of land. According to Patricia Seed "Like the English, the Spanish in the New World used a written document to ensure the legitimacy of imperial authority. For the English, authority was established by letter patent; for the Spaniards it was created by a papal bull. Inter caetera of Pope Alexander VI in 1493 gave Spain the exclusive right to present the Gospel to the natives of the New World and guaranteed Spain's right to rule the land in order to secure the right to preach" (Seed 200).

10 "This permitted John Cabot to investigate, *claim and possess any new lands* [my emphasis] so long as they did not intrude on Spanish or Portuguese territories" (*Patent Granted by King Henry VII to John Cabot and His Sons, March 1496*: Newfoundland and Labrador Heritage).

Bibliography

Illustrations

Figure 7.1 Thomas Cole 1827 from "*The Last of the Mohicans.*" Cora Kneeling at the Feet of Tamenund. Explore Thomas Cole. Thomas Cole Historical Site, 2010. Web. http://www.explorethomascole.org/gallery/items/33 accessed October 8, 2015.

Figure 7.2 Thomas Cole 1836 "*The Oxbow* (*View from Mount Holyoke, Northampton, Massachusetts, after a Thunderstorm*) (08.228)." In Heilbrunn Timeline of Art History. Metropolitan Museum of Art, Oct. 2006. Web. http://www.metmuseum.org/toah/works-of-art/08.228 accessed April 28, 2015.

Cases

Arnold v. Mundy N.J.L. 1, 1821 WL 1269 (N.J. Sup. Ct. 1821)

Brown v. Board of Education of Topeka, 347 U.S. 483 (1954)

Cherokee Nation v. Georgia, 30 1. U.S. (1831)

City of Sherrill v. Oneida Indian Nation of N.Y. (03-855), 544 U.S. 197. Supreme Court.

Gibbons v. Ogden, 22 U.S. 1 (1824)

Johnson & Graham's Lessee v. McIntosh, 21 U.S. 8 Wheat. 543 (1823)

Marbury v. Madison, 5 U.S. 137 (1803)

Marshall v. Clark, 8 VA 268. Virginia Supreme Court, 1791 WL 325

Oliphant v. Suquamish Indian Tribe, 435 U.S. 191 (1978)

Plessy v. Ferguson, 163 U.S. 537 (1896)

Tennessee v. Foreman, 6 Tenn. 256 (1835)

Thompson v. Johnston, 6 Binn. 68, 1813 WL 1243 (Pa. Sup. Ct. 1813)

Worcester v. Georgia, 31 U.S. 515 (1832).

Primary sources

"American Indians By the Numbers." Infoplease. Pearson Education, 2007. Web. http://www.infoplease.com/spot/aihmcensus1.html accessed March 19, 2016.

Barker, Martin and Roger Sabin. *The Lasting of the Mohicans: History of an American Myth.* Jackson: University Press of Mississippi, 1995. Print.

Bhabha, Homi K. *The Location of Culture.* London: Routledge, 1994. Print.

Boudinot, Elias. "New Echota." *The Cherokee Phoenix. Hunter Library*, n.d. Web. http://www.wcu.edu/library/DigitalCollections/CherokeePhoenix/Vol1/no01/pg3col2b-4.htm accessed October 21, 2015.

Bradford, William, and Worthington Chauncey Ford. *History of Plymouth Plantation, 1620–1647* [Boston]: Massachusetts Historical Society, 1912. Print.

Bryant, William Cullen, Henry C. Sturges, and Richard Henry Stoddard. *The Poetical Works of William Cullen Bryant.* New York: AMS, 1969. Print.

Burke, Edmund and Adam Phillips. *A Philosophical Enquiry into the Origin of Our Ideas of the Sublime and Beautiful.* Oxford: Oxford University Press, 1998. Print.

Byrd, William. *The Westover Manuscripts Containing the History of the Dividing Line Betwixt Virginia and North Carolina: A Journey to the Land of Eden, A.D. 1733*; and *A Progress to the Mines.* Petersburg [Va.] Printed by E. and J. C. Ruffin, 1841. Google Books. 11 Sept. 2006. Web. https://books.google.com/books?id=TMLpBsVTdWIC accessed April 28, 2013.

Clinton, DeWitt. *Discourse Delivered Before the New York Historical Society.* N.p.: James Eastburn, 1812. Google Books. Web. https://books.google.com/books?id=hxQTAAAAYAAJ accessed October 21, 2013.

Cooper, James Fenimore. *The Last of the Mohicans.* New York: Penguin, 1986. Print.

Foucault, Michel. *The History of Sexuality.* New York: Pantheon, 1978. Print.

——. "The Order of Discourse." *Untying the Text: A Post-Structuralist Reader.* Robert Young (ed.). Boston: Routledge & Kegan Paul, 1981. 48–78. Print.

——. "What Is an Author?" *The Foucault Reader.* New York: Pantheon, 1984. 101–20. Print.

——. *The Archaeology of Knowledge.* London: Routledge, 2002. Print.

Freneau, Philip. "Philip Freneau: 'The Indian Burying Ground.'" *Archiving Early America.* Fall 1996. Web. http://www.earlyamerica.com/review/fall96/freneau.html accessed September 20, 2015.

Frisbie, Levi. *A Discourse, Before the Society for Propagating the Gospel Among the Indians and Others in North America.* N.p.: Smith Ethridge, 1804. Google Books. Web. https://books.google.com/books?id=ZttEAAAAIAAJ accessed October 21, 2013.

Gadamer, Hans-Georg, Joel C. Weinsheimer and Donald G. Marshall. *Truth and Method.* London: Continuum, 2004. Print.

"General Assembly Adopts Declaration on Rights of Indigenous Peoples; 'Major Step Forward' Towards Human Rights for All." *UN News Center.* UN, 13 Sept. 2007. Web. http://www.un.org/News/Press/docs/2007/ga10612.doc.htm accessed May 4, 2015.

Goodrich, Peter. *Law in the Courts of Love: Literature and Other Minor Jurisprudences.* London: Routledge, 1996. Print.

Heckewelder, John G. E. *History, Manners, and Customs of the Indian Nations Who Once Inhabited Pennsylvania and the Neighboring States.* Philadelphia: Historical Society of Pennsylvania, 1881. The Internet Archive. Web. http://www.archive.org/stream/histmannerscust00heckrich/histmannerscust00heckrich_djvu.txt accessed May 2, 2013.

Irving, Washington. *"Introduction – A Tour on the Prairies – Washington Irving,* Book, Etext." Russell Taylor, n.d. Web. http://www.telelib.com/authors/I/Irving Washington/prose/touroftheprairies/introduction.html accessed March 10, 2016.

Jackson, Andrew. *Andrew Jackson to the Cherokee Tribe, 1835.* The Gilder Lehrman Institute of American History. Web. http://www.gilderlehrman.org/history-by-era/jackson-lincoln/resources/andrew-jackson-cherokee-tribe-1835 accessed October 9, 2013.

Jefferson, Thomas. *The Writings of Thomas Jefferson.* Albert Ellery Bergh and Andrew A. Lipscomb (eds). Vol. 17. Washington: Jefferson Memorial Assoc., 1904. Google Books. Web. https://books.google.com/books?id=_TEOAQAAIAAJ&pg=PP1#v=onepage&q&f=false accessed October 21, 2013.

Lewis, Meriwether, William Clark, and Bernard Augustine De Voto. *The Journals of Lewis and Clark.* Boston: Houghton, Mifflin, 1953. Print.

Locke, John. *The Second Treatise on Civil Government.* Class Club edition. New York: Roslyn, Walter J. Black: In, 1947. Print.

——. *Two Treatises of Government.* London: C. and J. Riverington, 1824. Google Books. Web. https://books.google.com/books?id=K1UBAAAAYAAJ accessed May 3, 2013.

Marshall, John and Charles F. Hobson. *Writings.* New York: Library of America, 2010. Print

Mather, Cotton. *Magnalia Christi Americana.* Vol. 1. Bedford: Applewood, 1823. Google Books Web. https://books.google.com/books?id=asShFz7MMSgC&lpg=PA26&dq=But%20we%20must%20therewithal%20ask%20your%20Prayers%2C%20that%20these%20%E2%80%9Cgolden%20Candlesticks%E2%80%9D&pg=PA26#v=onepage&q=But%20we%20must%20therewithal%20ask%20your%20Prayers,%20that%20these%20%E2%80%9Cgolden%20Candlesticks%E2%80%9D&f=false accessed August 29, 2015.

Mather, Cotton. *Magnalia Christi Americana.* Vol. 2. Hartford: Slas Andrus & Sons, 1853. Google Books. Web. http://books.google.com/books?id=f0Y5s7bsqDQC&pg=PP7#v=onepage&q&f=false accessed April 30, 2013.

Naipaul, V. S. *The Mimic Men.* 1st edition. Canada: Vintage, 2001. Print.

"*Profile.*" Benetton Group. Web. http://www.benettongroup.com/group/profile/glance accessed October 5, 2013.

Rabinow, Paul (ed.). "Nietzsche, Genealogy, History." *The Foucault Reader.* New York: Pantheon, 1984. 76–99. Print.

——. "The Repressive Hypothesis." *The Foucault Reader.* New York: Pantheon, 1984. 301–29. Print.

Said, Edward W. "*Orientalism.*" New York: Vintage, 1979. Print.

——. Moustafa Bayoumi, and Andrew Rubin (eds). *The Edward Said Reader.* New York: Vintage, 2000. Print.

——. *Culture and Imperialism.* New York: Vintage, 1994. Print.

Willston, Ebenezer Bancroft. *Eloquence of the United States.* Vol. 2. Middletown, CT: E. & H. Clark, 1827. Google Books. Web. https://books.google.com/books?id=dOInAQAAIAAJ accessed May 3, 2013.

Secondary sources

About the Revolutionary War Bounty Warrants. Web. http://www.lva.virginia.gov/public/guides/opac/bountyabout.htm accessed March 5, 2016.

Ahmad, Aijazuddin. *In Theory.* London: Verso, 2008. Print.

Alvey, Jim. *Adam Smith's Optimistic, Teleological View of History.* Palmerston North, N.Z.: Dept. of Applied and International Economics, Massey University, 2003. Print.

Aristodemou, Maria. *Law and Literature: Journeys from Her to Eternity.* Oxford: Oxford University Press, 2000. Print.

Arnold, Mary. *The Romantic Idealization of American Indians in Early American Literature.* Earthpages.org. N.p., 19 Oct. 2010. Web. http://epages.wordpress.com/2010/10/19/the-romantic-idealization-of-american-indians-in-early-american-literature/ accessed June 1, 2013.

Asad, T. "Review of Said's Orientalism." *The English Historical Review* 95 (1980): 648–9.

Axtell, James. *The European and the Indian: Essays in the Ethnohistory of Colonial North America.* Oxford: Oxford University Press, 1981. Print.

Banner, Stuart. *How the Indians Lost Their Land: Law and Power on the Frontier.* Cambridge, MA: Belknap of Harvard University Press, 2005. Print.

Baron, Jane B. "Law, Literature, and the Problems of Interdisciplinarity." *The Yale Law Journal* 108.5 (1999): 1059–085. JSTOR. Web. http://www.jstor.org/stable/797370 accessed May 1, 2013.

Benetton. *Benetton – A Global Fashion Brand, Based in Treviso, Italy.* N.p., n.d. Web. http://corporatelane.com/page/Benetton.htm&or=040243a09c0f73c2c3eadfe516fb1237 accessed March 12, 2016.

Berkhofer, Robert F. *The White Man's Indian: Images of the American Indian from Columbus to the Present.* New York: Knopf, 1978. Print.

Beya, Abdennebi Ben. "Mimicry, Ambivalence, and Hybridity." *Postcolonial Studies@Emory.* July 12, 2012. Web. https://scholarblogs.emory.edu/postcolonialstudies/2014/06/21/mimicry-ambivalence-and-hybridity/ / accessed March 12, 2016.

Bierce, Ambrose. *The Devil's Dictionary.* N.p.: The Project Gutenberg, n.d. 4 Nov. 2012. Web. http://www.gutenberg.org/files/972/972-h/972-h.htm accessed April 28, 2013.

Billington, Ray Allen. *Land of Savagery/land of Promise: The European Image of the American Frontier in the Nineteenth Century.* New York: Norton, 1981. Print.

Black, Henry R. *Black's Law Dictionary.* 6th edition. St. Paul: West, 1990. Print.

Boorstin, Daniel. *The Mysterious Science of Law.* Gloucester: Peter Smith, 1973. Print.

Botham, Fay. *Almighty God Created the Races: Christianity, Interracial Marriage, and American Law.* 1st edition. Chapel Hill: University of North Carolina Press, 2009. Print.

Bradbury, John. *Travels in the Interior of America, in the Years 1809, 1810, and 1811.* N.p.: Sherwood, Neeley and Jones, 1817. Google Books. Web. https://books.google.com/books?id=Gw5UAAAAcAAJ accessed October 21, 2013.

Bradbury, John and John Bywater. *Travels in the Interior of America.* Ann Arbor: University Microfilms, 1966. Print.

Bross, Kristina. *Dry Bones and Indian Sermons: Praying Indians in Colonial America.* Ithaca: Cornell University Press, 2004. Print.

"*The Bull Romanus Pontifex (Nicholas V) January 8, 1454.*" Doctrine of Discovery. Doctrine of Discovery Study Group, n.d. Web. http://www.doctrineofdiscovery.org/ accessed December 5, 2015.

Burke, Joseph C. "The Cherokee Cases: A Study in Law, Politics, and Morality." *Stanford Law Review,* 21.3 (1969): 500. Print.

Burroughs, Bryson. "The Hudson River School of Painting." *The Metropolitan Museum of Art Bulletin,* 12.10 (1917): 3–11. Print.

Butler, Brian. "Law as an Aesthetic Subject." *Aesthetics On-Line.* American Society for Aesthetics, n.d. Web. http://www.aesthetics-online.org/articles/index.php?articles_id=16 accessed May 1, 2013.

Cherokee Nation v. Georgia. 30 1. U.S. 1831. *Justia*. Web. http://supreme.justia.com/cases/federal/us/30/1/case.html accessed April 28, 2013.

Churchill, Ward. *A Little Matter of Genocide: Holocaust and Denial in the Americas, 1492 to the Present*. San Francisco: City Lights, 1997. Print.

City of Sherrill v. Oneida Indian Nation of N.Y. (03–855). 544 U.S. 197. *Supreme Court*. 29 Mar. 2005. FindLaw. Web. http://caselaw.lp.findlaw.com/scripts/getcase.pl?court=us&vol=544&invol=197 accessed May 4, 2013.

Cleary, Edward L. and Allen D. Hertzke. *Representing God at the Statehouse: Religion and Politics in the American States*. Lanham, MD: Rowman & Littlefield, 2006. Print.

Clinton, Dewitt. "Encyclopædia Britannica." *Encyclopædia Britannica Online*. Encyclopaedia. Britannica, Inc., 2015. Web. http://www.britannica.com/biography/DeWitt-Clinton-American-politician accessed December 6, 2015.

Conser, Walter H., Jr. "John Ross and the Cherokee Resistance Campaign, 1833–1838." *The Journal of Southern History*, 44.2 (1978): 191–212. JSTOR. Web. http://www.jstor.org/stable/2208301 accessed October 21, 2013.

Cormack, Bradin. "Practicing Law and Literature in Early Modern Studies." *Modern Philology*, 101.1 (2003): 79–91. JSTOR. Web. http://www.jstor.org/stable/10.1086/382815 accessed October 21, 2013.

Cotterill, R. S. "Federal Indian Management in the South 1789–1825." *The Mississippi Valley Historical Review*, 20.3 (1933): 333–52. JSTOR. Web. http://www.jstor.org/stable/1886843 accessed October 8, 2015.

Cuddon, J. A. and Claire Preston. *The Penguin Dictionary of Literary Terms and Literary Theory*. London: Penguin, 1999. Print.

Cutcher, Catherine, and Siphokazi Madadla. "*AVATAR: Noble Savages Meet the White Messiah in Colonial Struggle*." N.p.: Bokamoso Leadership Forum. 2 Feb. 2010. Web. http://bokamosoafrica.org/2010/02/avatar-noble-savages-meet-white-messiah-colonial-struggle.html accessed October 24, 2013.

Cutler, Charles L. *O Brave New Words: Native American Loanwords in Current English*. N.p.: University of Oklahoma Press, 1994. Print.

Dawn, Ernest C. "Review: Orientalism by Edward W. Said." *American Historical Review*, 84.5 (1979): 1334+. Print.

Demos, John. *The Unredeemed Captive: A Family Story from Early America*. Vintage edition. New York: Alfred Knopf, 1994. Print.

Dippie, Brian W. *The Vanishing American: White Attitudes and U.S. Indian Policy*. N.p.: University of Kansas Press, 1982. Print.

Domnarski, William. "Law and Literature." *Legal Studies Forum*, 27.1 (2003): 109–29. Print.

Douzinas, Costas and Adam Gearey. *Critical Jurisprudence: The Political Philosophy of Justice*. Oxford: Hart, 2005. Print.

Drinnon, Richard. *Facing West: the Metaphysics of Indian-hating and Empire-building*. New York: New American Library, 1980. Print.

Easton, John, Richard Hutchinson, Mary White Rowlandson, and Cotton Mather. *Narratives of the Indian Wars, 1675–1699*. Charles H. Lincoln (ed.). Vol. 15. New York: Charles Scribner's Sons, 1913. Print.

Eaton, Rachel Caroline. *John Ross and The Cherokee Indians*. Menasha, Wisconsin: George Banta, 1914. Google Books. Web. https://books.google.com/books?id=RlJCAAAAIAAJ accessed October 21, 2013.

Echo-Hawk, Walter R. *In the Courts of the Conqueror: The Ten Worst Indian Law Cases Ever Decided*. Golden, CO: Fulcrum Pub., 2012. Print.

"Edward Said: On 'Orientalism" Interview by Sut Jhally. Media Education Foundation. MEF, 24 Jan. 2005. Web. http://www.mediaed.org/assets/products/403/transcript_403.pdf accessed June 18, 2013.

"El Requierimento: Spain Demands Subservience." *Native Voices.* National Institutes of Health and Human Services, n.d. Web. http://www.nlm.nih.gov/nativevoices/timeline/178.html accessed April 30, 2013.

Elkins, James R. "A New Strain of Law and Literature." *Lawyers and Literature,* 1 (2015): n.p. Web. https://web.archive.org/web/20080705212011/http://myweb.wvnet.edu/~jelkins/lawyerslit/images-pdf/first_week_lecture.pdf accessed March 26, 2016.

Encyclopedia Britannica. "Hudson River School." *Encyclopedia Britannica Online.* Encyclopedia Britannica, n.d. Web. http://www.britannica.com/art/Hudson-River-school accessed March 10, 2016. Re. Thomas Cole (1801–1848), the founder of the Hudson River School.

Engle, Patricia. "The Origins and Legacy of Justice Marshall's "New Rule" of Conquest in *Johnson v. M'Intosh.*" *The Literature of Justification – Supreme Court – Essays.* N.p., n.d. Web. http://digital.lib.lehigh.edu/trial/justification/court/essay/ accessed December 5, 2015.

Felker, Tracie. "First Impressions: Thomas Cole." *American Art Journal,* 24 (1992): 66–93. Print.

Ferraro, Vincent. *John Winthrop's City upon a Hill, 1630.* Vincent Ferraro. N.p., n.d. Web. https://www.mtholyoke.edu/acad/intrel/winthrop.htm accessed May 4, 2013.

Fletcher, Matthew L. M. "The Iron Cold of the Marshall Trilogy." *North Dakota Law Review,* 82 (2006): 627–96. Print.

Foreman, Grant. *Indian Removal.* Norman: University of Oklahoma Press, 1972. Print.

Francis, Robert. *Two Kinds of Beings: The Doctrine of Discovery.* Manataka American Indian Council. N.p., n.d. Web. http://www.manataka.org/page94.html accessed May 3, 2013.

Fritzell, Peter A. "The Wilderness and The Garden: Metaphors For The American Landscape." *Forest History,* 12 (1968): 16–23. Print.

Frost, J. William. "William Penn's Experiment in the Wilderness: Promise and Legend." *The Historical Society of Pennsylvania,* 107.4 (1983): 577–605. JSTOR. Web. http://www.jstor.org/stable/i20091803 accessed April 28, 2013.

Galvin, William Francis. "The History of the Arms and Great Seal of the Commonwealth of Massachusetts." *Public Records.* N.p., 2012. Web. http://www.sec.state.ma.us/pre/presea/sealhis.htm accessed October 1, 2013.

Garrison, Tim Alan. *The Legal Ideology of Removal: The Southern Judiciary and the Sovereignty of Native American Nations.* Athens, GA: University of Georgia Press, 2002. Print.

Gates, W. B. "Cooper's Indebtedness to Shakespeare." *Modern Language Association,* 67.5 (1952): 716–31. JSTOR. Web. http://www.jstor.org/stable/460023 accessed May 4, 2013.

Gearey, Adam and John Gardner. *Law and Aesthetics.* Oxford: Hart Pub., 2001. Print.

Gibbons v. Ogden. 22 U.S. 1. Supreme Court. 1824. *Justia.* N.p., n.d. Web. http://supreme.justia.com/cases/federal/us/22/1/case.html accessed April 30, 2013.

Golder, Ben and Peter Fitzpatrick. *Foucault's Law.* Milton Park, Abingdon: Routledge, 2009. Print.

Goodrich, Peter. *Law in the Courts of Love: Literature and Other Minor Jurisprudences.* London: Routledge, 1996. Print.

Graham, Linda J. "Discourse Analysis and the Critical Use of Foucault." *Australian Association for Research in Education.* Sydney, Australia. N.p.: n.p., 2005. 1–15. Eprints Queensland University of Technology. Web. http://eprints.qut.edu.au/2689/1/2689.pdf accessed April 28, 2013.

Hacker, David J. and Michael R. Haines. "American Indian Mortality In The Late Nineteenth Century: The Impact Of Federal Assimilation Policies On A Vulnerable Population." *Annales De Démographie Historique,* 2nd ser. (2005): 17–45. Web. http://www2.binghamton.edu/history/docs/hacker-haines_american_indian.pdf accessed October 24, 2013.

Haldar, Piyel. *Law, Orientalism, and Postcolonialism: The Jurisdiction of the Lotus Eaters.* Abingdon UK: Routledge-Cavendish, 2007. Print.

Hall, Anthony J. "The Royal Proclamation of 1763." *The Canadian Encyclopedia.* N.p., 7 Feb. 2006. Web. http://thecanadianencyclopedia.com/en/article/royal-proclamation-of-1763/ accessed October 8, 2015.

Heimert, Alan. "Puritanism, The Wilderness and The Frontier." *The New England Quarterly,* 26.3 (1953): 361–82. JSTOR. Web. http://www.jstor.org/stable/362849 accessed April 24, 2013.

Hollander, Jocelyn A. and Rachel L. Einwohner. "Conceptualizing Resistance." *Sociologica Forum,* 19.4 (2004): 533–54. JSTOR. Web. http://www.jstor.org/stable/4148828 accessed October 21, 2013.

Huddart, David. *Homi K. Bhabha.* N.p.: Routledge, 2007. Print. Routledge Critical Thinkers.

Jackson, Helen Hunt. *A Century of Dishonor: The Early Crusade for Indian Reform.* New York: Harper & Row, 1965. Print.

"Jacksonian Democracy and Modern America." *U.S. History Pre-Columbian to the New Millennium.* The Independence Hall Association in Philadelphia, n.d. Web. http://www.ushistory.org/us/23f.asp accessed April 30, 2013.

Jahoda, Gloria. *The Trail of Tears: The Story of the American Indian Removals 1813–1855.* New York: Holt, Rinehart & Winston, 1975. Print.

Kades, Eric. "History and Interpretation of the Great Case of *Johnson v. M'Intosh.*" *Law and History Review,* 19.1 (2001): 67. Web. http://scholarship.law.wm.edu/facpubs/50 accessed March 26, 2016.

Kennedy, Valerie. *Edward Said: A Critical Introduction.* Cambridge, UK: Polity, 2000. Print.

Kingfisher, Pamela J. "Just One Dress To Walk 800 Miles." *Eating Fire, Tasting Blood: Breaking the Great Silence of the American Indian Holocaust.* MariJo Moore (ed.). New York: Thunder's Mouth, 2006. 201–15. Print.

Klages, Mary. *Literary Theory: A Guide for the Perplexed.* London: Continuum, 2006. Print.

Kohn, Margaret. "Colonialism." *Stanford Encyclopaedia of Philosophy.* N.p., 19 Apr. 2012. Web. http://plato.stanford.edu/archives/sum2012/entries/colonialism accessed April 19, 2012.

Laurence, David. "William Bradford's American Sublime." *Modern Language Association,* 102.1 (1987): 55–65. JSTOR. Web. http://www.jstor.org/stable/462492 accessed October 21, 2013.

Leonard, John. "Novel Colonies." *Nation*, 22 (Mar. 1993): 383–90. Print.

Lewis and Clark in Kentucky: Kentucky Connections: Newspaper Reports. N.p., n.d. Web. http://www.lewisandclarkinkentucky.org/connections/newspapers.shtml accessed October 3, 2013.

Lincoln, Charles Henry, John Easton, S. N., Richard Hutchinson, Mary White Rowlandson, and Cotton Mather. *Narratives of the Indian Wars, 1675–1699.* New York: C. Scribner's Sons, 1913. Print.

Loewen, James W. *Lies My Teacher Told Me: Everything Your American History Textbook Got Wrong.* New York: Touchstone, 1995. Print.

Loomba, Ania. *Colonialism–postcolonialism.* 2nd edition. London: Routledge, 2005. Print.

Magliocca, Gerard N. "The Cherokee Removal and the Fourteenth Amendment." *Duke Law Journal*, 53.3 (2003): 875–965. Duke University School of Law. Web. http://scholarship.law.duke.edu/dlj/vol53/iss3/1 accessed May 3, 2013.

Marsden, George M. *Jonathan Edwards: A Life.* New Haven: Yale University, 2003. Print.

"Marshall Trilogy (1823–1832)." *Federal Indian Law For Alaska Tribes.* Interior-Aleutians Campus, n.d. Web. http://tm112.community.uaf.edu/unit-1/marshall-trilogy-1823-1832 accessed April 28, 2013.

Martin, Matthew J. "The Nature and Extent of the Exercise of Criminal Jurisdiction by the Cherokee Supreme Court." *North Carolina Central Law Review*, 32.1 (2009): 27–64. Print.

Mather, Cotton. *"Decennium Luctuosum." Narratives of the Indian Wars 1675–1699.* Charles H. Lincoln (ed.). New York: Charles Scribner's Sons, 1913. 169–297. Print.

Mcloughlin, William G. "Thomas Jefferson and the Beginning of Cherokee Nationalism." *The William and Mary Quarterly*, 32.4 (1975): 547–80. Print.

McLoughlin, William G. *Cherokees and Missionaries.* 1st edition. Norman: University of Oklahoma Press, 1995. Print.

Meyer, Kinereth. "Landscape and Counter-Landscape in the Poetry of William Cullen Bryant." *Nineteenth-Century Literature*, 48.2 (1993): 194–211. JSTOR. University of California Press. Web. http://www.jstor.org/stable/2933890 accessed April 30, 2013.

Miller, Perry. *Errand Into the Wilderness.* N.p.: Harvard University Press, 2009. Print.

Miller, Robert J. "The Doctrine of Discovery in American Indian Law." *Idaho Law Review*, 42 (2005): 1–96. Print.

Miller, Robert J. and Elizabeth Furse. *Native America, Discovered and Conquered: Thomas Jefferson, Lewis and Clark, and Manifest Destiny.* Westport, CT: Praeger, 2006. Print.

Moulton, Gary E. *John Ross, Cherokee Chief.* Athens: University of Georgia Press, 1978. Print.

Murray, Keat. *Proc. of 2008 Conference of the American Literature Association in San Francisco, Cooper Panel No. 2 (Cooper's Indians).* James Fenimore Cooper Society Website, May 2008. Web. http://external.oneonta.edu/cooper/articles/ala/2008ala-murray.html accessed September 20, 2013.

Nash, Roderick. "*The Cultural Significance of the American Wilderness.*" *Wilderness and the Quality of Life.* Maxine McCloskey and James P. Gilligan (eds). San Francisco: Sierra Club, 1969. 66–73. Print.

Nash, Roderick. *Wilderness and The American Mind.* 4th edition. New Haven: Yale University Press, 2001. Print.

"Native Blood: The Myth of Thanksgiving." *Revolutionary Worker Online.* N.p., 24 Nov. 1996. Web. http://rwor.org/a/firstvol/883/thank.htm accessed October 24, 2013.

The New Encyclopedia Britannica. 15th edition. Vol. 2. N.p.: Encyclopedia Britannica, 1995. Print.

Newcomb, Steven. *Five Hundred Years of Injustice: The Legacy of Fifteenth Century Religious Prejudice.* Indigenous Law Institute. N.p., n.d. Web. http://ili.nativeweb.org/sdrm_art.html accessed May 24, 2013.

Newcomb, Steven T. *Pagans in the Promised Land: Decoding the Doctrine of Christian Discovery.* Golden, CO: Fulcrum Pub., 2008. Print.

Norgren, Jill. *The Cherokee Cases: Two Landmark Federal Decisions in the Fight for Sovereignty.* Norman, OK: University of Oklahoma Press, 2004. Print.

Nuttall, Thomas. *A Journal of Travels into the Arkansas Territory.* Philadelphia: Thos B. Palmer, 1821. Google Books. Web. accessed May 3, 2013.

O'Brien, Jean M. *Dispossession by Degrees: Indian Land and Identity in Natick, Massachusetts, 1650–1790.* Cambridge: Cambridge University Press, 1997. Print.

"Papal Bulls Burning." *Restore World Peace.* Matsunaga Institute for Peace, n.d. Web. http://bullsburning.itgo.com/Papbull.htm accessed October 24, 2013.

Parry, Ellwood C. "Overlooking the Oxbow: Thomas Cole's 'View from Mount Holyoke' Revisited." *American Art Journal,* 34 (2003–2004): 7–61. Print.

"Patent Granted by King Henry VII to John Cabot and His Sons, March 1496." Patent Granted by King Henry VII to John Cabot. N.p., n.d. Web. http://www.heritage.nf.ca/articles/exploration/1496-cabot-patent.php accessed November 12, 2015.

Perdue, Theda. "Rising from the Ashes: The Cherokee Phoenix as an Ethnohistorical Source." *Ethnohistory,* 24.3 (1977): 207–18. JSTOR. Web. http://www.jstor.org/stable/481695 accessed October 21, 2013.

Perdue, Theda. "Clan and Court: Another Look at the Early Cherokee Republic." *American Indian Quarterly,* 24.4 (2000): 562–9. JSTOR. Web. http://www.jstor.org/stable/1185890 accessed October 21, 2013.

Perdue, Theda and Michael D. Green. *The Cherokee Nation and the Trail of Tears.* New York: Viking, 2007. Print.

Porsdam, Helle. "Doing What Comes Naturally?—Fish, Posner, and the Law and Literature Enterprise." *American Quarterly,* 44.3 (1992): 494–505. JSTOR. Web. http://www.jstor.org/stable/2712992 accessed October 21, 2013.

Posner, Richard A. "Against Ethical Criticism." *Philosophy and Literature,* 21.1 (1997): 1–27. Print.

"Proclamation of 1763." *USHistory.org.* Independence Hall Association, 1995. Web. http://www.ushistory.org/declaration/related/proc63.htm accessed May 27, 2013.

Prucha, F. P. "Andrew Jackson's Indian Policy: A Reassessment." *The Journal of American History,* 56.3 (1969): 527–39. JSTOR. Web. http://www.jstor.org/stable/1904204 accessed October 21, 2013.

Prucha, Francis Paul. *American Indian Treaties: The History of a Political Anomaly.* Berkeley: University of California Press, 1997. Print.

Remini, Robert Vincent. *Andrew Jackson and His Indian Wars.* New York: Viking, 2001. Print.

Rensink, Brenden. "Genocide of Native Americans: Historical Facts and Historiographic Debates." 2011 Dissertations, Theses, and Student Research, Department of History. Paper 34. Web. http://digitalcommons.unl.edu/historydiss/34 accessed March 26, 2016.

"Revoking the Bull 'Inter Caetera' of 1493." Manataka American Indian Council, n.d. Web. http://www.manataka.org/page155.html accessed May 4, 2013.

Reynolds, Guy. "The Winning of the West: Washington Irving's 'A Tour on the Prairies.'" *The Yearbook of English Studies, Nineteenth-Century Travel Writing,* 34 (2004): 88–99. JSTOR. Modern Humanities Research Association. Web. http://www.jstor.org/stable/3509486 accessed April 30, 2013.

Reynolds, Jerry. *Revoking the Papal Bull of 1493.* Indigenous Law Institute, n.d. Web. http://www.manataka.org/page155.html accessed May 4, 2013.

Richter, Daniel K. *Facing East from Indian Country: A Native History of Early America.* Cambridge, MA: Harvard University Press, 2001. Print.

Robert Arnold v. Benajah Munday. 6 NJL 1. *Supreme Court of New Jersey.* 1821. Print.

Robert Arnold v. Benajah Munday. 6 NJL 1. *Supreme Court of New Jersey.* 1821. Rutgers History. N.p., n.d. Web. http://fas-history.rutgers.edu/clemens/NJLaw/arnold1821.html accessed April 30, 2013.

Robertson, Lindsay Gordon. *Conquest by Law: How the Discovery of America Dispossessed Indigenous Peoples of Their Lands.* Oxford: Oxford University Press, 2005. Print.

Romero, Lora. "Vanishing Americans: Gender, Empire, and New Historicism." *American Literature,* Sep., 63.3 (1991): 385–404. JSTOR. Web. http://www.jstor.org/stable/2927239 accessed October 21, 2013.

Rondthaler, Rev. Edward. *Life of John Heckewelder.* B. H. Coates (ed.). Philadelphia: Townsend Ward, 1847. Google Books. Web. https://books.google.com/books?id=ByATAAAAYAAJ accessed October 21, 2013.

Rosen, Deborah A. "Colonization through Law: The Judicial Defense of State Indian Legislation, 1790–1880." *The American Journal of Legal History,* 46.1 (2004): 26–54. JSTOR. Web. http://www.jstor.org/stable/3692417 accessed October 21, 2013.

Routh, E. C. *Early Missionaries to the Cherokees.* Oklahoma Historical Society's Chronicles of Oklahoma. N.p., n.d. Web. http://digital.library.okstate.edu/chronicles/v015/v015p449.html accessed May 4, 2013.

Rubin, Andrew N. "Edward W. Said (1935–2003)." *Arab Studies Quarterly,* 26.4 (2004): 37–55. Print.

Ruskola, Teemu. "Legal Orientalism." *Michigan Law Review,* 101.1 (2002): 179–234. JSTOR. Web. http://www.jstor.org/stable/1290419 accessed October 21, 2013.

Russell, Steve. "The Cherokee Nation: A Colonial Morality Play in Three Acts." *Eating Fire, Tasting Blood: Breaking the Great Silence of the American Indian Holocaust.* Marijo Moore (ed.). 1st edition. New York: Thunder's Mouth, 2006. 128–69. Print.

Sachidananda, Mohanty. "Literary Review." *The Hindu.* N.p., July 3, 2005. Web. http://www.hindu.com/lr/2005/07/03/stories/2005070300020100.htm accessed April 30, 2013.

"Samuel Worcester." *Cherokee Nation.* N.p., n.d. Web. http://www.cherokee.org/AboutTheNation/History/Biographies/SamuelWorcester.aspx accessed May 3, 2013.

Schirato, Tony, Geoff Danaher, and Jen Webb. *Understanding Foucault: A Critical Introduction.* Thousand Oaks, CA: SAGE Publications, 2012. Print.

Schlag, Pierre. "The Aesthetics of American Law." *Harvard Law Review,* 115.4 (2002): 1047–1118. JSTOR. Web. http://www.jstor.org/stable/1342629 accessed October 21, 2013.

Schueller, Malini Johar and Edward Watts. *Messy Beginnings: Postcoloniality and Early American Studies.* New Brunswick, NJ: Rutgers University Press, 2003. Print.

Seed, Patricia. "Taking Possession and Reading Texts: Establishing The Authority of Overseas Empires." *William and Mary Quarterly*, 49 (1992): 183–209. JSTOR. Web. http://www.jstor.org/stable/2947269 accessed October 24, 2013.

Segal, Charles M. and David C. Stineback. *Puritans, Indians, and Manifest Destiny.* New York: Putnam, 1977. Print.

Shatzman, Aaron M. *"The Old World, the New World, and the Creation of the Modern World, 1400–1650: An Interpretive History"* N.p.: n.p., 2013. Print.

Sheehan, Bernard W. *Seeds of Extinction: Jeffersonian Philanthropy and the American Indian.* New York: W. W. Norton, 1974. Print.

Silver, Peter Rhoads. *Our Savage Neighbors: How Indian War Transformed Early America.* New York: W. W. Norton, 2008. Print.

Solove, Daniel J. Law and Literature Syllabus. N.p., Spring 2010. Web. http://docs.law.gwu.edu/facweb/dsolove/Law-Humanities/Law-Literature-Syllabus.htm accessed October 4, 2013.

Staff, History.com. "James Monroe." *History.com.* A&E Television Networks, 2009. Web. http://www.history.com/topics/us-presidents/james-monroe accessed December 6, 2015.

Stannard, David E. *American Holocaust: Columbus and the Conquest of the New World.* New York: Oxford University Press, 1992. Print.

Stevens, Laura M. *The Poor Indians: British Missionaries, Native Americans, and Colonial Sensibility.* Philadelphia: University of Pennsylvania Press, 2004. Print.

Stodala, Katheryn Z. D. *Woman's Indian Captivity Narratives.* New York: Penguin, 1998. Print.

Totten, Samuel and Robert K. Hitchcock. *Genocide of Indigenous Peoples.* New Brunswick, NJ: Transaction, 2011. Print.

Tuitt, Patricia. *Race, Law and Resistance.* London: GlassHouse, 2004. Print.

Ushistory.org. "Jacksonian Democracy and Modern America." *U.S. History Online Textbook.* Independence Hall Association, n.d. Web. http://www.ushistory.org/us/23f.asp accessed May 3, 2013.

Van Zandt, Franklin K. "Article." *Expansion And Growth Of The United States.* United States Department of the Interior, 14 Jan. 2013. Web. http://nationalatlas.gov/articles/history/a_expansion.html accessed May 1, 2013.

Varisco, Daniel Martin. *Reading Orientalism: Said and the Unsaid.* Seattle: University of Washington Press, 2007. Print.

Vaughn, Karen I. "John Locke and The Labor Theory of Value." *Journal of Libertarian Studies*, 2.4 (1978): 311–26. Ludwig Von Mises Institute. Web. http://mises.org/journals/jls/2_4/2_4_3.pdf accessed October 21, 2013.

Weisburg, Richard. *Wigmore, and the Law and Literature Movement.* Cardozo (2006): 1–15. Social Science Research Network. Web. http://papers.ssrn.com/sol3/papers.cfm?abstract_id=951700## accessed October 21, 2013.

Wendell, Barrett A. *A Literary History of the United States.* 1st edition. London: T. Fisher, 1901. Print.

West, Robin. "Authority, Autonomy, and Choice: The Role of Consent in the Moral and Political Visions of Franz Kafka and Richard Posner." *Harvard Law Review*, 99.2 (1985): 384–428. JSTOR. Web. http://www.jstor.org/stable/1341128 accessed October 21, 2013.

Wilkins, David E. *American Indian Sovereignty and the U.S. Supreme Court: The Masking of Justice.* Austin: University of Texas Press, 1997. Print.

Williams, David Ross. *Wilderness Lost: The Religious Origins of the American Mind.* Selinsgrove: Susquehanna University Press, 1987. Print.

Williams, Robert A. *The American Indian in Western Legal Thought: The Discourses of Conquest.* New York: Oxford University Press, 1990. Print.

Williamson, Peter. "A Captive's Account of the Cruelty of Indians." *Native Americans: Opposing Viewpoints.* William Dudley (ed.). San Diego, CA: Greenhaven, 1998. 35–44. Print.

Windschuttle, Keith. "Edward Said's Orientalism." *The New Criterion,* 17.5 (1999): 30–38. Web. http://ontology.buffalo.edu/smith/courses01/rrtw/Windschuttle.htm accessed October 8, 2015.

Windschuttle, Keith. "Edward Said's Orientalism." *The New Criterion,* 17.5 (1999): 30–38. Print.

Worcester v. Georgia. 31 515. Supreme Court. 1832. Justia. N.p., n.d. Web. http://supreme.justia.com/cases/federal/us/31/515/case.html accessed April 30, 2013.

Wright, Ronald. *Stolen Continents: Five Hundred Years of Conquest and Resistance in the Americas.* Boston: Houghton Mifflin, 2005. Print.

Young, Mary. "The Cherokee Nation: Mirror of the Republic." *American Quarterly,* 33.5 (1981): 502–24. JSTOR. Web. http://www.jstor.org/stable/2712800 accessed October 21, 2013.

Young, Robert. *Postcolonialism: An Historical Introduction.* Oxford, UK: Blackwell, 2001. Print.

Index

a prioris 10, 156n4, 172, 173
Adams, John 23n6, 203
Adams, John Quincy 92–3
Ahmad, Aijaz 183–4
Alexander VI, Pope 28, 221n9
Alfonso V, King of Portugal 25, 32
Alloway, John 136
ambivalence 178–9, 184, 185, 187, 191, 198–9, 200, 206–7n6
American Exceptionalism 80
'Americans' defined 22n1; *see also* Native Americans
amnesia, theory of 83, 84, 128, 156n4, 169, 177n12–13
Anderson, Benedict 188
anxiety 131, 179, 198–200, 201, 203, 204–5
archive 10, 14, 20, 57, 62
Aristodemou, Maria 161, 168, 175
Arkansas 46
Arnold, Mary 96
Arnold v. Mundy (1821) 31
art: and the conquest of the Americas 80–2; landscapes 99, 103n2, 139, 148, 149, 149*f*, 150–1, 150*f*, 154, 157–8n19; and wilderness 71, 126, 148–52
Asad, Talal 76
assimilation 109, 119, 127–8, 142, 199, 207n11; *see also* Cherokee resistance
Austen, Jane: *Mansfield Park* 74, 80, 110, 123n11
Avatar (film) 220n4

Bakhtin, Mikhail 78–9
Baldwin, Henry 64–5
Banner, Stuart 86, 91
Barker, Martin 99
Baron, Jane B. 162, 168
beauty and the sublime 145–6, 147–8
Berkhofer, Robert F. 98
Bhabha, Homi K. 4n1, 18, 20, 51, 162, 206n2; on colonial discourses 178–9, 184, 188; criticism of *Orientalism* 181, 184–90; on hybridity 4n1, 189; on mimicry 4n1, 178–9, 185–90, 197; theory of ambivalence 178–9, 184, 185, 187, 200, 206–7n6; theory of anxiety 200, 201
Bierce, Ambrose 19
Billington, Ray Allen 127
bio-power 18, 78
Black, Henry R. 19, 23n9, 23n10, 157n13
Blackstone's *Commentaries* 143, 144, 145, 147
Bleecker, Ann Eliza 138
Blount, William 60
Boorstin, Daniel 143, 144–5, 147–8, 157n14
Botham, Fary 123n8
Boudinot, Elias 195
bounty land system 52n8; *see also* Virginia–Kentucky militia bounty problem
Brackenridge, Hugh Henry 73, 105–6
Bradbury, John 91–2
Bradford, William 127, 131–2, 158n22
Bross, Kristina 213, 214, 215
Brown v. Board of Education of Topeka (1954) 219

Bryant, William Cullen 55, 60, 100–1, 103n9, 137, 138–40, 157n10, 214
Burke, Edmund 143, 144
Burke, Joseph C. 46, 145–7
Butler, Brian 171, 172
Byrd, William 133–4

Cabot, John 30, 57, 216–17, 221n10
Caldwell v. Alabama (1831) 52n6
Camus, Albert 164, 167, 176n5
capacity 8, 14, 161
captive narratives 58, 65n4, 90–1, 106, 115–16, 122n4, 123n7
Cardozo, Benjamin 172
Catlin, George 100–1
Charles II, King of England 156n9
Charter of Cabot (1496) 30, 57
Cherokee Nation 109, 123n6, 123n9, 212; clan based system 193–5; Constitution (1828) 186, 190, 193, 195; and missionaries 190, 196–7, 202, 207n9–10; National General Council 193, 195, 207n9; nationalism 195; Supreme Court 190, 197–8; territory 36; treaties 60, 205, 208n15; *see also Cherokee Nation v. Georgia* (1831); Cherokee resistance; *Worcester v. Georgia* (1832)
Cherokee Nation v. Georgia (1831) 15, 22–3n2, 33–5, 39, 48, 49, 52n4, 124; conquest of the wilderness 140; Indian right of occupancy 28; structure of legal judgment 55–6, 60–2, 63–4, 196–7, 198; *see also* Marshall Trilogy cases; *Worcester v. Georgia* (1832)
The Cherokee Phoenix 36, 190, 195
Cherokee resistance 178–81, 206n3; American ambivalence to 198–9; judicial resistance 196–7; loci of Cherokee resistance 192–3; nature of resistance 190–2; Orientalism to mimicry 182–90; political replication as resistance 193–5, 207n8; Trail of Tears 65, 220n3
Cheyenne Nation 91
Chickasaw Nation 44, 93, 200, 212
Choctaw Nation 39, 212
Christianity *see* divine purpose; Doctrine of Discovery; missionaries; Papal Bulls; religious domination
Churchill, Ward 211–12, 215, 220n2, 221n7
civilization policy 108, 110, 118, 120, 122–3n5, 123n9, 129, 134, 148, 202–3, 207n11; *see also* Cherokee resistance
Clark, William *see* Lewis and Clark Expeditions
Clinton, DeWitt 58, 65n3, 65n4, 73, 94
cognitive theory 31
Cole, Thomas 32, 94–5n2, 148, 149–51, 157n17; *The Last of the Mohicans* 99, 149*f*, 150; *The Oxbow* 71, 150*f*, 151, 154, 157–8n19
Cole, William 157n18
colonial archive 22, 65n4, 70, 179, 211; and Marshall Trilogy 14–15, 18, 20, 57, 59, 128, 180
colonial conquest 12, 25–7, 59; *see also The Last of the Mohicans*
colonial discourses 14, 178–9, 184, 188; unity of 21–2, 54–5, 57; *see also* Doctrine of Discovery
colonial knowledge 3, 54–5; structure of legal judgment 55–65
colonized subjects 24–5, 38–9
Columbus, Christopher 32, 211–12
Commerce Clause 41–2, 43
Compact Treaty (1802) 34
Congressional Act (1819) 63
Conser, Walter H., Jr. 199, 201, 205–6
Constable, John 151
Constitutional Convention (1789) 40–1, 42
Continental Congress 52n9
Cooper, James Fenimore 95n4, 98, 100–1, 103–4n10, 137, 141, 157n10, 214; *Leatherstocking* novels 77, 102, 126; *see also The Last of the Mohicans*
Corrington, John William 167
Cotterill, R. S. 201
Cotton, John 32, 125
Courts of First Instance 19
Crawford, Col. William 73
Crawford, William H. 202

Creek people 201, 202; *see also* Red Sticks
Crisp, Steven 136
Cuddon, J. A. 103n3
culture and imperialism 71–3, 77, 78–80; *see also* Said, Edward W.
custom, as basis of legal opinion 58–9
Cutcher, Catherine 220n4
Cutler, Charles L. 103

Danforth, Samuel 134, 135
Dawn, Ernest C. 155
de novo 19, 23n9
De Tocqueville, Alexis 133, 156n7, 175
De Vitoria, Francisco 88–9, 95n6
Demos, John 123n7
Derick, Gertrud 136
Derrida, Jacques 165, 166, 167, 169
Dexter, Pete 167
Dickens, Charles 164
Dippie, Bryan W. 99–100
discourse 8–9; capacity 8, 14; and discursive formations 8, 9–10, 15; early 19th century public discourse 91–4; from formation to dispersal 11–14; power relations 12–13; *see also* colonial discourses; discourse in colonial context; discourse theory; Said, Edward W.; statements
discourse in colonial context 69–71; culture, imperialism and Said 71–3; the Other 74–8
discourse theory: and the American wilderness 124–6; *see also* Foucault, Michel: theory of discourse
discursive formations 8, 9–10, 15, 17
discursive 'policing' 16
divine purpose 97–8, 125, 136, 213–14, 221n5
Dobyns, Henry R. 221n7
Doctrine of Discovery 207n14; Cherokee claim 33; international law 25–7, 29, 30; Jefferson's claim 153–4; Marshall's interpretation 26, 27–30, 36–8, 44–6, 52n3, 55, 56–7, 59, 70–1, 169, 204–5, 207–8n14; *New York vs. Oneida Indian Nation of New York* (2005) 217–19; religious basis of 25–6, 28, 32–3, 215–17; *terra nullius* 154
Domnarski, William 164
Dostoevsky, Fyodor 164, 176n5
Douzinas, Costas *et al.* 83
Drinnon, Richard 153, 199, 200
Dryden, John 157n14
Duston, Hannah 65n4
Dwight, Theodore, Jr. 151
Dworkin, Ronald 165

Eaton, Rachel Caroline 202
Echo-Hawk, Walter R. 219
Edwards, Jonathan 32, 125, 133
Elkins, James 166–7
Elliott, John 100(n6)
Engle, Patricia 28
English Common Law 19, 26–7, 145, 147, 155
Enlightenment 74, 99, 144
enunciations *see* statements
enunciative system 9, 18, 161, 176n1, 180
episteme 11, 21
essentialism 183, 206n4

facts 19; *see also* findings of fact
Fanon, Franz 206–7n6
farmers, Indians as 15, 49, 73, 77, 91–2, 154, 196
Federal tariffs 39
Federal Treaties 60–2, 63, 65n6; *see also treaties by name*
Federalism 15, 16, 23n6, 24, 40–1, 43, 46–8; interpretation 48–51
fee simple title 20, 37, 38, 51, 62, 64
Ferdinand, King of Spain 216
findings of fact 11, 49, 163, 169; as historical presumptions 167–8; in Marshall Trilogy cases 12, 15, 20, 22, 34–5, 49–50, 51, 56, 59–60, 62, 63, 84, 171; and wilderness 125–6
Fish, Stanley 165
Fitzpatrick, Peter 13
Five Nations 105, 122n2
Fletcher, Mathew L. M. 24, 49–50
Foucault, Michel: enunciative system 9, 18, 161, 176n1, 180; and the Marshall Trilogy 24–5, 171; on power relations 12–14, 20–1, 74, 76–7, 78; resistance

178; statements 176n1, 179–80; theory of discourse 2–3, 7, 8–10, 11, 15–16, 17–18, 21–2, 23n3, 23n4, 54–5, 57, 62, 176, 179; 'will to truth' 15–16, 125
Freeman's Journal 73, 105
Frelignhuysen, Theodore 207n8
Freneau, Philip 98, 100–1
Frisbie, Levi 30, 87, 89
Fritzell, Peter 139, 157n11
Frost, J. WIlliam 136–7
Furse, Elizabeth 93

Gadamer, Hans-Georg 81, 148, 165, 167, 176
Garrison, Tim A. 16, 17, 33, 39, 41, 43, 46, 48, 53n11, 65n6
Gay, Hunter 90
Gearey, Adam 172, 173, 174
Geneva Bible 156n6
genocide 211–12, 214, 215, 220n2, 221n7
George III, King of England 51–2n2
Georgia v. Tassels (1830) 34, 41
Gerish, Sarah 132–3, 156n5
Gibbons v. Ogden (1824) 41–2
Gilbert, Sir Humphrey 32–3, 57
Ginsburg, Ruth 217–19
Golder, Ben 13
Goodrich, Peter 18, 83, 128, 156n4, 158n22, 161, 169, 170, 171, 174, 176, 177n12–13
Graham, Linda J. 22
Gramsci, Antonio 206n1
Green, Michael 122–3n5, 123n6, 123n9

Halder, Piyel 176n4, 183
Hale, Nathan 100(n5)
Hall, Anthony J. 51–2n2
Hall, Basil 157n19
Hall, Kermit L. 48
Hamilton, Alexander 23n6
Hanson, Elizabeth 65n4
Harrison, William 153
Hawks, Benjamin 199
Heckewelder, John 33, 101–2, 103–4n10
Hegel, G.W.F. 81, 148–9
Heimert, Adam 134–5
Henry VII, King of England 216
hermeneutics 81, 148–9, 157n16, 164, 165, 167
Hicks v. Ewhartonah (1860) 46
historical horizons 148–9, 150, 157n16
historical presumptions 167–8
Hobson, Charles F. 13
Holy See 25–6, 27
Houston, Sam 190–1
Howe, Jemima 65n4
Huddart, David 4n1
Hudson River School 94n2, 149–51, 157n15
humane policy 127–8, 142, 153, 199, 203, 204, 205–6
hunters, Indians as 49, 56, 73, 77, 86, 87, 91–2, 94, 154
Huron Indians 106, 108, 110, 112, 113–14
hybridity 4n1, 189

imperialism *see* culture and imperialism
Inden, Ronald 81
Indian Removal Act (1830) 37, 40, 52n4, 65, 140, 196, 207n8, 213
Indian right of occupancy 20, 28, 29, 37, 44–5
Indian sovereignty 30–1, 36, 37–8, 39, 41, 43, 50
institutional contexts 17; *see also* legal judgment
international law 25–7, 29, 30, 88, 93
Irving, Washington 33, 55, 98, 100–1, 102–3, 137, 140–1, 157n10
Isabella, Queen of Spain 216

Jackson, Andrew 39, 40, 44, 50, 52n7, 60, 64, 140, 191, 192, 202, 220n3; humane theme 205–6, 212–13
Jahoda, Gloria 56, 65, 87, 88
Jefferson, Thomas 73, 109; quest for Indian land 93–4, 125, 152–5, 191, 199–204
Jemison, May 65n4
Jennings, Francis 65n6

Johnson v. M'Intosh (1823) 12, 17, 20, 23n5, 53n15, 71, 124; alive and well 217–20; Doctrine of Discovery 26, 27–8, 29–33, 44–5, 52n3, 80, 114, 142, 207–8n14; Marshall's anxiety 204–5; reflections 209–11; structure of legal judgment 55, 56, 58–9, 61, 62, 64–5, 168–9, 176–7n6, 198; *see also* Marshall Trilogy cases
Johnson, William 64
judicial resistance 196–7
judicial review 15, 23n6, 24

Kades, Eric 45
Kafka, Franz 163, 164, 169, 176n5
Kant, Immanuel 81, 148
Kennedy, Valerie 183, 184
Kentucky *see* Virginia-Kentucky militia bounty problem
Kingfisher, Pamela J. 203, 207n14
Kinnan, Mary 58, 65n4, 90
Kiowa Nation 91
Kipling, Rudyard 78, 188
Klages, Mary 74, 78–9
Knickerbocker Group 138, 157n10
knowledge and power 12–13, 15, 17–18, 20–1, 74, 76, 78, 155
Knox, Henry 60, 120, 122–3n5, 123n9, 207n11
Kollock, Shepard 58
Komie, Lowell B. 167
Kupperman, Karen 213

Lacan, Jacques 186, 189
Lake, Handsome 153
land rights 24, 55, 61, 87–8, 91, 92, 109, 123n6; *see also* Doctrine of Discovery
language (*langue*) 23n3
The Last of the Mohicans 33, 55, 71, 96, 103, 105–6, 149*f*, 220n4; Chingachgook 106, 107, 110, 111, 114–15, 118, 119–20, 121; civilization policy 109; early modern English 118–22; Hawkeye 105, 106, 107, 110, 111–13, 114–15, 119, 121; Magua 106, 107–8, 110, 114, 115–18; race 106–9, 110–18; vanishing Indian theme 35, 85, 98, 99; wilderness 32, 71, 108, 112–13, 128–9
Laurence, David 132
law 8; black letter law 144, 157n13; English Common Law 19, 26–7, 145, 147, 155; equity 144; genre of law 83–4, 128–9; international law 25–7, 29, 30, 88, 93; natural law 34, 89; and power 169; the sublime as 143–5, 147; *see also* Doctrine of Discovery; findings of fact; Law of Nations; legal capacity; legal discourse; legal judgment; U.S. Federal Indian Law
Law and Aesthetics 171–4
law and literature 18, 82–4, 161–3; knowledge and power 17–18; law as literature 164–5, 166–7, 176n3; law in literature 164, 165–6, 167, 176n3; and Marshall Trilogy 82–4, 163, 167–71; *see also* Law and Aesthetics; Legal Orientalism
Law of Nations 27, 88–9
Lee, Eliza 100
Lee, Harper 167
legal capacity 8, 15, 20, 23n5, 30–1, 51, 57, 85, 179, 191
legal discourse 9, 24–5
legal judgment 15, 79, 128, 163, 173, 176, 177n14; historical presumptions in 167–8; in Marshall cases 30, 55–65, 82–4, 168–71, 196–7, 198; structure of 19–21, 49, 173
Legal Orientalism 174–6
Leonard, John 72
Leopold, Aldo 134
Lewis and Clark Expedition (1804–1806) 60, 73, 91, 93, 125, 152, 153–5, 158n20, 158n21
Lewis, Meriwether *see* Lewis and Clark Expeditions
Lincoln, Charles Henry 132–3
literature 7; 18th century archive 22, 58, 59, 85–6; after 1776 73, 86–91; early 19th century public discourse 91–4; post-colonial literature 80, 85, 96–7; captive narratives 58, 65n4, 90–1, 106, 115–16, 122n4, 123n7; culture and imperialism

71–3; defined 73; Marshall Trilogy and 20, 82–4, 98, 163, 167–71; and metropolitan dominance 78–80; missionary journals 101–2; novels 69, 70, 71–3, 74–5, 77–9, 84, 188–9; poetry 77, 79, 83, 98, 100–1, 138–9, 146–7; Romanticism 98, 99, 100–1, 103n2, 124, 125; the silent fiction 18; the sublime 142–8, 157n12; and unity of discourses 59, 65n5, 125; the vanishing Indian 80, 96–103; wilderness theme 85, 124, 129–33; *see also* Austen, Jane: *Mansfield Park*; law and literature; *The Last of the Mohicans*
Locke, John 87–8, 92–3
Long, Stephen 73, 91
Loomba, Ania 75–6, 192
Louisiana Purchase (1803) 152, 158n20, 200, 203, 207n12

McLean, John 64–5
McLoughlin, William G. 195, 207n9–10, 207n11
Madison, James 56
Magadla, Siphokazi 220n4
Magliocca, Gerard N. 207n11
majority opinion 20, 23n10
Manifest Destiny 80, 138, 150, 151, 211
Marbury v. Madison (1803) 23n6
Marie, Henry 73
Marsden, George M. 133
Marshall, John 24, 40; anxiety in legal discourse 204–5; and Cherokee resistance 178, 179, 191; Federalism 15, 16, 23n6, 40, 46; on the Native American 54–5, 113–14, 116; death of 64–5; *see also Cherokee Nation v Georgia* (1831); Doctrine of Discovery; *Johnson v M'Intosh* (1823); Marshall Trilogy; *Worcester v Georgia* (1832)
Marshall Trilogy cases 3, 11–12, 24–5, 158n22, 177n6; and the colonial archive 14–15, 18, 20, 57, 59, 128, 180; Constitutional and political context 39–43, 45–6; conventional interpretations 15, 16–17, 20; discursive 'policing' 16; Doctrine of Discovery 26, 27–33, 36–8, 44–6, 52n3, 55, 56–7, 59, 70–1, 80, 114, 142, 169, 204–5, 207–8n14; Federalism 46–51; findings of fact 12, 15, 20, 22, 34–5, 49–50, 51, 56, 59–60, 62, 63, 84, 171; as literature 20, 82–4, 98, 163, 167–71; structure of legal judgment 30, 55–65, 82–4, 168–71, 196–7, 198; and the sublime 142–4, 157n12; reflections 209–11; moving forward 211–15; *see also Cherokee Nation v. Georgia* (1831); Cherokee resistance; *Johnson v. M'Intosh* (1823); *Worcester v. Georgia* (1832)
Martin, J. Matthew 197–8
Massachusetts Bay Colony 201
Mather, Cotton 31, 32, 57, 80, 85–6, 125, 128–30, 132–3
Mather, Increase 129
Mayhew, Experience 97
Melville, Herman 95n4, 164, 167, 176n5
metropolitan dominance 78–80
Meyer, Kinereth 138
Miller, P. 134, 135
Miller, Robert J. 50, 93
Milton, John: *Paradise Lost* 146–7
mimicry 4n1, 178–9, 185–90, 192–5, 197
missionaries 73, 87, 88, 89, 97–8, 126–7, 130, 137; and the Cherokee 190, 196–7, 202, 207n9–10; and the civilization policy 110, 129, 134, 207n11; and the Natick 201–2
missionary journals 101–2
Mitchel v. United States (Mitchel I) (1835) 65n7
Monroe Doctrine 65n2
Monroe, James 56, 65n2, 87
Morse, Jedediah 88
Muir, John 134
Mullanphy, John 158n21
murmurs 11, 12, 126, 156n4
Murray, Keat 102, 103–4n10

Naipaul, V. S. 188–9
Nash, Roderick Frazier 128, 130, 132, 156n3
Natick Indians 201–2

Native Americans 7, 11–12; discursive formations of 15, 20, 55, 65n1, 211; as 'domestic dependent nations' 20; judicial omissions 12; legal capacity of 15, 20, 23n5, 30–1, 51, 57, 85, 179, 191; resistance 20; unity of discourses 54–5
natural law 34, 89
Neoclassical period 99, 103n3, 157n14
New York Historical Society 73
New York vs. Oneida Indian Nation of New York (2005) 217–19
Newcomb, Steven T. 26, 28, 31, 32–3, 56, 207–8n14, 215–16
Nicholas V, Pope 25–6, 32, 33, 57
Nietzsche, Friedrich 182, 183
nomads, Indians as 73, 77, 82, 84, 86, 91, 94, 154, 212
Non-Conformist Christianity 134
Norgren, Jill 39, 40–1, 48, 50
novels 69, 70, 71–3, 74–5, 77–9, 84, 188–9; *see also* Austen, Jane: *Mansfield Park*; *The Last of the Mohicans*
Nuttail, Thomas 73, 92

O'Brien, Jean 201–2
Oliphant v. Suguamish Indian Tribe (1978) 198
Olmsted, Frederick Law 134
Oneida Nation 217–19
ordering of objects 7, 17–18
Orians, G. Harrison 98
the Orient 72, 94n1
Orientalism 18, 20, 21–2, 74, 94n1, 155, 174, 182–5, 192; *see also* Legal Orientalism
the Other 72, 94n1; discourse and 74–8, 95n3, 154, 171, 183–4

Palladium Newspaper 158n21
Papal Bulls 25–6, 28, 32, 33, 211, 215–17, 221n9
Penn, William 57, 82, 136–7, 156n9
Pennsylvania 82, 136–7, 156n9
Peqot Indians 213
Percy, Walker 167
Perdue, Theda 123n9, 194–5
persuasion 72
Plato 83
Plessy v. Ferguson (1896) 219
Poe, Edgar Allan 137
poetry 77, 79, 83, 98, 100–1, 138–9, 146–7
political replication as resistance 193–5, 207n8
Pope, Alexander 157n14
Porsdam, Helle 170–1
Porter, Katherine Anne 167
Posner, Richard 83, 163, 170
post colonial theory 50–1, 103n1
power relations 12–14, 124–5; bio-power 18, 78; dispersal of 76–7; and knowledge 12–13, 15, 17–18, 20–1, 74, 76, 78, 155; and law 169; as productive 13, 77
pre-emption rights 86, 91
precedent 19, 23n8
Preston, Claire 103n3
Prucha, Francis Paul 203, 207n13
Purchas, Samuel 127
Puritans 85–6, 115, 116, 125, 126–7, 129–31, 134–5

Quakerism 136, 137, 156n9

race: discourses of 35, 55–6, 60, 219–20; in *The Last of the Mohicans* 106–9, 110–18
racism 49, 50
Raleigh, Sir Walter 33, 37, 57, 216
Randolph, John 190
rational man theory 170
reason 144
Red Sticks 212; *see also* Creek people
Reed, Luman 157n19
Reese, Sally 122–3n5
religious domination 25–7, 56–7; and Doctrine of Discovery 25–6, 28, 32–3, 215–17
Rensink, Brenden 220n2
research 2–3, 14–17
resistance 20, 178–9, 206n3; *see also* Cherokee resistance
Reynolds, Guy 141
Reynolds, J. 215–16
Richter, Daniel K. 212

Ridge, John 190
right of possession 55, 61, 87–8, 92
right to the soil 30–1, 37–8, 64, 88, 91; *see also* Indian right of occupancy
Robertson, Lindsay G. 37–8, 44, 45, 64, 65n7, 176–7n6, 210
Romanticism 55, 96, 133–4, 138; in art 150–1; in literature 98, 99, 100–1, 103n2, 124, 125
Romero, Lora 99
Rose, Salley 123n9
Rosen, Deborah A. 41, 42–3, 46–7, 53n11
Ross, John 52n4, 193, 202
Rowlandson, Mary 65n4
Royal Proclamation (1763) 27, 29, 33, 37, 52n2
Rubin, Andrew 74–5
Ruskola, Teemu 174, 175
Russell, Steve 1

Sabin, Roger 99
Said, Edward W. 7, 15, 206n2; contraptional approach 76, 78–9, 192; culture and imperialism 69–70, 71–3, 81, 95n4, 109, 110, 120, 121, 123n11, 173–4; discourse 78, 84; discourse and the Other 72, 74–5, 79, 84, 94n1, 95n3, 113, 115, 125, 155, 171, 183–4; Orientalism 18, 20, 21–2, 74, 76, 94n1, 155, 174, 179, 181, 182–5, 192, 206n5
Satz, Ronald N. 203, 207n13
savages, Indians as 15, 20, 33, 54, 73, 82, 92, 94, 115; in captive narrative accounts 90–1, 106; in *The Last of the Mohicans* 113–15; in Marshall cases 28, 31, 70, 71, 84, 211; and missionaries 87, 89; in pre-Cooper literature 105–6
Saye, Lord 213
Schirato, Tony 21
Schlag, Pierre 172–3
Schoolcraft, Henry 49
Sears, John 151
Seed, Patricia 221n9
separation of church and state 26, 56
Shatzman, Aaron M. 216
Shelby, Isaac 44
Sigourney, Lydia 77
Silver, Peter Rhoads 106
slavery 74, 123n11
Smith, Adam 60, 89, 94
Solove, Daniel J. Law 176n3
South Carolina Nullification Ordinance 39–40
Spivak, Gayatri Chakravorty 178, 206n1
Sprague, Peleg 37
Stanford Encyclopaedia of Philosophy 88–9, 95n6
Stannard, David E. 214, 215
stare decisis 19, 23n8
state courts 40, 41, 42–3, 46–7
state laws 23n6, 24, 33, 34
statements 8, 9, 10, 21–2, 23n3, 23n4, 48, 176n1, 179–80
states' rights 39–43, 46
Steele, William 130
Stevens, Laura 96–7
Stodola, Katheryn Z. D. 58, 90–1
Story, Joseph 27–8, 40
the sublime 142–9, 157n12
Suguamish Tribe 198
Sullivan, James 73, 82

Tanana Chiefs Conference 51n1
Taylor, Thomas 136
Tennessee v. Foreman (1835) 52n6
terra nullius 154
Thompson v. Johnson (1813) 30
Thornton, Russell 221n7
Tolstoy, Leo 167
trade 41, 89, 93–4, 105, 152–3, 200–1
tradition 20, 54, 55, 59, 62–3
Trail of Tears 65, 220n3
treaties 16, 34, 203–4, 208n15
Treaties of Holston (1791; 1794; 1798) 60, 208n15
Treaties of Washington (1806; 1816; 1819) 60–1, 202
Treaty of Echota (1838) 220n3
Treaty of Fort Jackson (1814) 202
Treaty of Hopewell (1785) 34, 35, 44, 60, 208n15
Treaty of Paris (1783) 82
Treaty of Philadelphia (1794) 60

Treaty of Tellico (1790) 60
Treaty of the Cherokee (1806) 208n15
Tudor, William, Jr. 100
Turner, J.M.W. 151

UAF Center for Distance Education 51n1
UAF Interior Aleutians Campus 51n1
Unger, Roberto 170
United States v. Kagama (1886) 42
Urofsky, Melvin I 48
U.S. Bureau of Indian Affairs 51n1
U.S. Department of Education 51n1
U.S. Federal Indian Law 24, 27, 29, 56, 65, 210, 217, 219

Van Zandt, Franklin K. 52n9
the vanishing Indian 80, 96–7; in missionary journals 101–2; in post-colonial America 101–3; Romanticism 98, 99, 100–1, 103n2; as validation of divine purpose 97–8; *see also The Last of the Mohicans*
Varisco, Daniel Martin 183, 184
Vico, Giambattista 75, 76
Virginia-Kentucky militia bounty problem 43–6, 52n8–9, 53n10

Washington, George 109, 120, 169, 177n7, 207n11
Wayne, John M. 64–5
Webster, Daniel 41–2
Weisberg, Richard A. 164–6, 171, 172, 176n5
Wendell, Barrett A. 129, 133
West, Benjamin 71, 80, 94–5n2
West, Robin 163, 170
White, John 80
Whitman, Walt 137
wilderness 126–9, 156n1; art as discourse 71, 126, 148–52; conquest: classifying the wilderness 152–6; from dark and barren to sublime 57, 126, 133–42, 148–9; and discourse theory 124–6; in early American literature 85, 124, 129–33; genre of law 83–4, 128–9; in *Johnson v. M'Intosh* 31–2, 125, 127; in *The Last of the Mohicans* 32, 71, 108, 112–13, 128–9; in *Worcester v. Georgia* 127–8
Wilkins, David E. 45–6
'will to truth' 15–16, 125
Williams, David Ross 131
Williams, Eunice 123n7
Williams, John 122n4, 123n7
Williams, Patricia 171–2
Williams, Robert A., Jr. 26–7
Williamson, Peter 106, 122n3
Williston, Ebenezer Bancroft 92
Windschuttle, Keith 72, 74
Winthrop, John 32, 125, 134, 135–6, 137, 213–14, 221n5
Wirt, William 29, 34
Woodson, Carter 123n8
Worcester, Samuel A. *see Worcester v. Georgia*
Worcester v. Georgia (1832) 17, 20, 34, 35–9, 40, 50, 52n6, 124, 206, 219; structure of legal judgment 63–5, 65n7; the wilderness 127–8; *see also* Marshall Trilogy cases
Wren, Christopher 157n14
Wright, Ronald 190, 192

Young, Mary 196–7
Young, Robert 21, 206n1